# In the Bog

## The ecology, landscape, archaeology and heritage of peatlands

## Part 2. Ecology, Management & Conservation

**Edited by Ian D. Rotherham and Christine Handley**

***Landscape Archaeology & Ecology* Vol. 13**

**January 2025**

Edited by Ian D. Rotherham and Christine Handley

ISBN: 978-1-904098-75-1
ISSN: 1354- 0262

**Published by:**
Wildtrack Publishing, Ash Tree Yard,
62-68 Thirlwell Road, Heeley, Sheffield S8 9TF

Typeset and processed by Christine Handley

**Supported by:**
Sheffield Hallam University.
British Ecological Society.
IUFRO.
JBA Consulting.
Thorne & Hatfield Moors Conservation Forum.
International Peat Society.
IUCN UK Peatland Programme.
South Yorkshire Biodiversity Research Group.
Landscape Conservation Forum.
HEC Associates.



Front cover picture by Bridie Hamilton
Back cover picture from the collection of Ian D. Rotherham

# Contents

# Foreword

The 2014 Sheffield conference addressed the themes of 'the ecology, landscape, archaeology and heritage of peatlands'. Contributions from around the world considered issues of:

1. The ecology of peatlands.

2. Their histories of utilisation and exploitation.

3. Their contributions to 'ecosystem services'.

And importantly,

4. Of their restoration.

Globally, peatlands have shrunk dramatically over perhaps 200 to 300 years, and this must be a major contribution to global environmental change. Furthermore, the removal and degradation of peatlands has severely compromised the planetary ability to respond to and mitigate problems such as climate change.

The book of the proceedings was delayed allowing for submission of chapters by various authors, but then for other reasons including workloads, university priorities, and ultimately COVID Lockdown. Nevertheless, the unique collection of contributions to the two books, '*In the Bog: The ecology, landscape, archaeology and heritage of peatlands Part 1: History & Heritage*', and '*In the Bog: The ecology, landscape, archaeology and heritage of peatlands Part 2. Ecology, Management & Conservation*', makes a remarkable contribution to the literature on peat and peatlands. The collections run from history and heritage and through to science and conservation management, and with a global coverage.

# Chapter 1. Restoration of afforested blanket bogs in Scotland

**Roxane Andersen[1], Richard Payne[2], Joshua Ratcliffe[1,2], Paul Gaffney[1]**
[1] Environmental Research Institute, University of the Highlands and Islands; [2]University of Stirling.

## Scottish blanket bogs and global carbon budget

In their pristine state, peatlands are the largest terrestrial carbon sink and have a net cooling effect on the climate; however, large scale degradation following land use and climate change can switch them from sink to sources of carbon to the atmosphere, thus fuelling global warming (Worrall *et al.*, 2007). It is estimated that up to 16,000 Mt C is stored in peatlands in the UK (ECOSSE 2007), and that approximately 400MT of C in the Flow Country, the vast expanse of blanket bog covering Caithness and Sutherland. Globally, damaged peatlands emit around 2 G tonnes of carbon dioxide per year – 10% of all carbon dioxide emissions (Joosten, 2009). In the UK, it is estimated that over 80% of the peatlands are degraded to some extent (Bain *et al.*, 2011). In the 1970s, plantation of non-native coniferous on "unproductive" land (Patterson & Anderson, 2000) was subsidised to fulfil post-war timber demand and led to afforestation of 20% of the total UK peatland resource (Artz *et al.*, 2014),with almost 80,000 ha (approx.16%) in the Flow Country.

Restoration of afforested peatlands back towards open blanket bog through combinations of drain blocking and tree removal started in the late 1990s and was mostly driven by habitat and biodiversity incentives. Since then, it has been recognised that peatland restoration, especially on the most degraded areas, is one of the most cost effective carbon abatement strategies, but it has been highlighted that data gaps and uncertainties remained significant (Chapman *et al.*, 2012). Here we present a short overview of the current state of knowledge on the impact of afforestation and restoration of blanket bogs on carbon stocks and greenhouse gas (GHG) fluxes and we present the key challenges and opportunities in peatland research in the North of Scotland, identified by the Flow Country Research Hub.

## The impact of afforestation on blanket bog on carbon stocks

Trees do not naturally grow on most British peatlands, thus ploughing, ditching and fertilisation are required for the establishment of conifer plantations. As a consequence of drainage and evapotranspiration, the water table drops, peat cracks and tree roots allow oxygen to reach previously anaerobic horizons. Nutrient inputs from fertilisation have the potential to alter biogeochemical cycling and decomposition processes (Bragazza *et al.*, 2012). Eventually, subsidence of the peat surface as well as losses of carbon to the atmosphere and watercourses occur (Shotbolt *et al.*, 1998). Although a lot of research has been done on peatlands drained for improved tree growth in Scandinavia (e.g. Minkkinen and Laine, 1998), it does not directly translate to treeless deep peat blanket bogs of Scotland. Similarly, conclusions reached previously about the projections of changes in carbon fluxes and stocks in Scotland are based on a number of questionable assumptions (e.g. Hargreaves *et al.*, 2003) and despite an agreement that forestry is a threat to carbon reserves, the impacts of afforestation on C stocks in plantation on deep peat remains almost entirely unquantified (Lindsay, 2010).

In response to this issue, we have developed a method using stratigraphic markers to quantify long-term carbon accumulation rates and compare C stocks accumulated in peat over known periods of time. Microscopic layers from volcanic ash, known as tephra, have long been known to occur in British peats where they are deposited after eruptions in Iceland (Figure 1). Their identification traditionally involved time-consuming microscopy (Dugmore *et al.*, 1995), but we have pioneered the use of multi-sensor core scanning technology (cf. Kylander *et al.*, 2012) to locate the larger layers very rapidly in peat cores.

Five of these layers should be readily identifiable in the Flow Country (Dugmore *et al.*, 1995). Using bulk density, loss on ignition and carbon content analyses we will compare soil carbon stocks within and between forested and open bog and with these tephra layers as markers, we will be able to identify for the first time where carbon loss occurs in the stratigraphic column, and complete carbon stock calculation by direct measurements of above-ground carbon.

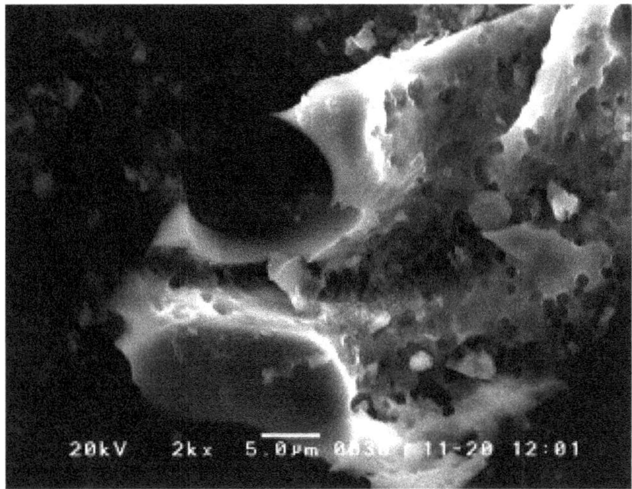


**Figure 1: Scanning Electron Microscope image of a tephra shard found in the peat column. Credit: J. Ratcliffe.**

## Carbon balance of afforested and restored blanket bogs

There are currently no complete greenhouse gas (GHG) budget studies on afforested and restored peatlands in the UK. While a number of studies have used chambers to assess impact of afforestation, the method fails to capture tree respiration and photosynthesis; thus, it only accounts for part of the emissions from these sites and renders the comparison with open, treeless blanket bog invalid (Artz *et al.*, 2013). Over the last two years, we have set up a network of Eddy Covariance towers equipped to measure $CO_2$, $CH_4$, $N_2O$ and water vapour, complimented with replicated measurements using closed chambers at different stages after restoration, to provide full GHG in a range of conditions including above-canopy $CO_2$ emissions from trees on deep peat for the first time. This will lead to a better understanding of whether and where GHG hotspots are likely to occur following drain blocking and tree removal, and to put these in the relevant context.

In addition to gaseous exchanges, aquatic concentration and downstream exports of carbon and nutrients need to be considered. It has been shown that in peatland dominated catchments, most of the export occurs during storms and related high flow events (Vinjinli, 2012) and that timing of exports can be altered following drain blocking (Armstrong *et al.*, 2010). However, there is a dearth of information about exports at the critical time immediately after felling, where changes in concentrations related to physical disturbance may occur. Similarly, the impact on other nutrients, metals and sediments *in situ* and all the way down to the larger rivers are currently not quantified. Ultimately, advances in restoration techniques such as whole-tree removal and furrow blocking could have a different impact on these exports than e.g. felling to waste which has been traditionally used in the Flow Country and which has been the focus of monitoring so far (e.g. Muller & Tankéré-Muller, 2012).

Using a large scale replicated design with open, afforested, restored (different methods) and open sub-catchments, we are testing the hypotheses that 1) felling will lead to a temporary increase in carbon export in comparison with pre-felling and undisturbed (forested and open bog) conditions because of increased concentrations 2) water chemistry (pH, N-P-K, conductivity, metals) will change a) over time, decreasing after an initial post-felling peak towards values found in open reference sub-catchments and b) along the catchment, with impacts most visible in drains and first order streams and c) between treatments, with enhanced blocking leading to the most rapid recovery. Pre-felling data were collected between 2013 and 2014 and add to other data gathered specifically in the Flow Country (Table 1). Post-felling data will cover the period between 2014 and 2016.

## Challenges and opportunities for restoration of afforested peatlands in Scotland

Restoration of peatlands is one of the most significant landscape-scale changes currently taking place in the UK and aims to deliver multiple benefits in terms of enhanced biodiversity, water storage and natural carbon capture/long-term storage. In addition to achieving a better quantification of the carbon benefits associated with peatland restoration, there are a number of challenges and knowledge gaps that will need to be addressed by future research. These were brought forward by the sixty-three delegates of the Second Flow Country Research Conference, held in Thurso in March 2014.

**Table 1. DOC concentration (mean ± std. dev.) in water collected from open water features and streams draining sub-catchments dominated by afforested, open or felled blanket bog.**

| Sub-catchment dominated by | Stream | DOC (mg $l^{-1}$) | Period | Reference |
|---|---|---|---|---|
| Plantation | AlltDailloisgate | 15.8 ± 6.3 | 2013-2014 | Gaffney, P. unpublished data |
| | Upper Dyke | 20.9 ± 9.5 | 2009-2011 | Vinjili, 2012 |
| | Sleach | 8.3 ± 2.7 | 2007-2008 | Muller &Tankéré-Muller, 2012 |
| Open blanket bog | Ewe Burn | 12.6 ± 7.1 | 2013-2014 | Gaffney, P. unpublished data |
| | Garb allt burn | 21.3 ± 7.7 | 2009-2011 | Vinjili, 2012 |
| | Open water components to Sleach | 41.0 ±33.3 | 2007-2008 | Muller &Tankéré-Muller, 2012 |
| | Sleach | 9.7 ±4.0 | 2007-2008 | Muller &Tankéré-Muller, 2012 |
| Felled plantation | Upper Dyke | 47.2 ±13.1 | 2009-2011 | Vinjili, 2012 |
| | Open water components to Sleach | 56.2±46.5 | 2007-2008 | Muller &Tankéré-Muller, 2012 |
| | Sleach | 8.9±3.2 | 2007-2008 | Muller &Tankéré-Muller, 2012 |

## Developing restoration techniques in response to different disturbances and different objectives

Understanding which peatland management and restoration methods are optimal for biodiversity conservation and/or for carbon storage and sequestration is necessary to allow informed decisions, especially where trade-offs may be required. Determining optimal and cost-effective restoration approaches is essential both for the ongoing management of afforested peatland areas, and to inform government grant schemes supporting bog restoration. To achieve this, the practitioners, researchers and policy makers need to align their strategies and work together to ensure that restoration and monitoring on the ground is underpinned by science-based evidence.

## Cost-benefit of restoration in economic terms

Restoration of peatlands often requires a large upfront capital investment that is expected to translate into benefits arising from ecosystem services (e.g. reduction in carbon emissions). Quantifying other benefits in economic terms has the potential to influence future investment in peatland restoration. For instance, we know relatively little about the potential impact of peatland restoration and management on the surrounding aquatic system, which is likely to show a significant response in terms of water quality, quantity and aquatic ecosystem functioning. Given that many peatland streams and rivers are also prime salmon habitat, understanding the downstream impacts on ecosystem functioning of restoration activity has a particularly high socio-economic relevance.

## Monitoring blanket bog restoration

In order to assess the "success" of blanket bog restoration, adequate monitoring needs to be undertaken, comparing the pre- and post-restoration status and setting them in context using a reference system. However, the costs associated with adequate monitoring of ecosystem functions are often prohibitive and, in many cases, monitoring is not undertaken, is limited to the restored site (i.e. does not encompass a reference site) or isn't comprehensive enough for statistical analyses and comparisons.

In addition, there is often a significant mismatch in assessments of the responses to peatland restoration of environmental and biochemical responses compared to measurements of biotic responses, which are often severely lacking (Lindsay, 2010). Developing faster, cheaper and comprehensive methods, for instance using remote sensing and proxies, is even more critical for monitoring large-scale restoration projects – often covering several hundreds of hectares – where ground-based measurements would just not be deliverable. Long-term, decadal and multi-decadal monitoring programmes as part of peatland restoration work does not fit with traditional research programmes that support 2, 3 or at the most, 5 year projects. New or alternative funding schemes have to be developed and the view that monitoring is not a valuable activity has to change, it is indispensable for truly assessing restoration efforts, even more so where upfront costs are so significant.

## Future forecasting: linking past-present-future condition

With a combination of changes in management regimes and climate, how will peatland systems, degraded or not, respond in the future? Given that restoration aims to bring back peatlands in a climate now that is different than when they started to form in the early/mid-Holocene, what outcome is it reasonable to expect? We believe that a better integration of palaeoecological techniques and approaches with modern ecology would provide invaluable insight in some of those questions.

## Conclusions

The UK's northernmost blanket bogs are particularly underrepresented in current data sets, as a consequence of their remoteness from major centres where most researchers are based. Yet, the Flow Country peatlands of Caithness of Sutherland encompass a range of states, from near-pristine to highly degraded, includes several large-scale restoration sites, and span across a climatic gradient, with precipitations as high as 4,400 mm $yr^{-1}$ to the west, and as low as 500mm $yr^{-1}$ to the east. They provide an ideal setting to understand the influences of land use and climate change on carbon dynamics, biodiversity, water regulation both in peatlands and connected landscapes, but also to improve our capacity to predict the consequences of a changing climate upon those ecological functions. We believe that the Flow Country Research Network provides a framework within which collaborative research addressing those issues can thrive in the future and redress the balance across the UK.

## Acknowledgements

We would like to extend our thanks to all the partners within the Flow Country Research Network and in particular to the participants of the 2nd Flow Country Research Conference. The research presented here is supported by RSPB Scotland, The Carnegie Trust for the Universities of Scotland, the British Ecological Society, The Royal Society, MASTS, The Conservation Volunteers and Scottish Natural Heritage.

## References

Armstrong, A., Holden, J., Kay, P., Francis, B., Foulger, M., Gledhill, S., McDonald, A.T. and Walker, A. (2010) The impact of peatland drain-blocking on dissolved organic carbon loss and discolouration of water: results from a national survey, *Journal of Hydrology*, **381**, 112-120.

Artz, R.R.E.; Donnelly, D.; Andersen, R.; Mitchell, R.; Chapman, S.J., Smith, J., Smith, P., Cummins, R., Balana, B., and Cuthbert, A.(2014) Managing and restoring blanket bog to benefit biodiversity and carbon balance - a scoping study. *Scottish Natural Heritage Commissioned Report 562.*

Artz, R. R. E., Chapman, S. J., Saunders, M., Evans, C. D., and Matthews, R. B. (2013) Comment on " Soil CO 2, CH 4 and N 2 O fluxes from an afforested lowland raised peat bog in Scotland: implications for drainage and restoration" by Yamulki *et al.*(2013) *Biogeosciences*, **10** (11), 7623-7630.

Bain, C.G. *et al.* (2011) *IUCN UK Commission of Inquiry on Peatlands*. IUCN UK Peatland Programme, Edinburgh.

Bragazza L, Buttler A, Habermacher, J., Brancaleoni, L., Gerdol, R., Fritze, H. Hannajik, P., Laiho, R. and Johnson D. (2012) High nitrogen deposition alters the decomposition of bog plant litter and reduces carbon accumulation. *Global Change Biology,* **18** (3), 1163-1172.

Cannell, M.G.R., Dewar, R.C., and Pyatt, D.G. (1993) Conifer plantations on drained peatlands in Britain: a net gain or loss of carbon? *Forestry*, **66**, 353–369.

Chapman, S., Artz, R., and Donnelly, D. (2012) Carbon Savings from Peat Restoration. *Climate X Change enquiry*, (1205-02), 1-17.

Dugmore, A., Larsen, G., and Newton, A. (1995) Seven tephra isochrones in Scotland. *Holocene*, **5**, 257-266.

ECOSSE (2007) ECOSSE: *Estimating Carbon in Organic Soils - Sequestration and Emissions: Final Report*. Scottish Government, Edinburgh.

Hargreaves, K.J., Milne, R. and Cannell, M.G.R. (2003) Carbon balance of afforested peatland in Scotland. *Forestry*, **76** (3), 299-317.

Joosten H. (2009) *The Global Peatland CO2 Picture*, Wetlands International, Ede.

Kylander, M.E., Line, E.M., Wastegård, S. and Löwemark, L. (2012) Recommendations for using XRF core scanning as a tool in tephrochronology. *Holocene*, **22**, 371-375.

Lindsay, R.A. (2010) Peatlands and carbon: A critical synthesis, RSPB Scotland, Edinburgh.

Minkkinen, K, and Laine, J. (1998) Long-term effect of forest drainage on the peat carbon stores of pine mires in Finland. *Canadian Journal of Forest Research*, **28** (9), 1267-1275.

Muller, F. L., and Tankéré-Muller, S. P. (2012) Seasonal variations in surface water chemistry at disturbed and pristine peatland sites in the Flow Country of northern Scotland. *Science of the Total Environment*, **435**, 351-362.

Patterson, G. and Anderson, A.R. (2000) *Forests and peatland habitats*, Forestry Commission Guideline Note. Forestry Commission, Edinburgh.

Shotbolt, L., Anderson, A.R., and Townend, J. (1998) Changes to blanket bog adjoining forest plots at Bad a' Cheo, Rumster Forest, Caithness. *Forestry*, **71**, 311-324.

Vinjili, S. (2012) *Landuse change and organic carbon exports from a peat catchment of the Halladale River in the Flow Country of Sutherland and Caithness*. PhD Thesis, University of St Andrews

Worrall, F., Evans, M.G., Bonn, A., Reed, M.S., Chapman, D., and Holden, J. (2009) Can carbon offsetting pay for upland ecological restoration? *Science of the Total Environment*, **408** (1), 26-36.

# Chapter 2. Sphagnum restoration in the southern Pennines - problems and solutions

**Simon Caporn[1], Angus Rosenburgh[1], Josh Riggs[1], Karen Rogers[1], Stephanie Hinde[1, 2] and Neal Wright[3]**
Manchester Metropolitan University[1]; National Trust High Peak Estate[2]; Micropropagation Services (EM) Ltd[3]

## Introduction

In his Presidential address to the British Ecological Society in 1996, Professor J.A. Lee noted: 'The virtual absence of *Sphagnum* species from southern Pennine blanket peats and the loss of angiosperm species characteristic of *Sphagnum* carpets (e.g. *Andromeda* polifolia L. and *Drosera* spp.) remains a remarkable feature of British vegetation' (Lee, 1998). The wide scale demise of *Sphagnum* species almost certainly was the result of the close proximity of these peatlands to major centres of the Industrial Revolution and their emissions of atmospheric pollutants. Encouraging natural recovery and actively restoring *Sphagnum* on the southern Pennines (Figure 1) are now major goals of ecologists and conservation managers who recognise the very significant wider benefits for ecosystem services of actively growing *Sphagnum* peatlands.

## Recovery of *Sphagnum* in the southern Pennines

Over at least the past ten years, evidence has emerged that *Sphagnum* is recovering following the improvements in air quality although firm evidence is often limited by the poverty of good historical baseline survey data. To help address this, we revisited sites in the southern Pennines that had formed part of work by J.A. Lee and colleagues at the University of Manchester several decades earlier (Caporn *et al.*, 2006). In the 1980s, Studholme scoured the area for *Sphagnum* to use in population studies, but his field notebook recorded that very little was found on the ombrotrophic bog surfaces. In 2005-6, we revisited two of these sites with good bryophyte records and recorded in detail the changes in species composition. One site was near Holme Moss, and the other on Alport moor, where the monitored areas were both on relatively intact blanket bog with a reasonably high water table. Over a little more than twenty years, a marked increase in bryophytes was observed at both sites; at Holme Moss, *Sphagnum* species increased from two to six, while at Alport Moor they went from one to five species between 1983-5 and 2005-6.

**Figure 1: Typical eroding, partially re-vegetated peat mounds separated by deep, broad gullies on Black Hill in the southern Pennines in 2010. In the foreground are *Sphagnum* restoration trial plots.**

Caporn *et al.* (2006) also recorded the changes in a specific trial area near Holme Moss where Lee and colleagues in around 1980 introduced 30 cm blocks of six *Sphagnum* species and peat moved from north Cumbria. Success of the transplants within the initial 2-3 years was poor (Ferguson *et al.*, 1983) but by 2005 recovery was impressive for two of the most valuable hummock species *S. papillosum* and *S. capillifolium* and by 2010 all but *S. austinii* were recorded. These results and several anecdotal reports that *Sphagnum* appears to be on the increase prompted funding of a wider study of *Sphagnum* in the Peak District National Park by Carroll *et al.* (2009). They reported a good variety of species present in the Peak District and *Sphagnum*, largely in isolated patches, was recorded over many of the blanket bogs in the region. However, *Sphagnum* abundance in most areas of the Peak District moorlands is still very low and this is probably true of the entire southern Pennines region.

Understanding the factors that influence natural *Sphagnum* recovery will help decide strategies for restoration and habitat management and in recent transect studies on the heavily degraded Bleaklow area, K. Rogers (pers. comm.) provided detailed knowledge of the precise favoured locations of naturally recovering *Sphagnum* within different areas. In the area known as Joseph Patch near Bleaklow summit (a site with linear gullies and treated with lime, fertiliser and seed about 10 years ago), *Sphagnum* occurred only in the bottoms of gullies and depressions, particularly where standing or flowing water was available, while there was a complete absence of *Sphagnum* on the normal bog surface. In a contrasting nearby area of hydrologically intact blanket bog near to the Snake Pass summit there was much greater abundance of *Sphagnum* on the hydrated bog surface. The studies outlined above and other recent survey work by Moors for the Future Partnership show that *Sphagnum* is returning in this area of the southern Pennines although cover is still low, and distribution is patchy where its performance appears to be intimately linked to water. Although air pollution is now much improved it remains unclear if the legacy of air pollution in the soils, along with the continuing high levels of nitrogen deposition, are affecting the recovery of *Sphagnum* in general and true ombrotrophic species such as *Sphagnum capillifolium* in particular.

## Comparisons of southern Pennine and other British bogs

The quality of the southern Pennine bogs and their *Sphagnum* flora may be judged by comparison with other regions of Britain. Recent work of Rosenburgh compared *Sphagnum* growing in poor condition bogs of the southern Pennines (Bleaklow, Alport, Holme Moss, Black Hill) with a variety of bogs in much better state in England and Wales (Borth, Migneint, Glasson, Cranberry beds of Whixall) and Scotland (Moidach, Whim). In analysis of bog flora community composition, the southern Pennine sites were similar to each other while the other 'cleaner' sites formed another cluster quite different in species composition, both of *Sphagnum* and associated plant species. The clearest environmental drivers separating these two groups were high soil levels of nitrate and pollutant metals (aluminium, molybdenum and zinc), and depleted levels of base cations (magnesium and sodium). Rosenburgh showed that the Peak District moorland region of the southern Pennines have bog plant species and a peat chemistry that is still very different to bogs representative of less polluted regions of the UK (A. Rosenburgh, unpublished data).

## Managed restoration of *Sphagnum* on blanket bogs

The slow speed of natural *Sphagnum* recovery in the southern Pennines is being accelerated by managed introductions by various methods. The simplest approach, if a local *Sphagnum* source is available, is to transplant *Sphagnum* clumps directly into suitable receptor sites. Success using this targeted approach has been achieved near Chew Reservoir by RSPB and United Utilities who moved clumps into wet peat pans and cotton grass stands with a high water table. If the supply of *Sphagnum* is limited in volume it can be spread further if chopped and dispersed over a larger area. We tested this approach on both bare peats and treated areas (grass and heather – sown after liming and fertiliser applications) near Holme Moss. *Sphagnum* fragments entirely failed to establish on the bare peats but managed to take hold on the treated vegetated surfaces. The success was patchy and seemed to depend on the fragments contacting the areas of bare peat between the graminoid-heath patches (Rosenburgh, pers. comm.).

At the landscape scale in the southern Pennines, transplantation of whole clumps or chopped fragments of *Sphagnum* is limited by a lack of local source material and possibly biosecurity issues (pests, pathogens). Instead, a more sustainable approach developed by Horticultural firm *Micropropagation Services Ltd.* has been tested by our research group (Hinde *et al.*, 2009). Micro-propagation in agar and liquid culture enables tiny *Sphagnum* fragments selected from known populations and areas to be cultured and bulked up in to large volumes, which can potentially be spread over the landscape on a vast scale. So far, the majority of *Sphagnum* propagules raised by micropropagation have been spread in the form of beads of a gel-like material containing several young *Sphagnum* fragments known as 'Beadamoss®'. In moist greenhouse conditions, the Beadamoss typically grow into *Sphagnum* plants with 100 % success rate, but in the field the conditions are rarely as good, and establishment of the juvenile plants is frequently compromised by lack of moisture indicating that optimal conditions on the receptor site and suitable weather are vital to success.

Where the field environment is good, we have observed slow, sustained increase in cover of *Sphagnum* from beads. An example of results recorded in June 2014 is shown below (Table 1) for the oldest Beadamoss trials set up in 2008-2009 (Hinde *et al.*, 2009). The data reveal firstly that establishment on bare ground (the Holme Moss site) is very likely to yield poor returns compared with planting on treated, vegetated surfaces (Black Hill site). Secondly, addition of brash to protect beads will increase success; thirdly, the marked difference in establishment in different block positions appeared to reflect different underlying soil moisture or drying conditions between peat patches. The most successful plots in June 2014 contained over 400 *Sphagnum* capitula from the original planting of ninety beads. Understanding the best environments for *Sphagnum* growth and restoration will clearly be of great advantage in arriving at a high percentage of establishment of propagules and avoiding waste of costly resources.

## *Sphagnum* plug plants

A disadvantage of the *Sphagnum* beads is that their small size means they are difficult to see in the early years of growth so monitoring survival and establishment is hard. An alternative to the beads are *Sphagnum* plugs produced by *Micropropagation Services Ltd.*, equivalent in some ways to the plug plants of cotton grass and ericaceous shrubs used with much success on the southern Pennine moorlands. *Sphagnum* plugs are biodegradable paper tubes containing peat and sprayed with a suspension of micro-propagated fragments; these are grown on in the greenhouse until the moss covers the peat surface and is attached to the paper tube. By the time the *Sphagnum* plugs are fully established and hardened off (6-9 months) they provide a fairly robust module for planting out and, because of their size, growth can be easily monitored (Figure 2).The first field trials of the *Sphagnum* plugs only started in Spring 2014 and results by 3-4 months later show a high survival rate and, in the wetter sites, good establishment on the peat surfaces despite the dry summer.

**Table 1: Numbers of capitula of *Sphagnum fallax* in 0.5 m square experimental plots in June 2014, after planting on four dates in 2008-2009. Each data point refers to a plot in which 90 Sphagnum beads were added. Three blocks were set up on (a) bare ground at Holme Moss and (b) a treated area on Black Hill. Brash (*Calluna vulgaris* cut stems) was added to half the plots at each site. (unpublished data of S. Hinde and J. Riggs)**

(a) Holme Moss – bare

| | Block A | | Block B | | Block C | |
|---|---|---|---|---|---|---|
| | No brash | brash | No brash | brash | No brash | brash |
| Oct-2008 | 0 | 1 | 0 | 0 | 0 | 36 |
| Nov-2008 | 0 | 0 | 0 | 0 | 4 | 8 |
| Mar-2009 | 4 | 0 | 0 | 0 | 2 | 17 |
| May-2009 | 0 | 0 | 0 | 0 | 1 | 8 |

(b) Black Hill - treated

| | Block D | | Block E | | Block F | |
|---|---|---|---|---|---|---|
| | No brash | Brash | No brash | Brash | No brash | Brash |
| Oct-2008 | 0 | 2 | 12 | 14 | 0 | 195 |
| Nov-2008 | 0 | 0 | 0 | 49 | 0 | 50 |
| Mar-2009 | 0 | 0 | 115 | 127 | 73 | 436 |
| May-2009 | 0 | 9 | 26 | 1 | 151 | 240 |

**Figure 2: (left) Sphagnum plugs for planting; (right) mixed species planted 6th May 2014 into cotton grass in gully margins in the southern Pennines. Photograph after eleven weeks.**

## Conclusions

*Sphagnum* mosses are naturally recovering in many areas of the southern Pennines probably due to improvements in air quality in the last few decades. The extent and speed of *Sphagnum*'s return to the ombrotrophic vegetated bog surfaces appears to be influenced by the extent of the gullies affecting the local water table. Altered peat chemistry, the legacy of historical pollution in the southern Pennines is also strongly linked to the poverty of the bog vegetation, although which nutrient or pollutant is exerting the most influence is not easy to detect. Restoration of *Sphagnum* is in progress across the region using different techniques. The harvesting and spreading of local *Sphagnum* works well but is unlikely to be sustainable at the landscape scale. The bulking-up of *Sphagnum* using micro-propagation methods offers the potential to provide large volumes of *Sphagnum* from tiny fragments of source material but defining the optimal means of delivering this material in a cost-effective way and identifying the most favourable planting sites and weather conditions remains a work in progress.

## Acknowledgements

Matthew Buckler, Rachael Maskill, Brendon Wittram, and Jonathan Walker (Moors for the Future Partnership); Robin Sen, Nancy Dise and Chris Field (Manchester Metropolitan University); Tim Allott and Martin Evans (University of Manchester); many field work volunteers.

## References

Caporn, S.J.M., Carroll, J.A., Studholme, C. & Lee, J.A. (2006) *Recovery of ombrotrophic Sphagnum mosses in relation to air pollution in the southern Pennines.* Report to Moors for the Future. Edale, Derbyshire.

Carroll, J.A., Anderson, P., Caporn, S., Eades, P., O'Reilly, C. & Bonn, A. (2009) *Sphagnum in the Peak District: Current Status and Potential for Restoration*. Moors for the Future Report No 16. Edale, Derbyshire.

Ferguson, P. & Lee, J.A. (1983) The growth of *Sphagnum* species in the Southern Pennines. *Journal of Bryology*, **12**, 579-586.

Hinde, S., Rosenburgh, A., Wright, N., Buckler, M. & Caporn, S. (2010) *Sphagnum re-introduction project: A report on research into the re-introduction of Sphagnum mosses to degraded moorland.* Moors for the Future Research Report No. 18, Edale, Derbyshire.

Lee, J.A. (1998) Unintentional experiments with terrestrial ecosystems: ecological effects of sulphur and nitrogen pollutants. *Journal of Ecology*, **86**, 1–12.

# Chapter 3. Projected loss of climate space for active blanket bog in Ireland

**John Coll[1], David Bourke[2], Micheline Sheehy Skeffington[2], Michael Gormally[2], John Sweeney[1]**
[1] NUI Maynooth, Maynooth, Co Kildare, Ireland; [2] NUI Galway, Galway, Co Galway, Ireland.

## Summary

Active blanket bogs are ombrotrophic peatland systems of the boreo-temperate zones, although blanket peat tends to form only under the warmest and wettest of those conditions. In Europe, this is common only in Scotland and Ireland, coincident with the oceanic climate, and constitutes a significant global component of this ecosystem. Associated with this Atlantic distribution, Ireland has 50% of the remaining blanket bogs of conservation importance within the Atlantic Biogeographic Region of Europe. It is anticipated that future climate change will place additional pressure on these systems. Active blanket bog distributions in Ireland were modelled using two bioclimatic envelope modelling techniques, generalized linear modelling (GLM) and generalized additive modelling (GAM). The 1961 – 1990 baseline models achieved a very good agreement with the observed distribution and suggest a strong dependency on climate. The discrimination ability of the fitted models was assessed using the area under the curve (AUC; GLM = 0.927, GAM = 0.936) of a receiver operating characteristic (ROC) plot. A simple average of the probabilities from both models was computed to provide a consensus model (AUC = 0.930) which was calibrated against the observational data to further assess model performance. Using data from an A1B climate change scenario for 2031 – 2060 dynamically downscaled via a high resolution limited area model, the consensus model projects an overall loss of ~ 7.2% of suitable climate space at low elevations in the south and west of the country in particular. Small gains in climate space in the north and east of the country do not offset the projected losses.

**Key words:** Active blanket bogs, climate change, bioclimatic envelope models, GLM, GAM, climate space, vulnerability, uncertainty.

## Introduction

Globally, blanket bogs are rare, accounting for ~ 3% of the total peatland area, and their distribution is restricted to temperate maritime regions typified by cool summers, mild winters and year-round rainfall (Lindsay *et al.*, 1988; Warburton *et al.*, 2004; Boylan *et al.*, 2008; Kurbatova *et al.*, 2009). Within the climate space associated with temperate-boreal peatlands, blanket peat tends to form under the warmest and wettest conditions (Wieder & Vitt, 2006), where precipitation is around three times greater than potential evaporation (Pearsall, 1965) and there are no sustained dry periods (Moore & Bellamy, 1973). Globally, these areas typically occur in mid to high latitudes on the ocean fringes where precipitation is high and mean annual temperature range is low (Lindsay *et al.*, 1988).

In Europe, Atlantic blanket bogs are common only in Scotland and Ireland and constitute a significant global component of this ecosystem (Douglas, 1998; Sheehy Skeffington & O'Connell, 1998). This reflects the marked influence of the Atlantic for both countries where maritime influences dominate local climates (Coll *et al.*, 2005; Sweeney, 2014). Between 13.8 per cent (Connolly *et al.*, 2007) and 17 per cent (Hammond, 1984) of the Irish land area is peatland, containing an estimated soil carbon stock of between 53 and 62 per cent of the national soil carbon stocks (Tomlinson, 2005; Eaton *et al.*, 2008). Ireland's peatlands and wetlands are valued as a highly distinctive semi-natural habitat, and many have protective designations.

Given the close relationship between peat formation and climate, future climate change is likely to place additional pressure on these systems (Clark *et al.*, 2010; Coll *et al.*, 2011, 2013a, 2014). Climate change is expected to result in a decrease in the summer water table in peatlands through drier summers and alteration of pH, while modification of the nutrient cycle may lead to bogs becoming net emitters of carbon (Kurbatova *et al.*, 2009). Most bog burst and peat slide events are triggered by high magnitude rainfall events (Warburton *et al.*, 2004; Dykes *et al.* 2008) and UK and Irish data indicate that roughly half of all slippage events at present occur in the late summer months in relation to convective storm activity (Warburton *et al.*, 2004). Therefore, more frequent slippage events could be expected with climate change in the summer months if prior hotter and dryer conditions have increased surface cracking (Sweeney *et al.*, 2008).

Projected increases in winter rainfall may also lead to increased peat erosion, with losses of particulate and dissolved organic carbon from peat to surface waters (Freeman *et al.*, 2001; Freeman *et al.*, 2004; Monteith *et al.*, 2007; Clark *et al.*, 2010; Yallop *et al.*, 2010). The hydrological functioning of peat soils can influence peak river flows and flooding (Bonn *et al.*, 2009; Holden, 2009) through their influence on water retention. In addition, some of the thermal changes projected with elevation for maritime regions (Coll *et al.*, 2010) are likely to have implications for upland peat soils. However, projected changes in the frequency of more regionally severe winter storms are presently inconclusive (Coll *et al.*, 2013b), hence the implications for seasonal changes to slippage events are less clear. The interaction between pressures such as over-grazing, draining, burning, conifer plantation and climate change could further threaten the delivery of vital services from these ecosystems.

Various modelling approaches have been developed and used to convert point information of species distribution into predictive maps (e.g. Araújo & Guisan, 2006; Heikkinen *et al.*, 2006; Elith & Leathwick, 2009). Bioclimatic envelope models (BEMs) are an increasingly used class of models which can be considered as a special case of niche-based models or species distribution models (Guisan & Zimmermann, 2000; Guisan & Thuiller, 2005; Heikkinen *et al.*, 2006). BEMs correlate current species distributions with climate variables and may then be used to project spatial shifts in species climatic envelopes according to selected climate change scenarios (Berry *et al.*, 2002; Huntley *et al.*, 2004; Thuiller, 2004; Thuiller *et al.*, 2004).

The use of BEMs for habitats is novel and only a limited number of studies have applied the methods to consider landforms and habitats (e.g. Fronzek *et al.*, 2006; Parviainen & Luoto, 2007; Clark *et al.*, 2010). Recently however, there has been a more extensive application of these methods for Irish wetland habitats and many of their component species (Coll *et al.*, 2011, 2013a, 2014). A fundamental issue for the application of BEMs in the context of vulnerability analysis is that they can only give information about exposure to climate stress, not sensitivity (House *et al.*, 2010). Therefore, they do not provide process information, or information on feedback within ecosystems once the climate becomes unsuitable.

## Aims and objectives

The primary aim of this study was to model the impacts of climate change for the active blanket bog (ABB) priority habitat for the whole island of Ireland, using climate and elevation variables as predictors in a Generalized Linear Modelling (GLM) and Generalized Additive Modelling (GAM) framework. A secondary aim was to evaluate and refine candidate baseline models specified in the BIOMOD framework (Thuiller, 2003).

## Materials and Methods

## Study area

The study area is the whole island of Ireland and covers *ca.* 84,421 km$^2$ on the Atlantic margin of northwest Europe, between the latitudes of *ca.* 51° 00′ and 56 ° 00′ (Figure 1). Altitudes range up to 1038m a.s.l. (Corrán Tuathail, Co. Kerry). Much of the island is lowland, partly surrounded by mountains, with a characteristic temperate oceanic climate. Mean annual temperature (averaged over 1961–1990) is highest on the south-west coast (10.4 °C) and lowest inland (8.8 °C). On average, annual precipitation ranges from 750 mm to 1,000 mm in the drier eastern half of the country and over 3,000 mm per year in parts of the western mountains (Rohan, 1986). Active blanket bog is extensive in the west, as well as locally on mountains throughout the island (Figure 1).

## Data

Distribution data for Annex I priority habitats and species was provided by the Irish National Parks and Wildlife Service (NPWS) in a GIS format. The maps are based on a combination of habitat and species distribution maps supported by NPWS surveys (NPWS 2008). These data were complemented by data for Northern Ireland (NI) Annex I report from the Joint Nature Conservancy Council database (JNCC, 2007). While these are to some degree incomplete and none fully depict the national resource of habitats and species (NPWS, 2008); these data sources are highly reliable national repositories, and the geo-referencing of the data is likely to be excellent. Data of this resolution are appropriate for the modelling undertaken in the current study where these have been converted to binary presence (1) and absence (0) maps on a regular 10 x 10 km grid.

A quality controlled set of 1961–1990 climate data was used to test and construct the habitat BEMs for the baseline period. These 10 x 10 km resolution data are derived from observed monthly climate data for 560 precipitation stations and seventy temperature stations interpolated using a polynomial regression method with an inbuilt adjustment for elevation for the 1961-1990 baseline period (Sweeney and Fealy, 2002, 2003).

Met Éireann (The Irish Meteorological Service) supplied data from the HadCM3-Q16 GCM dynamically downscaled to a 14 x 14 km grid resolution via the regional atmospheric model (RCA3) (McGrath *et al.*, 2008). The output used for the impacts modelling here is for an A1B scenario from the above GCM and RCM combination. The A1B scenario projects a rise in annual temperature of 1.3 to 1.8° C, a decrease in summer precipitation by 5 to 10% and an increase in autumn and winter precipitation by 5 to 10% by 2021-2050 relative to the 1961-1990 baseline (McGrath *et al.*, 2008). The projected warming is greatest in the south and east of the country, whereas for precipitation there is no clear regional trend (McGrath *et al.*, 2008).

RCA3 simulated climate data for 1961-1990 and 2031-2060 were converted to daily and monthly mean values for temperature and precipitation variables, and R-based routines (R Development Core Team, 2011) used to re-interpolate these data to the 10 x 10 km modelling grid. The climate change signal derived with respect to the RCA3 simulated 1961-1990 baseline for each 10 x 10 km grid cell was then applied to the observed data for the variables of interest.

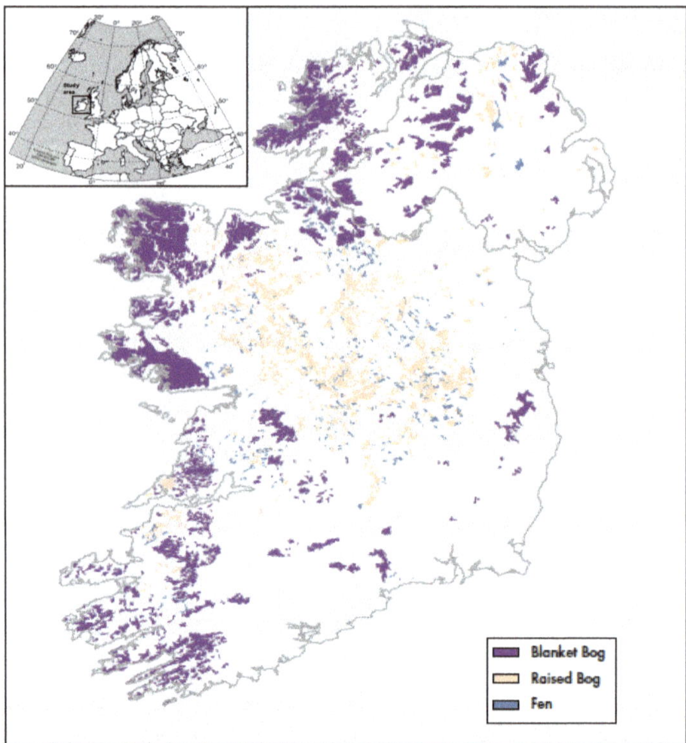


**Figure 1: Map showing the distribution of active blanket bog in Ireland and some other wetland habitat types. Purple shading denotes blanket bog; raised bog areas are denoted in light brown and fens in blue (Source: modified from the Irish Peatlands Conservation Council). Inset: map of the study area in European context.**

## Derivation of explanatory variables

Both the baseline climate data and the climate change signal data were converted to monthly and seasonal values for use in the BEMs. Eight climate variables were used, and included alongside these were four variables for topography (Table 1). The range of explanatory variables evaluated also overlap to some extent with those reported elsewhere (e.g. Fronzek *et al.*, 2006; Marmion *et al.*, 2008; Engler *et al.*, 2011).

Mean elevation for each 10 x 10 km grid cell (ArcGIS 9.3 software) was derived from a digital elevation model (DEM) (GTOPO30) with a horizontal grid spacing of 30 arc s (approximately 1km). The range in elevation variables (highest elevation – lowest elevation in the focal cell) was also calculated from the DEM, and the data referenced to the climatic datasets.

**Table 1: Candidate predictor variables screened**

| **Name** | **Definition** | **Unit** |
|---|---|---|
| **Climate** | | |
| ATR | Annual temperature range (maximum | |
| | temperature of the warmest month – | ° C |
| MAT | minimum temperature of the coldest | ° C |
| MST | month) | ° C |
| MTW | Mean annual temperature | ° C |
| | Mean summer temperature | |
| | Mean temperature of warmest month | |
| MWT | Mean winter temperature | ° C |
| NAP | Net annual precipitation | mm |
| MSP | Mean summer precipitation (June - August) | mm |
| MWP | Mean winter precipitation (December - | mm |
| | February) | |
| **Topography** | | |
| Min | Minimum elevation | m |
| Max | Maximum elevation | m |
| Mean | Mean elevation | m |
| Range | Elevation range | m |

## Bioclimatic envelope models

Candidate GLM and GAM covariate combinations specified in the BIOMOD modelling framework (Thuiller, 2003; Thuiller *et al.*, 2009) were explored for the ABB habitat. A secondary aim was to carefully evaluate the covariates used in the baseline models, this recognises that multiple regression-based approaches can be hampered by multicollinearity among predictors (Heikkinen *et al.*, 2004, 2006). BIOMOD can usefully specify non-linear terms for GLM in particular, thereby opening up many more candidate covariate possibilities. However, there is no screen for collinearity among predictors in BIOMOD *per se,* therefore some additional routines were used to scrutinise candidate models for collinearity. The finally selected models were calibrated using the R (version 2.13.0) environment software (R Development Core Team, 2011) and the Presence-Absence library (Freeman, 2011).

GLMs are mathematical extensions of linear models (McCullagh & Nelder, 1989); and they offer the advantage of fitting probability distributions to the variable being modelled. GLMs can also handle nonlinear relationships and different types of distributions characterising spatial data and are technically closely related to traditional practices used in linear modelling and analysis of variance (ANOVA) (Marmion *et al.*, 2009).

GAMs are non-parametric extensions of GLMs (Hastie & Tibshirani, 1990), and they are often used in biogeographical studies (Guisan *et al.*, 2002; Araújo *et al.*, 2005; Thuiller *et al.*, 2006; Marmion *et al.*, 2009). They provide a flexible data driven class of models that permit both linear and complex additive response shapes, as well as combinations of the two within the same model (Marmion *et al.*, 2009). The flexibility of their smooth functions confers an advantage to GAMs over GLMs in that they are able to 'fit' data more closely for a given number of degrees of freedom because they are not constrained to fit predefined parametric shapes (Bio *et al.*, 1998; Young *et al.*, 2011); but this comes with less transparency and interpretability (Hastie & Tibshirani, 1990; Wintle *et al.*, 2005).

The use of BIOMOD for habitat data and the application of variance inflation factors (VIFs) screening routines for BIOMOD-specified outputs in R, are also novel and not the same as the methods described previously for Ireland (Coll *et al.*, 2011); nor are they the same as recent ensemble forecasting in BIOMOD (Coll *et al.*, 2014). VIFs provide a measure of the multicollinearity in a regression design matrix and are more likely to reveal higher order collinearity than the pairwise collinearity determined from a correlation matrix (Velleman & Welsch, 1981; Neter *et al.*, 1990). BIOMOD allowed a wide set of candidate predictors to be evaluated and selected based on derived polynomial and power terms across a family of models.

The BIOMOD-specified and fitted GLM and GAM outputs were scrutinised in R using VIFs as a collinearity diagnostic before selecting a final model. For any regression-based model the VIF (and tolerance) is based on the proportion of variance the *i*th independent variable shares with the other independent variables in the model (O'Brien, 2007). Any collinear terms were dropped from the final fitted models, but in model building, the Akaike's Information Criterion (AIC) scores obtained at each stage were also used to guide final variable selection.

GLMs and GAMs enable the fitting of non-linear relationships between the dependent variable and the independent environmental variables. Despite not knowing *a priori* the form of a particular relationship (linear, quadratic, cubic or other), the variable selection routines enabled an evaluation of whether more complicated responses were ecologically sensible or justified by the data. We emphasise caution not to interpret too much in relation to which variables were included or not, as in any multivariate model-building process, producing a single model can be dubious (MacNally, 2000; Luoto *et al.*, 2004). This is particularly true when the candidate explanatory variables are numerous and the potential causal relationships between them and the response variable are not well known *a priori*.

Discrimination and calibration measure different aspects of model performance and are complementary, so it has been suggested that both should be used in combination (Harrel, 2001). The different discrimination measurements are subject to debate (e.g., Fielding & Bell, 1997; Foody, 2002; McPherson *et al.*, 2004; Guisan & Thuiller, 2005) and there is no generally accepted measure of performance for binary models (Guisan & Zimmermann, 2000; Pearce & Ferrier, 2000). Therefore, the discrimination ability of the finally fitted GLM and GAM was assessed with four different measures: (1) Sensitivity, (2) Specificity, and (3) the True Skill Statistic (TSS). (4) Model accuracy was also assessed with the area under the curve (AUC) from receiver operating characteristic (ROC) plots (Fielding & Bell, 1997).

Sensitivity is the proportion of occurrences accurately predicted by a model while Specificity is the proportion of absences accurately predicted (Fielding & Bell, 1997). TSS is equivalent to the Kappa statistic when frequencies of presence and absence points are equal; but, unlike Kappa, it is not sensitive to frequency (Allouche *et al.*, 2006; Jones & Reichar, 2009). AUC relates the proportion of correctly classified (true positive proportion) and incorrectly classified (false positive proportion) cells over a wide and continuous range of threshold levels and is therefore a threshold-independent measure (Pearce & Ferrier, 2000). The square of the residual deviance ($D^2$) was also calculated. $D^2$ is a measure of deviation of residual from the fitted model to the null model and is analogous to $R^2$ in normal regression models (Guisan & Zimmerman, 2000; Wintle *et al.*, 2005; Clark *et al.*, 2010).

## Results

## Final GLM and GAM models

For both GLMs and GAMs the screening in R resulted in more parsimonious models than the complex model term outputs from BIOMOD once the collinear and statistically insignificant terms were excluded. The finally selected models (ABB-GLM; ABB-GAM) (Tables 2 and 3) scored well on all the discrimination measures. GLM; Sensitivity = 0.85, Specificity = 0.85, TSS = 0.71, $D^2$ = 48.1. GAM; Sensitivity = 0.87, Specificity = 0.86, TSS = 0.73, $D^2$ = 53.2. For both models, the key controlling variables in accurately modelling the baseline habitat distribution are mean winter precipitation (MWP), mean summer temperature (MST) and elevation range (Range).

**Table 2: Generalized Linear Model (GLM) summary, climate and elevation variables. MST denotes mean summer temperature; MWP: mean winter precipitation; Range: elevation range (as per Table 1)**

| Variable | Regression coefficient | Std. Error | *z*-value | *p*-value |
|---|---|---|---|---|
| (Intercept) | 16.02 | 2.89 | 5.55 | <0.0001 |
| MST | -1.20 | 0.20 | -5.85 | <0.0001 |
| poly (MWP,2)1 | 38.58 | 3.77 | 10.22 | <0.0001 |
| poly (MWP, 2)2 | -17.89 | 0.20 | -4.46 | <0.0001 |
| I (Range^3) | $8.28 \times 10^{-8}$ | $1.08 \times 10^{-8}$ | 7.66 | <0.0001 |
| Null Deviance: 1,334.63 on 962 degrees of freedom<br>Residual Deviance: 692.93 on 958 degrees of freedom. AIC: 702.93 | | | | |

*Notes*: [1] poly denotes R standard term for a polynomial expression
[2] ^ denotes R standard term for a power expression

**Table 3: Generalized Additive Model (GAM) summary, climate and elevation variables. MST denotes mean summer temperature; MWP: mean winter precipitation; Range: elevation range (as per Table 1)**

| Variable | Parametric coefficients | Std. Error | *z*-value | *p*-value |
|---|---|---|---|---|
| (Intercept) | 0.25 | 0.13 | 1.87 | <0.0001 |
| | ~ Significance of smooth terms (edf) | Ref.df | Chi.sq | |
| s(MST) | 1.08 | 2.51 | 22.77 | <0.0001 |
| s(MWP) | 4.46 | 5.51 | 110.88 | <0.0001 |
| s(Range) | 1.78 | 2.26 | 115.46 | <0.0001 |
| Null Deviance: 1,334.63 on 962 degrees of freedom<br>Residual Deviance: 624.59 on 953 degrees of freedom. AIC: 644.59 | | | | |

*Notes*: [1]s denotes R standard term for a GAM smoother expression

## Averaging model probabilities

Consensus methods aim to decrease the predictive uncertainty of single-models by combining their predictions. They also encompass variation in the performance of different model families and are applied on the basis that averaging the results of individual models may increase the overall accuracy of predictions (Araújo & New, 2007; Crossman & Bass; 2008). Since only two model types were used here, a simple average of the probabilities from the ABB-GLM and ABB-GAM was computed for each grid cell to provide the final consensus model (ABB-GLAM).

Classification success rates for GLM and GAM are comparable and apply for both sensitivity (true present calls) and specificity (true absent calls) (Figure 2). However, the GLM recorded a residual deviance of 692.93 on 959 residual degrees of freedom compared to 624.06 and 953.78 respectively for each value in the better performing GAM. Finally, ROC was recomputed for ABB-GLAM and the new AUC (0.930 ± 0.01) and Kappa value (0.711 ± 0.02) obtained. Results are very close to the range of values reported by Fronzek *et al.* (2006) in the modelling of palsa mires in Finland using GLM and GAM alongside other model types.

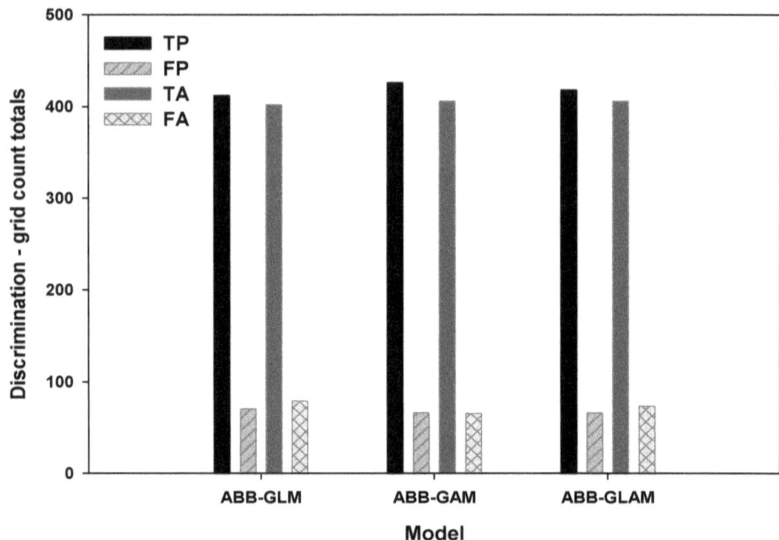


**Figure 2: Summary comparison of ABB-GLM, ABB-GAM and ABB-GLAM discrimination ability for the active blanket bog habitat distribution. TP denotes true present, FP: false present; TA: true absent, FA: false absent.**

## Comparison of model fit for the baseline climate and projected future changes in active blanket bog climate space

Mapped performance results for the two models, including correct and false predictions for each, for the baseline period (Figure 3) indicate that the general pattern of the spatial distribution of ABB is well captured in the models with incorrect predictions mainly occurring in individual grid cells at the edges of the observed ABB distribution. Boxplots for the GLM and GAM fitted to the baseline and the climate change data, show the clear shift in both the median and interquartile ranges for the future probability of occurrence compared to the baseline (Figure 4). Overall, GAM performs better than GLM, while the test scores associated with GLAM simply reflect the averaged probabilities from both models.

The combined ABB-GLAM projected changes for the ABB habitat indicate a potential loss and fragmentation of suitable climate space in the south and west in particular (Figure 5a).

These projected losses are offset by potential gains in the north and east of the country, especially in upland areas of the east and inland. However, these are smaller in number and are more fragmented, with overall gains recorded for forty-five grid squares compared to the baseline (Figure 5b).

The projected changes show the greatest loss of climate space to be in the south and west of the country and the most substantial losses are associated with low-elevation coastal cells. Overall, therefore, the models are projecting most losses of suitable climate space for low-lying southern and western cells in particular, whereas they indicate some preservation of suitable climate space for upland areas in these regions. However, an overall loss of 114 cells is recorded relative to the baseline distribution. The greatest projected expansions of climate space are in the east and north-east and are often associated with cells where the elevation range is greater. Overall, there is a net loss of sixty-nine cells or 7.17% of suitable climate space relative to the baseline.

## Discussion

### Modelling the current active blanket bog distribution

Climatic variables used to determine blanket peat bioclimatic space include temperature, growing degree days, precipitation and water balance (precipitation – potential evaporation) (Clark *et al.*, 2010). Precipitation has been shown to be more important than temperature in explaining blanket bog distribution in Fennoscandia (Parviainen & Luoto, 2007). In the UK, the number of days with rainfall was considered to be more important than total precipitation in explaining blanket peat distribution (Lindsay *et al.*, 1988; Clark *et al.*, 2010). This is most likely because the number of rain days has been linked with *Sphagnum* moss growth and primary production (Backeus, 1988; Lindsay, 1995). Maximum temperature is thought to be the main factor limiting the distribution of upland montane plant species in Britain (Rodwell *et al.*, 1992), though in the absence of maximum temperature data, mean temperature has been used to explain blanket peat distribution (Hossell *et al.*, 2000). Whereas in other recent work applying seven model families via BIOMOD to the habitat in Ireland, mean winter precipitation and elevation range emerged as the key variables in all the categories of model, although their relative importance in relation to the other covariates specified varied between the models (Coll *et al.*, 2014).

Overall, the results here provide good climate-based models for the distribution of active blanket bog which replicate the observed baseline distribution of active blanket bog across Ireland. Both GLMs and GAMs with the application of climatic-based variables, are useful predictors of active blanket bog distribution in Ireland. In general, climate is the primary controlling environmental factor in the distribution of active blanket bogs at the geographical scale modelled here, although elevation range through its influence on both temperature and precipitation is also an important variable in the models.

Temperature, precipitation and elevation range emerge as the key variables in both the GLM and GAM modelling framework here; this importance of elevation range supports results showing that the inclusion of topographical variables improves the predictive accuracy of models for this habitat (Coll *et al.*, 2011) and for European butterfly species (Luoto & Heikkinen, 2008). Climatic and topographical gradients are known to operate at different spatial scales, with the latter nested in the former (Bruun *et al.*, 2006). The inclusion of the elevation data in this study provides a more local component for GLM and GAM. Elevation range has been commonly used as a surrogate for environmental and climatic heterogeneity within grid cells in species richness modelling studies as topographical heterogeneity compresses biotic communities into more constricted vertical spaces (e.g. Richerson & Lum, 1980; Currie, 1991; Coblentz & Riitters, 2004) and effectively mingles habitat types and species that are otherwise often widely spatially separated.

The approach also enabled refinement of the covariates by allowing some of the polynomial and power terms specified by the outputs from BIOMOD to be retained, thereby allowing more flexibility in the model. Thus, for example, the polynomial terms for the GLM eliminate assumptions of linear responses along climatic gradients and allow the retention of more complex response surfaces (Guisan & Zimmerman, 2000). The use here of a simple average of the probabilities to provide the final consensus model (ABB-GLAM) can be considered as a simplified variant of consensus approaches applied over a wider range of model families as reported elsewhere (e.g. Araújo & New, 2007; Araújo *et al.*, 2011; Garcia *et al.*, 2012).

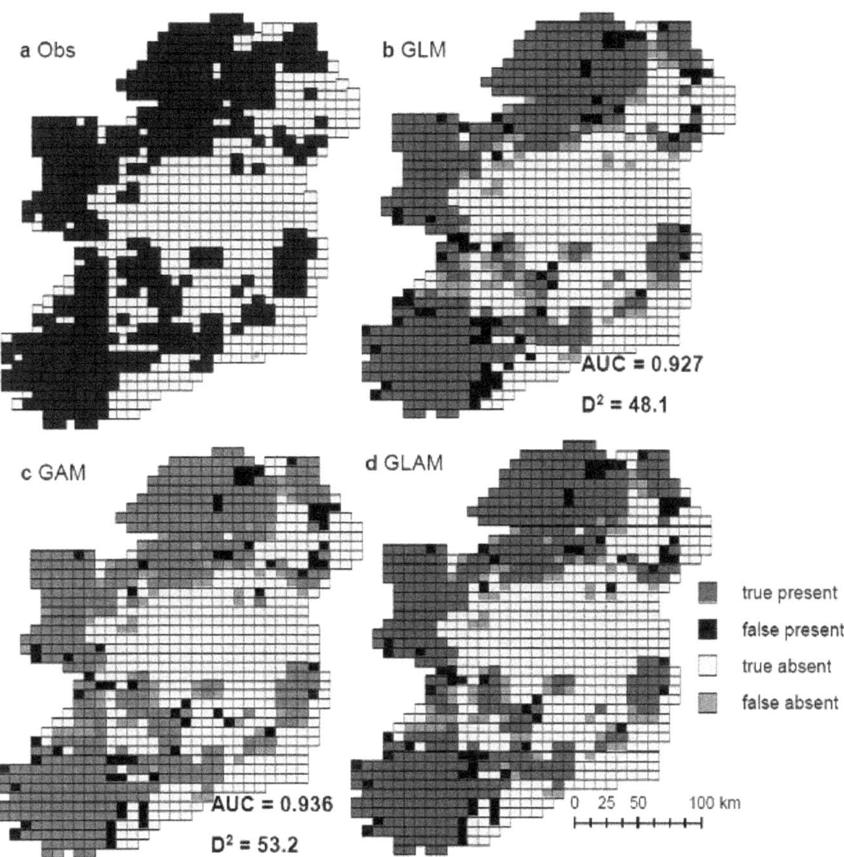


**Figure 3: Correct and false predictions of the current active blanket bog habitat distribution for the baseline period compared to the observed distribution based on National Parks and Wildlife Service data (Ireland) and Joint Nature Conservancy Council data (Northern Ireland). (a) Observed distribution (dark squares denote presence); (b) GLM; (c) GAM; and (d) GLM and GAM consensus model (GLAM). AUC = the area under the curve based on fourfold cross-validation, $D^2$ = percentage of explained deviance.**

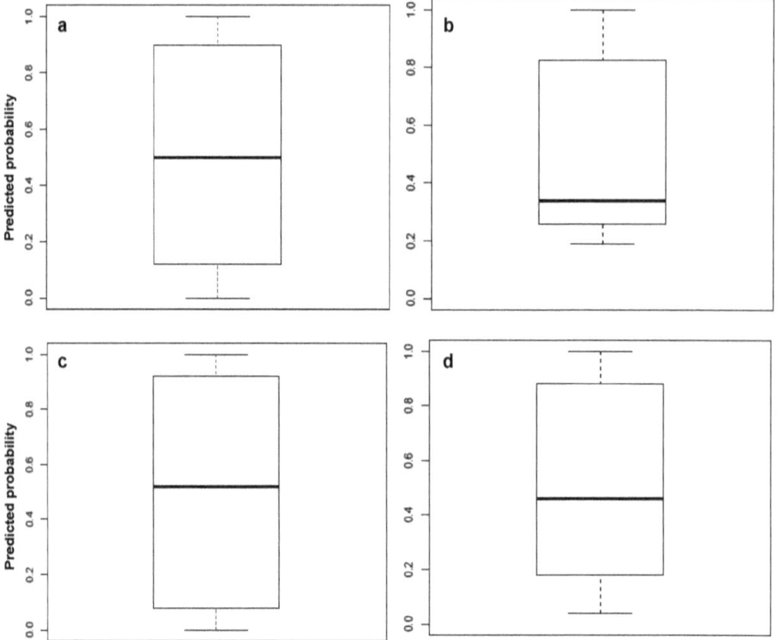


**Figure 4: Boxplots for the fitted GLM and GAM illustrating the probability distribution shifts associated with the climate change projections by comparison with the baseline. a) GLM 1961-1990; b) GLM 2031-2060; c) GAM 1961-1990; d) GAM 2031-2060. Boxes: interquartile range; whiskers 5th and 95th percentiles.**

Temperature and precipitation are known to be key controls on the habitat distribution in the present, and their importance as covariates in the models here reflect earlier findings in relation to the key controls on the active blanket bog habitat distribution (Jones *et al.*, 2006; Donnelly *et al.*, 2008). Hence the future changes in climate space projected for the habitats and their associated communities and species in response to the changes in temperature and precipitation make sense both biogeographically and topographically at the finer scale of analysis presented here for Ireland. This has major implications for the type of blanket bog most vulnerable to a loss of climate space, since the areas coincident with the greatest loss of suitable climate space are associated with the lowland blanket bog distribution along the western Atlantic seaboard.

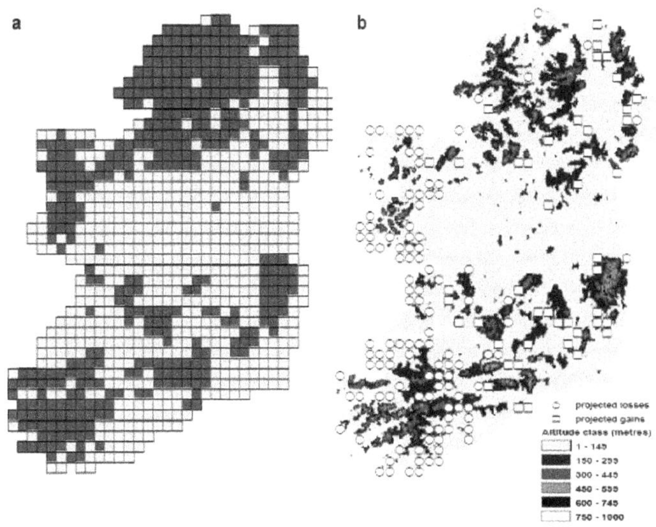


**Figure 5: a) Active blanket bog distribution according to the A1B climate scenario for 2031–2060, predicted with the GLAM consensus distribution model for the 10 x 10 km grid. The predicted occurrence of active blanket bog is shown with dark grey grid cells, the prediction of the habitat absence is shown with light grey grid cells. b) GLAM consensus distribution model with the projected losses and gains of climate space for each 10 x 10 km grid overlain on a digital elevation model (DEM) for the study region. White circles denote projected losses, and white squares denote projected gains.**

## Modelling the effect of climate change on active blanket bog distribution

A reduction in the climate space associated with blanket peat in the current study is consistent with projections using a GLM model based on mean temperature for the UK (Hossel *et al.*, 2000), but differs from other UK work, where BEMs based on artificial neural networks using measures of soil water deficit and surplus, as well as maximum and minimum temperature showed little overall change in blanket bog habitat under the same United Kingdom Climate Impacts Programme 1998 scenarios (Berry *et al.*, 2003). The importance of summer temperature in the models is consistent with palaeoecological studies, where reconstructions of the surface wetness of UK raised bogs have shown a relatively strong relationship with low summer temperature over the centennial time periods likely to be important for net peat accumulation (Barber & Langdon, 2007; Charman *et al.*, 2009).

In other words, summers with lower water deficits are associated with both higher precipitation and lower temperatures. Conversely, summers with higher temperatures and lower precipitation totals (as simulated in the A1B climate change scenario used here) are less likely to match the climate space associated with blanket peat formation. UK-based modelling also indicates that the combination of temperature and precipitation variables is important in BEMs for blanket peat. It was found e.g. that models which included measures of both hydrological conditions and maximum temperature provided a better fit to the mapped peat area than models based on hydrological variables alone (Clark *et al.*, 2010).

The significance of temperature in comparison to precipitation and water deficit in controlling peatland surface wetness has also been more widely debated recently, with contrasting views (Barber & Langdon, 2007; Charman, 2007; Charman *et al.*, 2009; Booth, 2010). Higher resolution reconstructions have shown that measures of water deficit, rather than temperature or precipitation alone, are more clearly correlated with surface wetness and reconstructed water table fluctuations over shorter 5- to 10-year time periods (Charman, 2007; Charman *et al.*, 2009; Booth, 2010). However, it remains unclear whether climatic variables driving shorter-term water table fluctuations (i.e. water deficit or annual accumulated monthly water deficit) or longer term measures of surface wetness (i.e. maximum or summer temperature) are more important for net peat accumulation in terms of the relative influence on peatland vegetation and structure relative to net organic matter decomposition (Clark *et al.*, 2010). Nevertheless, combinations of summer temperature and winter precipitation alongside the terrain variables parsimoniously captured the habitat distribution here.

## Limitations and assumptions of the methods

The limitations and assumptions involved in using a 10 x 10 km grid are recognised. Important controlling variables such as topographic and environmental heterogeneity will be lost at this resolution, together with important local micro-climatic controls. A key limitation is the lack of both data and resolution to discern the differences between lowland and upland blanket bog. This is critical, as the former is much rarer at a European scale (Moore & Bellamy, 1973; Sheehy, Skeffington & O'Connell, 1998). For similar scale-dependant reasons no account can be taken of the relative coherence or patchiness of the active blanket bog habitat within individual grids where the community presence is recorded. An obvious but important point in relation to the active blanket bog habitats, is that projected changes in the climate space associated with the current distribution of active blanket bog are not the same as projecting changes in the actual distribution of active blanket bog over the next century. It has been suggested that blanket peat habitats, even if not in a state of active growth, could well persist over decades or longer despite a reduction in climate space (Clark *et al.*, 2010).

The BEMs presented here are based on derived statistical relationships between the known mapped distribution of active blanket bog habitats and climatic variables; it is not known whether this mapped distribution represents active blanket bog in an equilibrium state with current climate. It is therefore possible that the baseline models do not fully capture the climate envelope reflecting sustainable conditions for the active blanket bog habitat presence. In addition, the caveat which applies to BEMs more generally must remain, i.e. compared to process-based simulation models, BEMs are intuitive but also simplistic (Jeschke & Strayer, 2008). BEMs couple presence-absence data to derive a multivariate and correlative characterisation of the abiotic ecological niche based upon current distributions and use this to predict the available climate space under scenarios of global warming. This assumes that distributions are principally determined by intrinsic physiological tolerances relating to temperature, moisture etc., a longstanding view in ecology captured in the fundamental niche concept, whereas the realised niche is essentially the net occupancy range after accounting for biotic effects (Hutchinson, 1957). However, as BEMs utilise observed ranges for their estimates, they are using realised distributions to predict future distributions.

The final variables selected in both the GLM and GAM reflect two primary properties of the climate (temperature and water) that are key factors affecting species and habitat distribution (e.g. Whittaker *et al.*, 2007; Araújo *et al.*, 2011). However, other important environmental information is omitted in the models. Therefore, there is scope to refine the models by the inclusion of more refined topography and land cover variables; obvious candidates for the active blanket bog habitats would be further information on slope angle and aspect, which through their controls on light regimes influence evapotranspiration. For example, differences in light regimes between north- and south-facing aspects in temperate latitudes can produce differences in temperature equivalent to a move of ~200 km polewards (Austin & van Neill, 2011). It has also been widely reported that the influence of local topography may create critical climatic refugia that are important even in studies of very large areas (e.g. Ohlemuller *et al.*, 2008; Coll, 2010; Austin & Van Neill, 2011). Consequently, there is scope to incorporate more refined measures in future models which better capture the influence of topography in creating the conditions necessary for the persistent rainfall which supports blanket bog formation.

## Implications of changing climate space for active blanket bog distributions

The projected decline in the climate space associated with active blanket bog areas can be expected to have significant implications for the ecology of these complex wetland ecosystems and their associated plant and animal species adapted to live in the wet, nutrient-poor, conditions. Seasonal drying for example may affect surface micro-topography and hydrology. This in turn will influence the plant composition and habitat suitability for birds and other species. Loss of unprotected high quality wetlands such as active blanket bog will result in the direct loss of wetland biodiversity by physical removal of the habitats and most plant and invertebrate species; while degradation may cause reduced species diversity and local extinction of rare or sensitive species (Scally *et al.*, 2010). Such a climate change-driven degradation and loss may have secondary impacts on the biodiversity value of the remaining bog areas through increased isolation and fragmentation of the remnant habitat.

## Conclusions and implications for future work

Our results indicate that the distribution of active blanket bog in Ireland is regionally sensitive to climate change, most notably for lower-lying areas in the south and west of the country. Increasing temperature and precipitation changes will reduce the area that is suitable for active blanket bog development. This could have major implications for the lowland blanket bog distribution along the western Atlantic sea-board where the projected losses are greatest. Offsetting these losses are the minor climate space gains and the retention of suitable climate space in upland areas in the south and west. These changes may proportionately affect lowland more than upland blanket bog, with important conservation policy implications. Further degradation as a result of climate change may also result in peatlands becoming carbon source ecosystems with the potential to lose carbon either as trace gases such as carbon dioxide ($CO_2$) and methane ($CH_4$) or fluvial dissolved organic carbon (Koehler *et al.*, 2010).

Incorporating more detailed information into the BEMs can further improve confidence and reduce uncertainty in model estimates for the future distribution of Irish blanket bogs. Specifically, information such as bog type and altitude at a finer scale could better inform us on ABB status and type. Other information concerning e.g. underlying drift, soil conditions, and slope angle and aspect may improve model results. The distribution models presented here should be applicable to blanket bog regions outside Ireland, if data for the evaluation of the estimates were available. An extension to the work reported here has already been undertaken for active blanket bog in Ireland using ensemble projections from some of the additional BEM families implemented in BIOMOD (Coll *et al.*, 2014).

Although only the downscaled output from one GCM and scenario has been used to project climate space changes here, the methods lend themselves to using different GCM and RCM outputs from a range of scenarios (e.g. Fronzek *et al.*, 2011; Garcia *et al.*, 2012) and from different sources (e.g. Fronzek *et al.*, 2012) to better encapsulate uncertainty. Overall, such a framework would allow the identification of adaptation strategies that are robust (i.e. insensitive) to climate change uncertainties and would allow more confidence in identifying and targeting vulnerable areas of blanket bog for priority conservation measures. However, future research could also integrate such a scenarios-impacts (top-down) approach alongside a vulnerability-thresholds (bottom-up) approach (Coll & Sweeney, 2013). Rather than trying to predict impacts through individual scenarios, such an integrated approach would help to better identify critical thresholds for climate change vulnerabilities alongside the multiple other drivers of change in these sensitive systems.

## Acknowledgements

We thank: the technical and scientific support staff at NPWS (Ireland) for supplying the GIS habitat maps for Irish priority habitats and species; Graham French at the National Biodiversity Network (UK) for supplying the GIS-enabled Irish Grid data and Steve Wilkinson at the Joint Nature Conservancy Council (UK) for the priority habitats and species database containing the NI records. We also thank Ray McGrath and Tido Semmler at *Met Éireann* for providing the c4i climate change data. Without all of their goodwill, assistance and support, our progress in the methods developed here for Ireland would not have been possible. This research was supported by the Irish Environmental Protection Agency (EPA) under grants 2007-CCRP-2.26 and 2010-CCRP-DS-2.3.

## References

Allouche, O., Tsoar, A. and Kadmon, R. (2006) Assessing the accuracy of species distribution models: prevalence, kappa and the true skill statistic (TSS). *Journal of Applied Ecology*, **43**, 1223-1232.

Araújo M.B, Alagador, D., Cabeza, M., Nogues-Bravo, D. and Thuiller, W. (2011) Climate change threatens European conservation areas. *Ecology Letters*, **14**, 484-492.

Araújo, M.B. and Guisan, A. (2006) Five (or so) challenges for species distribution modelling. *Journal of Biogeography*, **33**, 1677–1688.

Araújo, M. B., Whittaker, R.J., Ladle, R.J. and Erhard, M. (2005) Reducing uncertainty in projections of extinction risk from climate change. *Global Ecology and Biogeography*, **14**, 529-538.

Araújo, M.B. and New, M. (2007) Ensemble forecasting of species distributions. *Trends in Ecology and Evolution*, **22**, 42–47.

Austin, M.P. and Van Niel, K.P. (2011) Improving species distribution models for climate change studies: variable selection and scale. *Journal of Biogeography*, **38**, 1-8.

Backeus, I. (1988) Weather variables as predictors of *Sphagnum* growth on a bog. *Holarctic Ecology*, **11**,146–150.

Barber, K.E. and Langdon, P.G. (2007) What drives the peat-based paleoclimate record? A critical test using multiproxy climate records from northern Britain. *Quaternary Science Review*, **26**: 3318–3327.

Berry, P.M., Dawson, T.P., Harrison, P.A. and Pearson, R.G. (2002) Modelling potential impacts of climate change on the bioclimatic envelope of species in Britain and Ireland. *Global Ecology and Biogeography*, **11**, 453–62.

Berry P.M., Dawson, T.P., Harrison, P.A., Pearson, R. and Butt, N. (2003) The sensitivity and vulnerability of terrestrial habitats and species in Britain and Ireland to climate change. *Journal of Nature Conservation*, **11**,15–23.

Bio, A.M.F., Alkemande, R. and Barendregt, A. (1998) Determining alternative models for vegetation response analysis – a non-parametric approach. *Journal of Vegetation Science*, **9,** 5–16.

Bonn, A., Allott, T., Hubacek, K. and Stewart, J. (2009) *Drivers of environmental change in Uplands.* Routledge, Abingdon.

Booth, R.K. (2010) Testing the climate sensitivity of peat-based paleoclimate reconstructions in mid-continental North America. *Quaternary Science Review,* **29**, 720–731.

Boylan, N., Jennings, R. and Long, M. (2008) Peat slope failure in Ireland. *Quarterly Journal of Engineering Geology and Hydrogeology*, **41**, 93-108.

Bruun, H.H., Moen, J., Virtanen, R, Grytnes, J.A., Oksanen, L. and Angerbjorn, A. (2006) Effects of altitude and topography on species richness of vascular plants, bryophytes and lichens in alpine communities. *Journal of Vegetation Science*, **17**, 37–46.

Charman, D.J. (2007) Summer water deficit variability controls on peatland water-table changes: implications for Holocene palaeoclimate reconstructions. *Holocene*, **17**, 217–227.

Charman, D.J., Barber, K.E., Blaauw, M., Langdon, P.G. and others (2009) Climate drivers for peatland palaeoclimate records. *Quaternary Science Review*, **28**, 1811–1819.

Clark, J.M., Gallego-Sala, A.V., Allott, T.E.H, Chapman, S.J. and others (2010) Assessing the vulnerability of blanket peat to climate change using an ensemble of statistical bioclimatic envelope models. *Climate Research*, **45**,131–150.

Coblentz, D.D., Riitters, K.H. (2004) Topographic controls on the regional-scale biodiversity of the south-western USA. *Journal of Biogeography*, **31**, 1125-1138.

Coll, J. (2010) *Climate Change and Europe's Mountains*. In: Price, M.F. (ed.) *Europe's ecological backbone: recognising the true value of our mountains.* European Environment Agency (EEA) Report No 6/2010, pp252.

Coll, J., Bourke, D., Sweeney, J., Gormally, M. and Sheehy Skeffington, M. (2011) Developing a predictive modelling capacity for a climate change vulnerable blanket bog habitat: Assessing baseline climate relationships. *Irish Geography*, **44** (1), 27-60.

Coll, J., Bourke, D., Gormally, M., Sheehy Skeffington, M. and Sweeney, J. (2013) *Winners and Losers: Climate Change Impacts on Biodiversity in Ireland.* Environmental Protection Agency CCRP Report No. 19, Wexford.

Coll, J., Bourke, D., Gormally, M., Sheehy Skeffington, M. and Sweeney J. (2014) Projected loss of active blanket bogs in Ireland. *Climate Research*, **C1202**. doi: 10.3354/cr01202.

Coll, J., Gibb, S.W., Harrison, J. (2005) *Modelling future climates in the Scottish Highlands - an approach integrating local climatic variables and regional climate model outputs*. In: Thompson, D.B.A., Price, M.F. and Galbraith, C.A. (eds) *Mountains of northern Europe: conservation, management, people and nature*. TSO Scotland, Edinburgh, 103–119.

Coll, J., Gibb, S.W., Price, M.F., McClatchey, J. and Harrison, J. (2010) Developing site scale projections of climate change in the Scottish Highlands. *Climate Research*, **45**, 71–85.

Coll, J. and Sweeney, J. (2013) *Current and future vulnerabilities to climate change in Ireland.* Environmental Protection Agency CCRP Report No. 29, Wexford.

Coll, J., Woolf, D., Gibb, S. and Challenor, P. (2013b) Sensitivity of ferry services to the Western Isles of Scotland to changes in wave and wind climate. *Journal of Applied Meteorology and Climatology,* **52**, 1069–1084.

Connolly, J., Holden, N. and Ward, S. (2007) Mapping peatlands in Ireland using a rule-based methodology and digital data. *Soil Science Society of America Journal,* **71**, 492–499.

Crossman, N.D., and Bass, D.A. (2008) Application of common predictive habitat techniques for post-border weed risk management. *Diversity and Distributions,* **14**, 213–224.

Currie, D.J. (1991) Energy and large-scale patterns of animal-species and plant species richness. *American Naturalist,* **137**, 27-49.

Donnelly, A., Caffarra, A., Albanito, F. and Jones, M. (2008) *The Impact of Climate Change on Semi-Natural Ecosytems in Ireland.* In: *Climate Change in Ireland: Refining the Impacts.* Dublin, Environmental Protection Agency, 192pp.

Douglas, C. (1998) *Blanket bog conservation.* In: O'Leary G. and Gormely, F. (eds) *Towards a conservation strategy for the bogs of Ireland.* Dublin, Irish Peatland Conservation Council, 205-222.

Dykes, A.P., Gunn, J. and Convery, K.J. (2008) Landslides in blanket peat on Cuilcagh Mountain, northwest Ireland. *Geomorphology,* **102 (3-4)**, 325-340.

Eaton, J.M., McGoff, N.M., Byrne, K.A., Leahy, P. and Kiely, G. (2008) Land cover change and soil organic carbon stocks in the Republic of Ireland 1851–2000. *Climate Change,* **91**, 317–334.

Elith, J. and Burgman, M. (2002) *Predictions and their validation: rare plants in the Central Highlands, Victoria, Australia.* In: Scott, J.M., Heglund, P.J., Morrison, M.L., Haufler, J.B., Raphael, M.G., Wall, W.A., and Samson, F.B. (eds) *Predicting species occurrences. Issues of accuracy and scale.* Island Press, Washington DC, 303-313.

Engler, R., Randin, C.F., Thuiller, W., Dullinger, S. and others (2011) 21st century climate change threatens mountain flora unequally across Europe. *Global Change Biology*, doi: 10.1111/

Fielding, A.H. and Bell, J.F. (1997) A review of methods for the assessment of prediction errors in conservation presence/absence models. *Environmental Conservation*, **24**, 38–49.

Foody, G.M. (2002) Status of land cover classification accuracy assessment. *Remote Sensing of the Environment,* **80**,185–201.

Freeman, C., Evans, C.D., Monteith, D.T., Reynolds, B. and Fenner, N. (2001) Export of organic carbon from peat soils. *Nature*, **412**, 785.

Freeman, C., Fenner, N., Ostle, N.J., Kang, H. and others (2004) Export of dissolved organic carbon from peatlands under elevated carbon dioxide levels. *Nature*, **430**, 195–198.

Freeman, E. (2011) Presence-Absence Model Evaluation. CRAN R Library repository. Available at: http://cran.r-project.org/. Last accessed 09/03/11.

Fronzek, S., Carter, T.R. and Jylhä, K. (2012) Representing two centuries of past and future climate for assessing risks to biodiversity in Europe. *Global Ecology and Biogeography*, **21**, 19-35.

Fronzek, S., Luoto, M. and Carter, R.C. (2006) Potential effect of climate change on the distribution of palsa mires in subarctic Fennoscandia. *Climate Research*, **32**, 1-12.

Garcia, R.A., Burgess, N.D., Cabeza, M., Rahbek, C. and Araújo, M.B. (2012) Exploring consensus in 21st century projections of climatically suitable areas for African vertebrates. *Global Change Biology*, **18 (4),** 1253-1269.

Guisan, A. and Zimmerman, N.E. (2000) Predictive habitat distribution models in ecology. *Ecological Modelling*, **135**, 147-186.

Guisan, A., Edwards, T.C. and Hastie, T. (2002) Generalized linear and generalized additive models in studies of species distributions: setting the scene. *Ecological Modelling*, **157**, 89-100.

Guisan, A. and Thuiller, W. (2005) Predicting species distributions: offering more than simple habitat models. *Ecology Letters*, **9**, 993-1009.

Hammond, R.F. (1984) *The Classification of Irish peats as surveyed by the National Soil Survey of Ireland*. 7th International Peat Congress, Dublin, Ireland.

Harrell, E.E. (2001) *Regression Modeling Strategies*. Springer-Verlag, New York, NY.

Hastie, T. and Tibshirani, R. (1990) *Generalized Additive Models.* Chapman and Hall, London.

Heikkinen, R.K., Luoto, M., Araújo, M.B., Virkalla, M., Thuiler, W. and Sykes, M.T. (2006) Methods and uncertainties in bioclimatic envelope modelling under climate change. *Progress in Physical Geography*, **30**(6), 751-777.

Heikkinen, R.K., Luoto, M., Kuussaari, M. and Poyry, J. (2004) Effects of habitat cover, landscape structure and spatial variables on the abundance of birds in an agricultural-forest mosaic. *Journal of Applied Ecology*, **41**, 824-835.

Holden, J. (2009) *Upland hydrology*. In: Bonn, A., Allott, T., Hubacek, K. and Stewart, J. (eds) *Drivers of environmental change in uplands.* Routledge, London, 113–134.

Hossell, J.E., Briggs, B., Hepburn, I.R. (2000) *Climate change and UK nature conservation: a review of the impact of climate change on UK species and habitat conservation policy.* Department of the Environment, Transport and the Regions, London.

House, J.I., Orr, H.G., Clark, J.M., Gallego-Sala, A.V., Freeman, C., Prentice, I.C., Smith, P. (2010) Climate change and the British Uplands: evidence for decision-making. *Climate Research*, **45**, 3-12.

Huntley, B., Green, R.E., Collingham, Y.C., Hill, J.K., Willis, S.G., Bartlein, P.J., Cramer, W., Hagemeijer, W.J.M. and Thomas, C.D. (2004) The performance of models relating species geographical distributions to climate is independent of trophic level. *Ecology Letters*, **7**, 417–26.

Hutchinson, G.E. (1957) Concluding remarks. Population studies: Animal ecology and demography. *Cold Spring Harbor Symp. Quantative Biology*, **22**,415-427.

Jeschke, J.M. and Strayer, D.L. (2008) Usefulness of Bioclimatic Models for Studying Climate Change and Invasive Species. *Annals of the New York Academy of Science*, **1134**, 1-24.

JNCC (2007) *Second Report by the UK under Article 17 on the implementation of the Habitats Directive from January 2001 to December 2006.* Peterborough, Joint Nature Conservation Committee, pp20.

Jones, M.B., Donnelly, A. and Albanito, F. (2006) Responses of Irish vegetation to future climate change. *Biology and Environment: Proceedings of the Royal Irish Academy,* **106B** (3), 323-334.

Jones, C.C. and Reichard, S. (2009) Current and Potential Distributions of Three Non-native Invasive Plants in the Contiguous USA. *Natural Areas Journal*, **29** (4), 332-343.

Koehler, A., Sottocornola, M. and Kiely, G. (2010) How strong is the current carbon sequestration of an Atlantic blanket bog? *Global Change Biology*, **17**, 309–319.

Kurbatova, J., Li, C., Tatarinov, F., Varlagin, A., Shalukhina, N. and Olchev, A. (2009) Modelling of the carbon dioxide fluxes in European Russia peat bogs. *Environmental Research Letters*, **4** (4), 1-5.

Lean, J.L., Rind, D.H. (2009) How will Earth's surface temperature change in future decades? *Geophysical Research Letters*, **36**, L15708, doi:10.1029/2009GL038932.

Lindsay, R.A. (1995) *Bogs: the ecology, classification and conservation of ombrotrophic mires*. Scottish Natural Heritage, Battleby.

Lindsay, R.A., Charman, D.J., Everingham, F., O'Reilly, R.M., Palmer, M.A., Rowell, T.A. and Stroud, D.A. (1988) *The flow country: the Peatlands of Caithness and Sutherland.* Nature Conservancy Council, Peterborough.

Luoto, M., Fronzek, S. and Zuidhoff, F.S. (2004) Spatial modelling of palsa mires in relation to climate in northern Europe. *Earth Surface Processes and Landforms*, **29**, 1373–1387.

Luoto, M. and Heikkinen, R.K. (2008) Disregarding topographical heterogeneity biases species turnover assessments based on bioclimatic models. *Global Change Biology,* **14**, 483-494.

MacNally, R. (2000) Regression and model-building in conservation biology, biogeography and ecology: the distinction between - and reconciliation of - 'predictive' and explanatory models. *Biodiversity and Conservation*, **9**, 655-671.

Marmion, M., Luoto, M., Heikkinen, R.K. and Thuiller, W. (2009) The performance of state-of-the-art modelling techniques depends on geographical distribution of species. *Ecological Modelling*, **220**, 3512–3520.

Marmion, M., Parviainen, M., Luoto, M., Heikkinen, R.K. and Thuiller, W. (2008) Evaluation of consensus methods in predictive species distribution modelling. *Diversity and Distributions*, **15**, 59-69.

McCullagh, P. and Nelder, J. (1989) *Generalized Linear Models.* Chapman and Hall, London

McGrath, R. and Lynch, P. (eds) (2008) *Ireland in a Warmer World: Scientific Predictions of the Irish Climate in the Twenty-First Century*. Community Climate Change Consortium for Ireland (C4I), Dublin, pp118.

Monteith, D.T., Stoddard, J.L., Evans, C.D., de Wit, H.A. and others (2007) Dissolved organic carbon trends resulting from changes in atmospheric deposition chemistry. *Nature*, **450**, 537–540.

Moore, P.D. and Bellamy, D.J. (1973). *Peatlands.* Unwin Brothers, Woking.

McPherson, J.M., Jetz, W. and Rogers, D.J. (2004) The effect of species' range sizes in the accuracy of distribution models: ecological phenomenon or statistical artefact? *Journal of Applied Ecology*, **41**, 811–823.

Neter, J., Wasserman, W. and Kutner, M.H. (1990) *Applied Linear Statistical Models.* 3rd Edition, Irwin, Boston.

NPWS (2008). *The Status of EU Protected Habitats and Species in Ireland.* Dublin, National Parks and Wildlife Service, Department of the Environment, Heritage and Local Government**:** pp135.

O'Brien, R.M. (2007) A Caution Regarding Rules of Thumb for Variance Inflation Factors. *Quality and Quantity,* **41**, 673-690.

Ohlemuller, R., Anderson, B.J., Araújo, M.B., Butchart, S.H.M., Kudrna, O.R. Ridgely, R.S. and Thomas, C.D. (2008) The coincidence of climatic and species rarity: high risk to small-range species from climate change. *Biology Letters,* **4**, 568-572.

Parviainen, M., Luoto, M. (2007) Climate envelopes of mire complex types in Fennoscandia. *Geografiska Annaler Series A Physical Geography*, **89A**,137–151.

Pearce, J. and Ferrier, S. (2000) Evaluating the predictive performance of habitat models developed using logistic regression. *Ecological Modelling*, **133**, 225-245.

Pearsall, W.H. (1965) *Mountains and moorlands.* Bloomsbury Books, London.

R Development Core Team (2011). CRAN R Library repository. Available at: http://cran.r-project.org/.

Richerson, P.J. and Lum, K.L. (1980) Patterns of plant species diversity in California: relation to weather and topography. *American Naturalist*, **116**, 504-536.

Rodwell, J.S., Pigott, C.D., Ratcliffe, D.A., Malloch, A.J.C. and others (1992) *British Plant Communities, Vol 3. Grasslands and Montane Communities.* Cambridge University Press, Cambridge.

Rohan, P.K. (1986) *The climate of Ireland.* The Stationery Office, Dublin.

Scally, L., Waldren, S., Atalah, J., Brown, M. and others (2010) *Biodiversity and Environmental Change an Integrated Study Encompassing a Range of Scales, Taxa and Habitats (Biochange).* Draft Technical Project Report, EPA, Wexford.

Sheehy Skeffington, M.J. and O'Connell, C. (1998) Peatlands of Ireland. *Studies in Irish Limnology.* In: Giller, P. (ed.) *Societas Internationalis Limnologiae* (SIL). Dublin, 39-66.

Sweeney, K., Fealy, R., McElwain, L., Siggins, L., Sweeney, J. and Trinies, T. (2008) *Changing Shades of Green: The environmental and cultural impacts of climate change in Ireland.* The Irish American Climate Project & Rockefeller Family Fund, California, pp48.

Sweeney, J. (2014) Regional weather and climates of the British Isles – Part 6: Ireland. *Weather*, **69(1)**, 20-27.

Sweeney, J. and Fealy, R. (2002) A preliminary investigation of future climate scenarios for Ireland. *Biology and Environment: Proceedings of the Royal Irish Academy*, **102B(3)**, 121-128.

Sweeney. J. and Fealy, R. (2003) *Establishing Reference Climate Scenarios.* In: Sweeney, J. (ed.). *Climate Change Scenarios and Impacts For Ireland.* Dublin, Environmental Protection Agency. ERTRI Report 15, pp 247.

Thuiller, W. (2003) BIOMOD - optimizing predictions of species distributions and projecting potential future shifts under global change. *Global Change Biology*, **9**, 1353-1362.

Thuiller, W., Albert, C., Araújo, M.B. and others (2008) Predicting global change impacts on plant species' distributions: future challenges. *Perspectives in Plant Ecology, Evolution and Systematics*, **9**, 137–152.

Thuiller, W. (2004) Patterns and uncertainties of species' range shifts under climate change. *Global Change Biology*, **10**, 2020–2027.

Thuiller, W., Araújo, M.B. and Lavorel, S. (2004) Do we need land-cover data to predict species distributions in Europe? *Journal of Biogeography*, **31**, 353–361.

Thuiller, W., Broennimann, O., Hughes, G.O., Alkemade, J.M.R., Midgley, G.F. and Corsi, F. (2006) Vulnerability of African mammals to anthropogenc climate change under conservative land transformation assumptions. *Global Change Biology*, **12**, 424–440.

Tomlinson, R.W. (2005) Soil carbon stocks and changes in the Republic of Ireland. *Journal of Environmental Management*, **76 (1)**, 77-93.

Velleman, P.F. and Welsh, R.E. (1981) Efficient computing of regression diagnostics. *The American Statistician*, **35(4)**, 234–242.

Warburton, J., Holden, J. and Mills, A.J. (2004) Hydrological controls of surficial mass movements in peat. *Earth-Science Reviews*, **67(1-2)**, 139-156.

Whittaker, R.J., Nogues-Bravo, D. and Araújo, M.B. (2007) Geographic gradients of species richness: a test of the water-energy conjecture of Hawkins *et al.* (2003) using European data for five taxa. *Global Ecology and Biogeography*, **16**, 76–89.

Wieder, R.K. and Vitt, D.H. (2006) *Boreal peatland ecosystems*. Springer, Berlin.

Wintle, B.A., Elith, J. and Potts, J.M. (2005) Fauna habitat modelling and mapping: A review and case study in the Lower Hunter Central Coast region of NSW. *Austral Ecology*, **30**, 719-738.

Yallop, A.R., Clutterbuck, B. and Thacker, J. (2010) Increases in humic dissolved organic carbon export from upland peat catchments: the role of temperature, declining sulphur deposition and changes in land management. *Climate Research*, **45**, 43–56.

Young, R.L., Weinberg, J., Vieira, V., Ozonoff, A. and Webster, T.F. (2011) Generalized additive models and inflated type I error rates of smoother significance tests. *Computational Statistics and Data Analysis*, **55**, 366-374.

# Chapter 4. Recent Work of the Thorne & Hatfield Moors Conservation Forum

**Helen R. Kirk**
Executive Secretary, Thorne & Hatfield Moors Conservation Forum

## Introduction

Formed in 1989, Thorne & Hatfield Moors Conservation Forum acts as an umbrella for a wide range of like-minded organisations. Its extensive network is drawn from voluntary organisations and natural history societies, and it has observers from statutory agencies and local authorities. The rationale behind creating an organisation, which might discuss and debate key issues relating to the conservation of Thorne and Hatfield Moors and then act as a separate entity whilst remaining collaborative, made sense. The Executive Committee could act in a timely manner as it was not constrained by internal protocols which might prevent or water down the message if each organisation acted individually. Collective action was powerful and there was benefit from working together.

The Forum has on occasions taken on a campaigning role (for example in 1997 when English Nature proposed to de-notify parts of Thorne & Hatfield Moors of their protective SSSI status). This aspect of its work has always been underpinned by robust science, and research, survey and monitoring remain key activities. The Forum is administered by an Executive Committee.

Many of the founding members from organisations with paid staff, have since moved on, or are sadly no longer with us. The Forum has however continued to keep a local focus whilst still working with the national network; it undertakes and commissions surveys, monitoring and publishes its findings extensively in a variety of media. See http://www.thmcf.org/home.html and also http://thmcf.wordpress.com/

The posters presented at the 2014 conference provided resumes of two substantive invertebrate surveys, a 'predictive' analysis of *Thorne and Hatfield Moors Past, Present and Future Irretrievably lost or potentially recoverable? Invaders and residents, welcome and unwelcome.* The fourth poster was produced by Lauren Mansell a student of Dr Nicki Whitehouse (then Queen's University Belfast) and provides a report on her *"Recent palaeoecological Research in the Humberhead Levels".*

## Thorne and Hatfield Moors Past, Present and Future Irretrievably lost or potentially recoverable? Invaders and residents, welcome and unwelcome.

These two illustrated posters raise questions and discuss issues which the management of Thorne and Hatfield Moors will have to address as the world faces warming and where rainfall becomes more intense and less predictable in some areas. The question was posed about the removal of birch and whether it could have the opposite effect to that desired and lead to further desiccation? The question is asked, should the slightly raised area at Hatfield Moors be managed as wet heath or bog? A case is presented that any future management strategy needs to address the whole, rather than just the lowland raised mire aspects. Any plan needs to take account of the manifold complexities, from the ecology of single species (including little understood invertebrates to the autecology of wetland plant species) to landscape-scale issues including the record preserved in the peat and other sediments in the Humberhead Levels.

## Recent Palaeoecological Research in the Humberhead Levels

Mire and floodplain deposits hold useful records of past environmental and climatic changes. Floodplain and mire ecosystems have been infrequently investigated within the same landscape setting. The research aimed to identify threshold events using fossil beetle remains in floodplain and mire deposits. Beetles were chosen as they are considered as excellent indicators of past climatic and environmental changes (e.g. they can indicate flooding events). Testing whether or not the systems react to change in a similar manner allows review of Holocene (11,700 years ago to present) climate change in greater detail. More detail is provided in **Volume 8** (2011) of the *Thorne & Hatfield Moors Papers "Recent palaeoecological research on Hatfield Moors and the River Torne Floodplain".*

## Inkle Moor Invertebrate Survey 2012

The findings from the Inkle Moor Invertebrate Survey undertaken in 2012 were reported at a Seminar on 23rd September 2013 although not all determinations had been completed at this point and further research is continuing. This collaborative venture was made possible consequent upon a successful funding application to Defra through the IDB Grant Scheme as detailed above. Appreciation is extended to Kieran Sheehan (JBA) particularly and to officers of Natural England (NE) for their support and assistance. The fieldwork and sorting was undertaken by Helen Kirk and Peter Kendall with assistance from Ian McDonald. The final determinations for the report were received and the final text was produced as a Forum Technical Report. Some 64 species of Arachnids, 19 of Auchenorrhyncha (frog, plant and leafhoppers), 248 of Coleoptera, around 60 of Diptera, 21 of Heteroptera (aquatic and terrestrial true bugs), 46 of Hymenoptera: Aculeate, 24 of Hymenoptera: Parasitica, 25 of Opilionids, Myriapoda and isopoda, around 170 species of Lepidoptera are also known from the site; there are 16 species of Mollusca. The survey was able to confirm the continued presence of many quality habitat indicators, and one determiner wrote of [Inkle Moor fen] that it is clearly one of the most important water beetle habitats on the Humberhead Peatlands, with a fauna dominated by scarce and localised species. Perhaps the most significant find was that of a UK first for the bug *Streptanus okaensis.* The Forum Executive place on record their appreciation to all the specialists who painstakingly worked through volumes of material, much of it in poor condition, largely because of the chosen pitfall trap methodology.

## The Yorkshire Triangle Invertebrate Survey 2013

This project was initiated, with NE approval to inform JBA and the LWT about the status of target species of invertebrates which were known historically from the area known as the Yorkshire Triangle. An update on target species would inform the implementation of the Water Level Management Plan. The fieldwork and sorting was undertaken by Helen Kirk with determinations being made by a range of specialists. Identifications of Coleoptera were completed and the contrast with Inkle Moor was instructive, particularly in the total dominance of the ground beetle *Pterostichus rhaeticus*, over 400 of which were painstakingly dissected by Peter Kendall!

## The Forum, our aims:

1. To conserve the biodiversity, and the geological, palaeoecological, archaeological and historic features of Thorne and Hatfield Moors and the wider Humberhead Levels,

2. To promote Thorne and Hatfield Moors as a natural and cultural resource, at all levels.

3. To encourage high quality research to provide a scientific basis for the conservation of Thorne and Hatfield Moors.

4. To disseminate knowledge and understanding of Thorne and Hatfield Moors, and of the issues affecting them.

5. To facilitate communication and co-operation between organisations that share the above objectives.

6. To encourage understanding and enjoyment of wildlife and the countryside through education programmes aimed at the community.

# Chapter 5. Farming on the peatlands of the Falkland Islands

**Jim McAdam**
Agri Food and Biosciences Institute, Queen's University Belfast and the United Kingdom Falkland Islands Trust

## Summary

The Falkland Islands (Long 57-62°W; Lat 51-53°S), land area 12,200km$^2$ have a cool temperate (2.2°C - 9.4°C), oceanic climate. Rainfall varies between 400-800mm and is lowest in spring. The islands were glaciated only on the highest ground with surrounding land affected by a periglacial environment. During the Post-glacial period acid, organic soils have formed mainly because of low temperature and the impervious clay-rich subsoil creating conditions which favour waterlogging. Upland peat, lowland peat or tussac (coastal) peat cover a large area of the entire land surface. Vegetation is typically 'dwarf shrub heath' on drier soils and magellanic moorland on wetter soils. Agriculture is confined to extensive sheep farming in large enclosures (89% > *c.* 2000 ha).

In the early days of the Colony (early 1800s) cattle roamed the islands and sheep were first introduced in the 1860s. They quickly became the main source of income on the (approx. 30) large farms which existed up until the early 1980s. Lord Shackleton's Economic Survey (1976) recommending subdivision of the large farm units and transferring land ownership to local owners transformed the agricultural industry on the islands. Subsequently, the building of a certified abattoir in the early 2000s created further major opportunities. Traditionally, pasture improvement through reseeding and fertilising was practiced only on a very small scale. Recently the development of pastures with improved grasses and legumes coupled with rotational grazing has received much greater priority than previously. There are concerns that climate change predictions have indicated a steady temperature rise resulting in an unfavourable precipitation-evapotranspiration balance and other factors may contribute to the instability of the peatlands. Now and in the future, agricultural management practices will play a key role in ecosystem services delivery and climate change mitigation in the islands.

**Keywords:** climate change, overgrazing, farm restructuring, ecosystem services

## Introduction

### (i) Background

The Falkland Islands are an archipelago of 782 islands (Woods, 2001) situated in the South Atlantic Ocean between latitudes 51°S and 53°S and longitudes 57°W and 62°W. They cover an area of *c.* 12,200km$^2$ and are approximately 500 kilometres from the nearest point on mainland South America. The climate is cool/ temperate/ oceanic, mean January temperature is 9.4°C, mean for July 2.2°C, and ground frosts can occur throughout the year. Rainfall is low with a mean annual precipitation at Stanley of 640 mm. Rainfall is unevenly distributed across the islands, is lowest in spring and this, combined with strong winds, reduces plant growth (McAdam, 1985; Summers & McAdam, 1993). Climatic variation across the Falkland Islands archipelago is poorly understood. Recent climate change predictions estimate approximately 3°C increase in mean annual air temperature over the next 80 years and no appreciable change in rainfall though given such a temperature rise, change in frequency and severity of rainfall can be predicted (Jones, Harpham & Lister, 2014).

### (ii) Soils and Peatlands

Soil formation and vegetation cover have been described in McAdam (2013). A typical Falkland soil comprises a shallow (usually no deeper than 30cm) peaty horizon overlying a compact, poorly drained, silty clay subsoil (Figure 1). Mineral soils occur in areas wherever the underlying geology is exposed, particularly on mountain tops and in eroded and coastal areas. Most Falkland soils are shallow peats (less than 30cm deep and too shallow to qualify as Histosols) but in places deposits of 11-12m have been recorded. They have a pH in the range 4.1 to 5.0 and are deficient in calcium and phosphate (Cruickshank, 2001).

The IUCN define peatlands as 'areas of land with a naturally accumulated layer of peat formed from carbon-rich dead and decaying plant material under waterlogged conditions'. Joosten & Clarke (2002), define peats as 'sedentarily accumulated material consisting of at least 30% (dry mass) of dead organic material'. Most soils in the Falklands come under the definition of peat as they have a fibric surface horizon >20% (OC organic carbon) in upper layers (this is more than the 30% definition of organic material above); deeper layers tend to be sapric. The International Mire Conservation Group Global Peatland Database (Joosten, 2010) cites the Falklands as having 11,408 ha of peatlands (93.7% of total land cover). In reality no proper soil survey of the Falklands has been carried out. The peatlands of the Falklands have been described by McAdam & Upson (2012) and McAdam (2013) among others.

**Figure 1: Typical soil profiles from the Falkland Islands (photographs courtesy of R. Burton).**

King *et al.* (1968) carried out a Land Systems Analysis of the Falkland Islands. This involved some soil description and depth profiling. Apart from a brief scientific visit by Etcheverere (1975) and Cruickshank (2001), Maltby & Legge (2003) and Burton & Leeds-Harrison (2007), have been the only soil scientists/surveyors to attempt to describe the soils. There is no comprehensive soil map available. Burton & Leeds-Harrison (2007) characterised the Islands' minefields, a legacy of

Argentine occupation in 1982, for a feasibility study, recording 186 profiles for texture, depth, pH but not OC or bulk density. Burton, McAdam (T) and Marengo have recently been trying to construct a soil map based on surface drift geology, the Land Systems Analysis (see above) and soil profiling from a limited range of sources. This work was part of a larger (EU funded) project to determine the potential impact of climate change on the terrestrial ecosystems of the Falklands (Upson & McAdam, 2014). This work will have significant impact on the future development of farming on the islands.

### (iii) Vegetation

The main vegetation types, acid grasslands dominated by *Cortaderia pilosa* and dwarf shrub heathland dominated by *Empetrum rubrum* (Ericaceae), have been little altered over the vegetation history of the islands, but scrub communities dominated by *Chiliotrichum diffusum* (Asteraceae) or *Hebe elliptica* (Plantaginaceae) would have been much more widespread before the introduction of livestock as was a coastal community dominated by the tall grass, *Poa flabellata* which today survives mainly on small offshore islands. There is no native tree cover. Peatland types and vegetation cover have been described by McAdam & Upson (2012), and McAdam (2013). Some reseeding has been carried out using introduced European forage species but most of the grassland is extensively grazed throughout the year without serious impact as much of the material is indigestible.

## Land use and Farming in the Falklands

### (i) Early development

The islands had no indigenous human population and human impact on the landscape only began with the first settlement approximately 250 years ago, when cattle, pigs, sheep and goats were introduced by French settlers (Summers & McAdam, 1993). The earliest attempts to farm sheep in the islands were by the Whittington brothers who, in East Falkland between 1835 and 1840, successfully introduced Leicester rams from England for crossing with ewes from Montevideo in Uruguay. This was done in an attempt to produce a breed suitable for the Falkland Islands.

However, G. Rennie, Governor of the Falkland Islands in a letter to *The Times* 21 January 1857, wrote "Up to the present time no settler in the Falkland Islands has ever maintained himself by agriculture alone and the numerous experiments I made – convince me that it is impossible to do so". Despite Rennie's pessimism, sheep were farmed commercially from the 1860s (in 1874 the status of the colony was officially described as "sheep farming") numbers increasing up to a maximum of 800,000 in the early 1900s. This population was probably too large, and overgrazing of the better pastures may have led to the reduction in numbers of sheep after the turn of the century. Stock numbers declined to about 600,000 by 1930 and remained relatively constant (at a mean stocking density of approximately 1 sheep per 2ha) until early in the 1980s when a programme of farm sub-division was introduced (McAdam, 1984a; Summers & McAdam, 1993).

**Figure 2: Farming in the Falklands is based on sheep production for wool.**

The total wool clip over the years followed the trend in numbers but when the population declined after 1900, the wool clip remained static at around 2,100 tonnes because improvements in individual wool yield compensated for the reduction in numbers.

Gibbs (1946) stated that the approximate average density of sheep "varies from 1.09 acres (0.44 ha) per sheep on the best estate to 7.43 acres (3.01 ha) per sheep on the worst". At present, sheep density is roughly one sheep per two hectares although this varies enormously from area to area. Adie (1951, reprinted 2012) gave one of the first published descriptions of the traditional nature of sheep farming in the islands.

The sheep are mainly Corriedale and Polwarth breeds, but other breeds, particularly pure Romney and pure Merino, have been crossed with the stock (Figure 2). Both the Corriedale and Polwarth have proved suitable for the islands for they can withstand the rigours of the climate and produce a fine wool which fetches a good price. The climate is not suited to pure-bred Merinos but the crossing of Merino blood with Corriedale has greatly improved the wool quality. The Department of Agriculture continues to test alternative breeds for the changing market demands in the Falklands.

The development of the present flocks progressed by trial and error during the early years and a number of unsatisfactory cross-bred sheep resulted. However, following the detailed recommendations of Munro (1924), the first agriculturalist to visit the islands, some attempt was made to improve the stock by importing pedigree rams. This resulted in an increase in wool yield between the 1920s and 1966. The mean wool yield per sheep, which was 2.39 kg over the years 1890-1900, increased to 3.08 kg by 1919, 3.47 kg by 1940, was 3.88 kg in 1966, 3.46 kg in 1972, 3.75 kg in 1983, 3.90 kg in 1993 and, 3.75 kg in 2013 (DoA Farming Statistics).

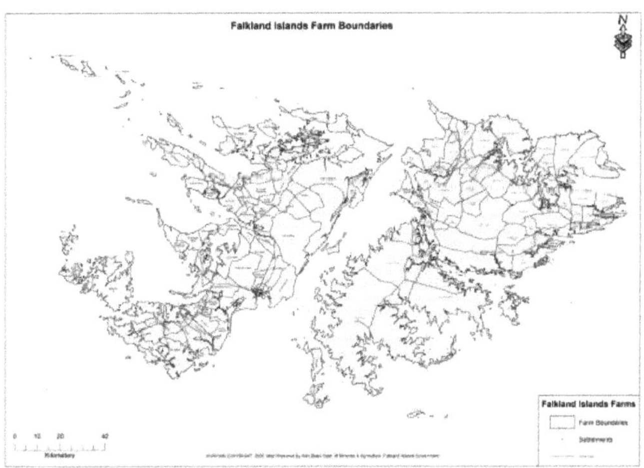


**Figure 3: Farm boundaries in the Falkland Islands.**

## (i) Farm structure

It is only since 1980, and particularly during 1984 to 1988, that the farming structure in the Falklands has undergone the first changes of any note in the entire history of the colony. Up until then, the estates were all large, with the ownership of the land divided amongst very few people. In 1979, there were thirty-six farms, seventeen on East Falkland, seven on West Falkland and twelve on the smaller islands. Of the total, nine were "sole traders" or partnerships, and another four could have been defined as owner-occupied in that the farm residents held more than 50 per cent of the company shareholding (Shackleton, 1976). The other twenty-three farms were owned by a total of fourteen companies: the Falkland Islands Company, with eight farms, being the biggest. Under this scheme, farms on East Falkland varied from 31,050 hectares to 161,000 ha in size. Those on West Falkland tended to be larger; most being in the 40,000 to 80,000 ha range. The majority of farms on the smaller islands were less than 2,000 ha (Theophilus, 1972). Each farm had a settlement (collection of owner's and workers' houses and farm buildings) in a sheltered coastal inlet so that goods could be brought in and wool taken out by sea to Stanley. Settlements were usually composed of a manager's house, houses for shepherds and navvies, a cook house, galley, social hall, garage, warehouses and shearing shed.

Peat has been the main fuel on farms until the 1970s. There are no figures available for the amount of peat used for fuel locally but because of the low population density and the dispersed nature of the farm settlements, the impact of peat extraction for fuel has been low. In 2012, peat was used to heat fewer than 2% of houses in Stanley but almost 20% of rural (mostly farm) houses (FIG, 2013). Increasingly, farm settlements use wind turbines for energy.

The only small paddocks on the farm tend to be those adjacent to the settlement where milk cattle, young stock, stud rams and working horses are kept. Hay was sometimes cut from these paddocks where fertility is high as a result of heavy stocking and application of artificial fertilisers. The rest of the farm was sub-divided into large enclosures, over 25% of which were over 2,000 ha. The siting of fence lines has been largely based on convenience, distribution of vegetation types and ease of gathering sheep. For example, fences are often sited on the isthmus of a large promontory. The whole farm of Port Stephens (before sub-division) was divided from its neighbour Fox Bay West, by a fence on an isthmus 2 km wide. Traditionally, the large farms employed staff to carry out all the tasks necessary to run that farm, resulting in relatively high manning levels. However, during the 1970s and up until 1982, a steady decline in the labour force through emigration or alternative employment (mainly in Stanley) led to a severe labour shortage on the farms, especially during shearing. There was little movement of labour between farms but from about 1977, itinerant shearing gangs have been an important development. Sub-division of many of the large farms into smaller one-man units did not appreciably alter this arrangement.

In his economic survey of the islands, Lord Shackleton (1976) recommended that the economy (which he presumed would continue to be based on agriculture) would only survive if farms were sub-divided and sold to the local people, i.e., transferred into local ownership. He also stressed the need to introduce some form of diversification into agriculture in the islands. At that time, the average farm size was 32,500 ha and only 4% of the sheep belonged to farms wholly in local ownership.

Lord Shackleton's recommendations, although slow to be implemented initially, had already started to come about several years before the Falklands Conflict in 1982 (McAdam, 1984a). The most significant change to the existing farm structure in the Falkland Islands has been fragmentation of the larger farms into a number of smaller 'one family' units.

**Table 1: Transfer of farms and stock to private ownership.**

| | **Company owned** | **Privately owned** | **Total** |
|---|---|---|---|
| **Number of farms** | | | |
| 1979 | 23 | 14 | 37 |
| 1988 | 9 | 75* | 84 |
| **% of total sheep** | | | |
| 1979 | 95.7 | 4.3 | |
| 1988 | 46.0 | 54.0 | |
| | | | |

(* Includes five Falkland Islands Co Ltd Share Farms)

The creation of small farm units was the most significant event in the history of farming in the Falklands, so it is worth considering its widespread ramifications. Initially, the industry, while recognising the social benefits of creating relatively small owner-managed or tenant farms, was concerned at the effect of sub-division on unit costs and, through fragmented breeding policies, on wool quality. Because some results of sub-division of sheep farms in South America were discouraging, early opinion in the Falkland Islands was divided. However, despite these reservations, the Falkland Islands Company – in response to the Shackleton recommendation (1976) – offered one of its major farms (Green Patch) to the Government for sub-division on an experimental basis. The offer was accepted, and the farm was sub-divided with the full co-operation of the company and on attractive financial terms arranged by the Falkland Island Government. Following this, two major farms on West Falkland were made available for sub-division. Since then, the process of sub-division proceeded at a rapid rate. The proportion of land in overseas ownership decreased from 76% in 1980 to 27% in 1988 (FIDC, 1988). There were, in 1988, 84 farms in the islands, with only a few more resulting from the sub-division of Port San Carlos planned (Table 1). In 1991, the Falkland Islands Company sold their remaining holdings to the Falkland Islands Government and almost all the Falkland Islands are now in local ownership (Figures 3 & 4).

### (ii) Performance and output

The performance of Falkland Islands' agriculture had not improved to any appreciable extent from the turn of the nineteenth century up until the radical structural change brought about by sub-division. The size of the sheep population declined gradually from the early 1900s until the 1950s but remained static over the next 20 years and although increases in the total wool clip occurred during 1971-76, these were not sustained and indeed, there was a slight decline in the late 1970s. One of the reasons for lack of progress was the lack of investment of profits in the farms. Also, profit margins had been reduced due to high costs and these have possibly contributed to the reduction in pasture improvement programmes on many farms between 1975 and 1980, which in turn may have checked output. In addition, the decline of the labour force was detrimental, although providing some saving in wages. Grassland improvement schemes, fencing, general building, and estate upkeep all suffered as a result of labour shortage.

It is interesting to consider the effect of the land reform on productivity and output from the farms. Green Patch farm was the first to be sub-divided; into six units in 1979/80 (Figure 5). The total output from the six individual family farms which replaced the one single unit, had increased substantially immediately after subdivision (Table 2).

The wool output increased from under 57 tonnes up to 77 tonnes representing a real increase (allowing for seasonal differences) from 4.7% to 6.2% of the wool produced from East Falkland. Figures from the other farm sub-divisions made during 1980-1985 indicate increased stocking rates of up to 23% and increased wool production of 27% (Figure 6; DoA, 1997; FIDC, 1988).

In the first ten years after subdivision sheep numbers increased by approximately 20% (Summers, Haydock & Kerr, 1993). This rate of increase slowed down over the next 10 years and by 2000, numbers were starting to decline. This was caused by a number of factors, principally a destocking of many of the outlying islands and the construction of an EU standard abattoir which made meat production an option and alternative to complete reliance on wool. Between 2004 and 2006 farming went through unprecedented change when farmers critically evaluated features such as sheep breed, flock structure, grazing management and product sales. They re-evaluated the age at which they could cull sheep for meat and, given the wool and meat prices at the time, most started to retain less sheep on the farm and cull at an earlier age. This resulted in a decline in total numbers of mature wethers (castrated male sheep) and a subsequent decline in overall stock numbers (Judd, 2006). Total sheep on farms was 485,937 in May 2013, down from approximately 650,000 at subdivision.

### (iii) The Abattoir

The construction of a Government funded and run abattoir to EU standards in the early 2000s was a hugely significant development as it meant that there was an alternative product to market. In its first full year of operation (2003-4), 21,466 sheep were killed. In 2012/13 this number had risen to 56,704. In addition, 490 cattle and 186 pigs were slaughtered.

### (iv) Other livestock

Given the very large paddocks in the Falklands, horses and dogs have been essential to gather sheep throughout most of the history of farming in the islands. There were typically up to 4000 horses in the islands up until the 1970s when use of motorcycles, improved fencing infrastructure and a decline in the farm labour force brought about a decline in their number. In 2013 there were 442 horses and 416 working sheepdogs. Cattle have been used for local meat and milk production and in the years leading up to subdivision there were approximately 10,000 cattle. Numbers steadily declined to below 5000 by the time the abattoir was constructed. Despite concerted efforts by the Department of Agriculture to improve stock genetics and create a National Beef Herd, there are still only 4,220 cattle (2013) on the islands.

A few farmers keep pigs, goats and reindeer, though numbers are very low (132, 133, and 243, respectively in 2012).

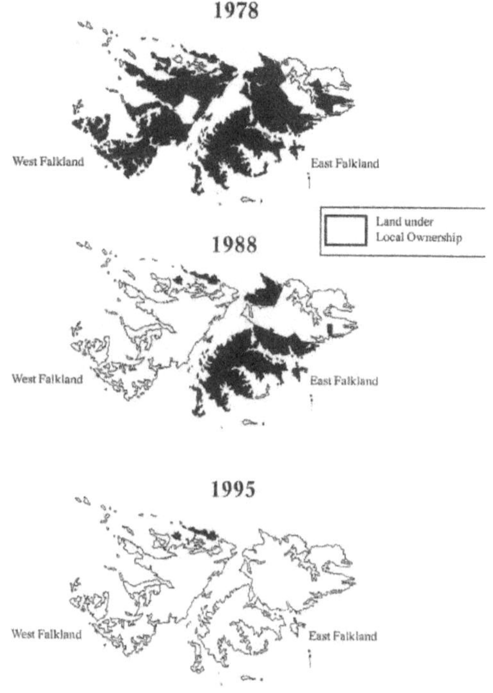


**Figure 4: Land reform in the Falkland Islands 1978-1995 (From: *Falkland Islands Farm Management Handbook and Statistical Review 1995*).**

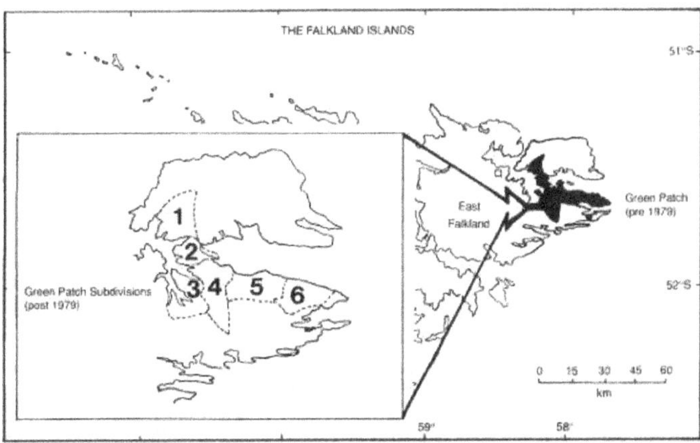


**Figure 5: The sub-division of Green Patch farm, 1979/80 (From Summers and McAdam, 1993).**

**Table 2: The productivity and output of Green Patch Farm in the last full year of operation before sub-division into six units (1979/80) and the total of the individual units in subsequent years following sub-division.**

| Year | Sheep (x 1000) | Wool (tons) | % of total East Falkland Sheep | % of total East Falkland Wool |
|---|---|---|---|---|
| 1977/78 | 15.42 | 58.47 | | |
| 1978/79 | 14.85 | 56.52 | | |
| 1979/80 | 14.86 | 53.70 | 4.38 | 4.71 |
| | | Sub-divided | | |
| 1980/81 | 17.49 | 61.51 | 5.75 | 7.10 |
| 1983/84 | 19.34 | 76.86 | 6.48 | 6.18 |
| 1984/85 | 21.58 | 73.93 | 5.96 | 6.22 |
| 1985/86 | 23.10 | 80.95 | 6.14 | 6.14 |
| 1986/87 | 22.03 | 76.66 | 5.60 | 6.10 |
| 1993/94 | 22.58 | 91.72 | 5.80 | 6.18 |
| 2011/12 | 15.85 | 63.30 | 6.65 | 6.65 |
| 2012/13 | 15.84 | 62.05 | 5.61 | 6.35 |

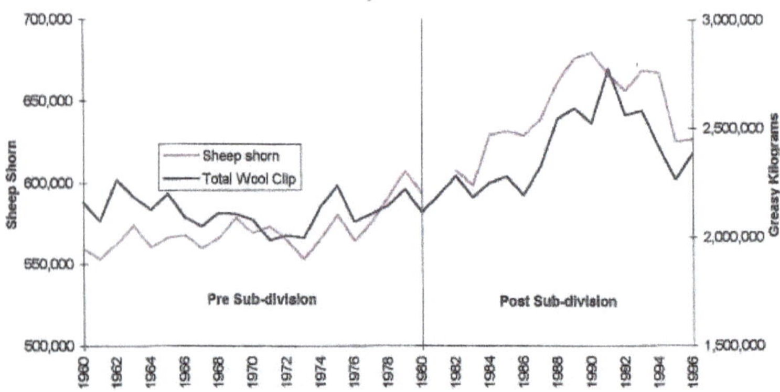


**Figure 6: Number of sheep shorn and annual wool production on all Falkland Island farms 1960-1996 (From DoA, 1997).**

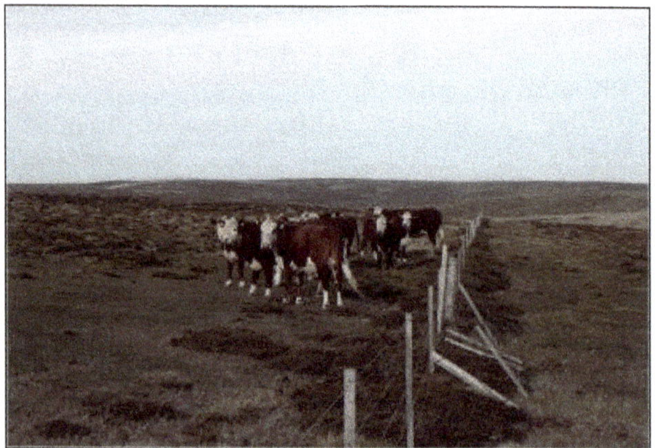

**Figure 7: Cattle numbers are low but there are moves to increase the beef herd.**

**Figure 8: Horses were traditionally used to gather sheep on the large farms.**

## (v) Sheep and grassland management

Generally, the sheep population on a farm includes the following approximate percentages of each class of sheep – 2% rams, 33% breeding ewes, 1% cast ewes (ewes at the end of their useful life), 9% maiden ewes (female sheep from about one year old until they produce their first lambs), 33% wethers and 22% hoggets (ewe, ram or wether from weaning to shearing). Ewes are generally at the end of their economically useful lives after five or six years. The non-breeding sheep tend to be the best wool producers.

Mating in April or May results in lambing in October and November. The degree of flock supervision at lambing is minimal, partly from lack of labour, but also because human disturbance can lead to lambs and ewes becoming separated. From four weeks before lambing to about six weeks afterwards, the energy demands of breeding ewes are greatest and yet pasture growth is still very slow. When the lambs are about eight weeks old, the ewes and lambs in each camp are driven into a pen for year marking (with an ear tag), castration, tail docking, counting and weaning. The timing of weaning involves balancing the needs of the growing lamb with the needs of their mothers, which must be allowed sufficient time to regain body condition before the next mating. Weather permitting, shearing commences in November and can last up to early February. Sheep under these free-ranging conditions have a cyclic reproductive pattern and, consequently, their energy demand varies over the season.

Each enclosure consist of a mosaic of vegetation types usually dominated by Whitegrass, a coarse, wiry tussock-forming grass of low livestock feed value, with only a small proportion of good quality pasture in valleys with short grazed, productive grass species("greens"), around ponds and on coastal greens. These greens tend to be overgrazed by sheep which largely ignore the poorer Whitegrass pasture, with the result that overall levels of utilisation of the pasture within enclosures are very low (only about 20% of pasture production is consumed by stock). Davies *et al.* (1971) estimated that the stocking rate for greens was 1.2 ha per ewe equivalent. This compared favourably with the poorer 'lax' Whitegrass associations – 2.1 ha per ewe – and 1.9 for uniform Whitegrass. In addition, such an uneven grazing pattern exacerbated the conflict between the sheep and an extremely numerous indigenous wild geese, as geese also tend to concentrate on the greens.

Sheep losses tend to be high, especially among young sheep. In general, from 100 ewes mated, 95 lambs will be born, 66 lambs will be marked, 59 will be weaned, 54 hoggets will be shorn and only 48 will reach 2½ years of age (Ferguson, 1980). Annual losses in adult sheep amount to 10%. The loss of 10% of the adult sheep each year is substantial since it is necessary to mate approximately four ewes to obtain one mature replacement ewe. Such a limitation on a sheep farm is obvious when one considers that the non-breeding sheep are the best producers. Diseases are not a significant problem and regular, compulsory dipping of sheep for skin parasites has eliminated these, and so dipping is no longer being practiced.

Mortality amongst lambs is primarily due to a combination of the adverse spring climate (high frequency of strong gusting winds), inability to get out of narrow gullies if they fall in and the fact that their mothers often cannot produce adequate milk from their meagre diet. Most losses in adult sheep are a result of poor nutrition and severe weather, particularly during late winter and early spring.

### (vi) Pasture improvement

Despite the problems of growing plants on the acid, peaty soils of the Falklands, the Department of Agriculture has done extensive trials on the suitability of a range of grass, legume, cereal and brassica crops (Figure 9). Depending on situation and season, these can prove economically viable, particularly to fatten stock to supply the abattoir. In 2013, 221 ha of reseeding were carried out in the Falklands, and total annual forage available on the farms was 639 ha.

The low soil pH limits growth substantially. There are limited stocks of Calcified Seaweed deposits and although these have the potential to enhance legume growth on the peat (Radic, 2010), they are limited in extent and location (Figure 10). There are huge seaweed resources in the waters around the Falklands and The United Kingdom Falkland Islands Trust (UKFIT) has supported a research programme on the potential for its use in the Falklands as stock feed and fertiliser (www.ukfit.org).

There is a need for shelter to reduce stock losses and improve plant and animal performance. UKFIT tested a range of conifer options (Figure 11) and the Department of Agriculture has demonstrated that these can be successfully grown on a range of sites though their economic viability remains unproven.

**Figure 9: Cereals, brassicas and legumes have been tested on most farms in selected areas.**

**Figure 10: Calcified seaweed deposits are the only local lime source. It has been used on a limited scale to increase soil pH (Department of Agriculture Falkland Islands).**

**Figure 11: Shelterbelt trials with Lodgepole Pine (*Pinus contorta*), West Falkland.**

**Figure 12: Burning of cultivated ground prior to reseeding. Pasture burning is largely falling out of favour but is still practiced (Dept of Agriculture, Falkland Islands).**

In the past, burning pastures in spring to reduce the standing fund of dead herbage and encourage fresh green growth was carried out (McAdam, 1984b; Figure 12). Given the fragility of the peatland ecosystem and the risk of fires getting out of control this practice is no longer encouraged.

## (vii) Research and Development

The history of agricultural research and development in the Falklands is a long one. The first official agricultural scientist to visit the Falklands (from New Zealand) was Munro (1924). Thereafter there were visits from Davies (1939) of the Welsh Plant Breeding Station and significant development and advances, often by trial and error, of individual farmers and land owners. All of these reached broadly the same conclusion - that the food resource (pasture) was not of sufficient quality to support productive livestock systems without improved grazing management or pasture improvement through fertilising and/or reseeding.

Probably the most significant visit of all was that funded by the then Overseas Development Administration in 1969 (Davies *et al.*, 1971). This was a very comprehensive visit, by a multi-disciplinary team which carried out field trials on farms. One of the main recommendations of the Davies team was to establish a permanent agricultural research unit in the Islands with the capacity to conduct field trials on which to base their advice. One of their main tasks was to test the emerging research carried out by the UK's Hill Farming Research Organisation (HFRO) in Scotland. Their work, particularly on integrating sheep nutritional requirements with pasture quality and growth into what became known as the "*two pasture system* of hill sheep management" was a huge advance in hill sheep farming in the UK and became the central core of the research unit established in the Falklands – the Grassland Trials Unit. Subsequently this became the basis for a fully equipped Department of Agriculture in the Falklands with responsibility for research, advice, plant and animal health.

(viii) Rural Life
The rural population is small (309 people in 2013) and though most are still engaged in agriculture, farm-based tourism has steadily increased in popularity in recent years and become economically more significant than sheep farming on several islands. A Government-run air service provides a vital link to outlying settlements on the few inhabited islands and to West Falkland, particularly during the summer (tourist) season. A rural roads programme, commenced in 1985, has made access to the countryside more widespread and a regular ferry service across Falkland sound in recent years has made a highly significant impact on agricultural and wider rural development.

## The future sustainability of farming on Falklands peatlands

In terms of ecosystem services delivery, the farmed peatlands of the Falkland Islands have a critical role in delivering the following services.

- *Provisioning* services - meat, wool, drinking water, land for renewable energy.
- *Regulating* services - climate change mitigation, carbon storage, water purification, flood control.
- *Supporting* services - peat accumulation, biodiversity, nutrient cycling.
- *Cultural* services - archaeology and heritage, tourism, sense of place, landscape, walking, fishing.

If farming is to have a sustainable future it must consider carefully how it delivers across the range of these services. Fundamental to delivering a balanced, sustainable land use is more knowledge of the peatland systems of the Falklands and how the biological processes they support will respond to changes in stocking and cultivation. Given that the peat cover in the Falklands is shallow and the climate harsh (cool, dry and windy), the peatlands can be considered a relatively fragile ecosystem. Hence an estimate of potential climate change and what it might mean for the components of the peatlands ecosystem and their capacity to deliver the range of ecosystem services listed above is critical. An EU-funded research project on this subject -TEFRA: Terrestrial Ecosystems of the Falklands – a Climate Change Risk Assessment (Upson, McAdam & Clubbe, 2014) has just commenced. Climate change predictions by the University of East Anglia are for a potential 3°C increase in temperature and little change in overall rainfall. This has highly significant implications for the seasonal balance of evapotranspiration from the shallow peat soils. Such a temperature rise would almost inevitably result in heavier rainfall episodes and in increased storminess. A workshop was held in the Falklands in May 2014 to enable the local population to have an input to the project and to prioritise impacts of climate change on agriculture. These were identified as having potential for:

- Increased soil erosion.
- Increased run-off/ erosion caused by high intensity rainfall events.
- Increased water use by animals in dry periods.
- Reduced water resources available for direct removal caused by changes to runoff and recharge.
- The need to increase national food security.
- The response of native grass species in pasture to increased temperature.

## Summary

Most soils in the Falkland Islands can be classed as peatlands of varying depths and, given the cool dry windy climate, grass growth is slow, highly seasonal and is of low nutritional value. Farming in the Falkland Islands consists basically of sheep grazing the peatlands in a free-ranging pattern over large enclosures which are made up of a mosaic of vegetation types. These vegetation types vary considerably in their productivity and quality but essentially most contain only a relatively small area of the more productive types – the greens, reseeded pasture and tussock-forming Whitegrass.

In the early days of the colony between 1850 and 1898, the numbers of sheep rose from just over 7,500 to 807,000. There was then a gradual decline, and numbers stabilised at around 630,000 by 1923, and remained at that level until the late 1970s. Following subdivision numbers rose to almost 700,000 and are now (2013) 485,937.

Stocking rates can be as low as 3.0 hectares per sheep. The stock are, mostly Corriedale, with Polwarths on some of the farms. Selective breeding has aimed for wool quality though now the abattoir is operational, carcass composition is of increasing importance.

Lambing rates are low, sheep mortality is generally high, but diseases are not a serious problem. Sheep have a cyclic pattern of energy demand and the high-energy demand in spring is not satisfied by the native pastures. Hence, in most cases, overall productivity of sheep is low.

As wool was the only feasible agricultural export up until 2004, as a result of poor world wool prices along with a shortage of re-investment of profits in the farms, there was some stagnation in the agricultural economy in the mid-1970s. The construction by the Government of an abattoir fundamentally altered the range of business options open to farmers.

Farm structure was characterised by large estates with the ownership of the land divided amongst relatively few people, a pattern of farming which changed little from about 1880 until the late 1970s. Since then, a radical programme of sub-division recommended by Lord Shackleton (1976) has resulted in the number of farms increasing from 36 to 84 with most of the land and sheep now in private ownership. Stocking rates and hence overall farm productivity increased in the early years of sub-division. They have fallen back in recent years, but this does not necessarily imply a decline in productivity, rather farmers adapting to the business potential of the abattoir in 2004 and restructuring their farms accordingly.

The farmed peatlands of the Falklands deliver a wide range of ecosystem services, and their sustainable development must be based on a thorough understanding of the resource and how to manage it under the potential climate change scenario of a 3°C increase in temperature over eighty years and inevitable changes in rainfall distribution and storminess.

## Acknowledgements

The author is grateful to Rodney Burton, David Ainslie, David Walton, Phil Stone, Christine Handley and Emma Jane Wells for helpful comments on, and additions to this paper. All photographs are the author's unless acknowledged otherwise. The author was a member of the Grasslands Trials Unit from 1976-78 and the United Kingdom Falkland Islands Trust (www.ukfit.org) funded the subsequent visits to the Falklands which led to the material presented in this paper.

## References

Adie, R. (1951-reprinted in 2012) The first modern account of sheep farming in the Falkland Islands. *Falkland Islands Journal*, **10** (1), 23-29.

Burton, R.G.O. and Leeds-Harrison, P.B. (2007) *Physical characteristics of the Islands' minefields*. Unpublished Field Survey Report 2007 Cranfield University, Bedford.

Cruickshank, J.G. (2001) *Falkland Soils – origins and prospects*. Unpublished Report to the Department of Agriculture, Stanley. Department of Agriculture for Northern Ireland, Belfast.

Davies, T.H., Dickson, I.A., McCrea, C.T., Mead, M. and Williams W.W. (1971) *The sheep and cattle industries of the Falkland Islands*. Overseas Development Administration, London.

Davies, W. (1939) *Grasslands of the Falkland Islands*. Government Printer, Stanley, Falkland Islands.

Department of Agriculture, (2012) *Agricultural Statistics, 2010-11*. Falkland Islands Government, Stanley.

Department of Agriculture (1997) *Falkland Islands Government, Department of Agriculture Annual Report 1996/97*. Falkland Islands Government, Stanley.

Etcheverere, P.H. (1975) Suelos y Geologia de la Islas Malvinas. *Anales de la Sociedad Cientifica, Argentina*, **Vol CXCIX** Entregas IV-VI April-June 1975, 81-98.

Ferguson, J.A. (1980) *Grasslands Trials Unit, Falkland Islands*. GTU Stanley, Falkland Islands.

FIDC (1988) *Falkland Islands Development Corporation, Annual Report 1988*. Falkland Islands Government, London Office, London.

FIG (2013) *Falkland Islands Census 2012: Statistics and data tables*. Falkland Islands Government Policy Unit, Stanley.

Gibbs, J.G. (1946) *Report of the Director of the activities of the Department of Agriculture from 1937-1946*. Unpublished Report, Falkland Islands Government, Stanley.

Jones P.D., Harpham, C. and Lister, D.H. (2014) *Construction of high spatial resolution climate scenarios for the Falkland Islands and Southern Patagonia*. Climate Research Unit, University of East Anglia, Norwich, 37pp.

Joosten, H. (2010) *The Global Peatland CO2 Picture: peatland status and drainage related emissions in all countries of the world*. Wetlands International. Available at: http://www.wetlands.org/WatchRead/tabid/56/mod/1570/articleType/ArticleView/articleId/2418/The-Global-Peatland-CO2-Picture.aspx

Joosten, H. and Clarke, D. (2002) *Wise use of mires and peatlands – Background and principles including a framework for decision making*. International Mire Conservation Group / International Peat Society, pp304.

Judd, N. (2006) *Wool and Livestock. Department of Agriculture Biennial Report 2004-2006*. Falkland Islands Government, Stanley.

Kerr, J.A. (2003) A history of grazing management in the Falkland Islands. *Falkland Islands Journal*, **8(2)**, 94-106.

King, R.B. Lang, D.M. and Blair Rains, A. (1969) *Land Systems Analysis of the Falkland Islands, with notes on the soils and grasslands*. Miscellaneous Report No 72. Land Resources Division, Directorate of Overseas Surveys, Tolworth, England.

Maltby, E. and Legg, C.J. (1983) *Problems of peatland mine clearance and site restoration on the Falkland Islands*. Report for Procurement Executive (MOD). Contract No 63997B. Dept of Geography, University of Exeter, Exeter.

McAdam, J.H. (1984a) Recent changes in Falkland Islands agriculture. *Interciencia*, **9**, 307-310.

McAdam, J.H. (1984b) The introduction of *Holcus lanatus* by direct drilling following burning of native grassland in the Falkland Islands. *Research and Development in Agriculture*, **1**, 165-169.

McAdam, J.H. (1985) The effect of climate on plant growth and agriculture in the Falkland Islands. *Progress in Biometeorology*, **2**, 155-176.

McAdam, J.H. (2013) *The Impact of the Falklands War (1982) on the Peatland Ecosystem of the Islands*. In: Rotherham, I.D. and Handley, C. (eds) *War and Peat*. Wildtrack Publishing, Sheffield, 143-162.

McAdam, J.H. and Upson, R. (2012) *Peatlands in the Falkland Islands – Origins, status and threats*. IUCN UK Peatland Programme/British Ecological Society Symposium, Bangor, Wales. p15.

McAdam, J.H. and Upson, R. (2013) *Climate Change in the Falkland Islands*. The Wool Press. Department of Agriculture, Falkland Islands Govt, April, 278,13-15.

Munro, H. (1924) *Report of an investigation into the conditions and practice of sheep farming in The Falkland Islands*. Waterlow and Sons Ltd, London. 57pp.

Radic, S. (2010) *Studies on calcified seaweed, legume yield and nitrogen fixation in acid soils in the Falkland Islands*. Unpublished PhD thesis, Queen's University of Belfast, Belfast.

Shackleton, E.A.A.S. (1976) *The economic development of the Falkland Islands*. H.M.S.O. London.

Summers, R.W. and McAdam, J.H. (1993) *The Upland Goose*. Bluntisham Books, Bluntisham.

Summers, O., Haydock, W.J.R. and Kerr, J.A. (1993) *Land subdivision in the Falkland Islands*. Proceedings of the XVII International Grassland Congress, Palmerston North, New Zealand, 812-814.

Theophilus, T.W.D. (1972) *The Economics Of Wool Production In The Falkland Islands*. Foreign and Commonwealth Office, Overseas Development Administration, London, pp38 plus Appendices.

Upson, R., McAdam, J.H. and Clubbe, C. (2014) Climate Change and the Falkland Islands. *Penguin News*, **Vol. 25**, No 49 22nd May, pp 8-9.

Woods, R.W. (2001) A survey of the number, size and distribution of island in the Falklands archipelago. *Falkland Islands Journal*, **7**(5), 1-25.

# Chapter 6. Blanket bog management and monitoring in the South Pennines

**Rachael Maskill and Jonathan Walker**
Moors for the Future Partnership

## Summary

In 2013, the Moors for the Future Partnership (MFFP) celebrated ten years of moorland conservation works. In this time, our public/private partnership worked to manage 2,700 ha of severely damaged blanket peat, including 1,500 ha of bare peat stabilisation (Dean *et al.*, 2014) across the South Pennines Special Area of Conservation. An extensive monitoring programme has been established to monitor the impact of this work on biodiversity and the ecosystem services provided by blanket bogs. Here we will present an overview of our management techniques and key findings from our most recent research and monitoring projects, as well as an insight into MFFP's science vision and strategy from 2015.

**Keywords:** blanket bog, conservation management, monitoring, ecosystem services

## Introduction

The blanket bog habitat of the Peak District and South Pennines has been severely degraded through a range of well-documented factors such as industrial pollution, wildfire, overgrazing and visitor pressures (Mackay &Tallis, 1996; Phillips, Yalden & Tallis, 1981; Tallis, 1987; Tallis, Meade & Hulme, 1997; Tallis, 1998). By the late twentieth-century, large areas of these moorlands had been lost leaving extensive areas of bare peat and extensive networks of erosion gullies that cut through the deep peat soils. Where vegetation remained intact, very few *Sphagnum* mosses were present.

Using methods developed and reviewed by Penny Anderson Associates (Anderson, Tallis & Yalden, 1997) as part of the Moorland Restoration Project, bare peat is stabilised using heather brash and geotextiles. These act as a protective layer that shields bare peat from the worst of the rain, wind and actions of freeze-thaw. The brash also acts as a source of bryophytes and heather seeds and provides a microclimate for them to germinate and grow. Lime and fertiliser are applied to raise the pH and provide nutrients to a level that will enable an application of seeds – largely composed of grasses – to act as a nurse crop. The grass species, often varieties used on sports pitches, are selected for their ability to resist drought conditions and their quick-growing roots, which knit the upper layers of the peat together. This combination of treatments stabilises the peat and therefore allows the more typical moorland species to gain a foothold in places where they have been absent for decades. Plug plants are used to aid the diversification of areas of species poor blanket bog.

Over the years MFFP has developed from a single project with integrated research and communications components, to a programme of several projects covering works, research and monitoring and awareness raising, capturing different catchments, ownerships and ecosystem services. Through in-house empirical data collection and analysis, collaborations with academic institutions and funding of research projects by means of PhDs, MFFP's monitoring programme accompanying the land management have sought to address knowledge gaps in the key areas of biodiversity (vegetation), erosion, carbon emissions, water tables, water flow and water quality.

## Evidencing the impacts of blanket bog restoration on ecosystem services

## Impact on biodiversity

The combination of treatments described above leads directly to revegetation of bare peat surfaces with an initial nurse crop of grass species such as *Lolium perenne*. MFFP uses a combination of fixed 2 x 2 m quadrats and fixed point photography to monitor the succession of vegetation from nurse crop to more typical moorland vegetation (Figure 1). Data from these surveys show rapid colonisation of blanket bog indicator species such as common heather (*Calluna vulgaris*), cotton grasses (*Eriophorum* spp) and *Vaccinium* species.

In addition, transect surveys of Black Hill indicate that revegetation works, in combination with improvements in air quality, are factors in the return of *Sphagnum* mosses to large areas of previously bare peat. The return of this key blanket bog species is an important next step in moorland restoration, and applications of *Sphagnum* propagules in various forms has been undertaken across several restoration sites within MFFP's EU-funded MoorLIFE project. *Sphagnum* 'bead' applications are monitored using 1 x 1 m quadrats to establish a baseline against which to assess the success of this treatment. MFFP has also been a key funder of a studentship, alongside The Cooperative and Manchester Metropolitan University, looking at the conditions required for *Sphagnum* reintroduction.

**Figure 2: fixed quadrats monitoring revegetation works on Kinder Scout in 2011 (top) and 2013 (bottom).**

## Impact on water-tables

A study of water-tables across Kinder Scout and Bleaklow in 2008 by the University of Manchester and MFFP described significant spatial and temporal variation in water table depth and variation across areas of differing restoration status (Allott *et al.*, 2009). Water-tables on revegetated sites were on average 80 mm higher than those of topographically similar, eroding sites. MFFP's monitoring programme has continued this work and has extended it across a wider area and a greater number of replicates. Pre-works monitoring has also been a key part of this extension and MFFP reported in March 2015 as to the impacts of revegetation on water-tables.

Early data gathered by MFFP as part of the monitoring of the National Trust's 'Peatlands for the Future' project has provided strong evidence for the raising of water-tables within close proximity of permeable timber gully blocks (Figure 2; Maskill, Walker & Allott, 2012).

**Figure 3: Automated dipwells monitoring water-table behaviour upstream of a permeable timber dam on Kinder Scout.**

## Impact on water flow

Moors for the Future are currently delivering a Defra funded Multiple Benefits Demonstration Catchment Project in the Upper

Derwent to study the impacts of gully blocking and revegetation on storm flow. Results presented by Allott *et al.* (2014) provided evidence of the extent to which these treatments have an effect on water flow. Firstly, restoration of monitored systems was shown to slow delivery of water from the headwaters. Lag times between peak rainfall and peak storm-flow is increased by approximately 20 minutes. In addition, the volume of water at peak storm flow is reduced by approximately 30%. Further work is ongoing to model the extent of the effects across a larger catchment area.

## Impact on erosion

Revegetation of bare peat effectively shuts down the erosion of peat into the fluvial system. Research funded by MFFP's Moorland Research Fund studied the sediment entering catchment systems at actively eroding, recently revegetated and intact moorland sites on Bleaklow (Shuttleworth, Evans & Rothwell, 2011). The study showed that the quantity of suspended sediment in water samples was greatly reduced in areas that had undergone revegetation works (26.06 mg $m^{-2}$ $week^{-1}$ pre- and 0.095 mg $m^{-2}$ $week^{-1}$ post-restoration). MFFP have extended the methodologies used within this study to monitor the impact of gully blocking and revegetation before and after works.

## Impact on carbon

Bare, eroding peatlands lose carbon through a number of pathways such as oxidation, surface erosion, and transfer of carbon into the aquatic system (e.g. dissolved organic carbon (DOC) and particulate organic carbon (POC)). Five years (2007-2011) of monitoring carbon fluxes from bare eroding, restored and 'intact' blanket bog on the Bleaklow Plateau in the Peak District was undertaken by the University of Durham and University of Manchester in collaboration with and support from MFFP, Defra and Natural England. This research showed that the carbon losses from bare peat sites can be as high as 522 ± 3 tonnes C/$km^2$/yr (Worrall *et al.*, 2011). The main benefit of restoration works is the avoided loss of carbon through the above pathways.

While there are clear carbon benefits to undertaking conservation works on blanket bog, the use of helicopters to deliver much of the works has its own implications for the carbon footprint of our projects. The MoorLIFE project is undertaking a carbon audit of all greenhouse gas emitting activities within the operational control of the project.

## Impact on water quality

Of particular concern to water companies and the Environment Agency is the quality of water in upland catchments that drain degraded peat. This is because of its high colour content and levels of heavy metals which puts pressure on water treatment processes and poses problems for implementation of Water Framework Directive standards. Since 2009, MFFP and collaborators have put considerable efforts into monitoring water quality before, during and after revegetation and gully blocking works. Monitoring work undertaken by Penny Anderson Associates on the Sustainable Catchment Management Programme have found significant, if small decreases water colour over a seven-year period following grip blocking (United Utilities, 2012).

Our empirical data collection currently involves the annual monitoring of over 700 vegetation quadrats; interval sampling from moorland gullies and streams to monitor water quality at fifty-one locations; water table measurements using over sixty automated dipwells and more than 700 manual dipwells; and monitor water flow at sixteen flow monitoring stations. Many of our projects are now entering their final year of data collection and many of the monitored sites are only just post-works. Key evidence gathered from the monitoring programme described above were presented in September.

## Towards March 2015 – Expected outputs

March 2015 will see the conclusion of several of MFFP's monitoring projects. At this time, we will be able to:

- Evidence the impact of revegetation on water tables and provide further evidence of the impact of gully blocking on water tables and sediment accumulation.
- Calculate the carbon footprint of capital works and its impact on the net carbon benefit gained through undertaking large-scale conservation management.
- Understand the impact of land management on flood risk.
- Inform the application of *Sphagnum* propagules at landscape scales.
- Produce trajectories of vegetation succession – from nurse crop to more typical moorland vegetation communities.

## Future strategy

Until now MFFP's science programme has largely been field–based data collection. Remote sensing is more applicable to monitoring restoration than traditional ground survey at a landscape scale. MFFP and Natural England supported a NERC CASE studentship at the University of Manchester investigating the use of high resolution remote sensing for landscape scale restoration of peatland. This work demonstrated the value and informed the operational use of remote sensing data for monitoring purposes (Cole, McMorrow& Evans, 2014a, b).

We will develop our use of remote sensing to evidence our future 'ecosystems approach' to upland conservation and land management through integration biodiversity conservation across habitats and evidencing the benefits of this approach. We will explore a range of remote sensing platforms and sensors to address our evidence needs at the appropriate spatial and temporal scales. Initially we plan to use remote sensing to inform the scoping of land management plans and move our existing field monitoring to remote sensing–based monitoring. We will then prioritise using remote sensing data to build on our collaborative work evidencing the threat that our uplands face from wildfire (McMorrow & Lindley, 2006) existing and emerging pathogens (Crouch & Walker, 2013) and inappropriate land use (Chapman *et al*, 2010). As well as evidencing the impact of conservation and land management on ecosystem services, a key objective of MFFP is to use the data and evidence gathered from our monitoring programme to undertake cost-benefit analyses for the works undertaken, and to develop case studies based on the sites treated.

## References

Allott, T.E.H., Evans, M.G., Lindsay, J.B., Agnew, C.T., Freer, J.E., Jones, A. and Parnell, M. (2009) *Water Tables in Peak District Blanket Peatlands*. Moors for the Future Report No 17, Edale, Derbyshire.

Allott, T., Evans, M., Agnew, C., Gorham, J., Mellor, J., Milledge, D., Pilkington, M. and Maskill, R. (2014) *Peat restoration reduces stormflow from headwater catchments: Results from the MS4W Peak District demonstration catchments*. Making Space for Water symposium, Part 1, Moors for the Future Partnership, Edale, Derbyshire. www.moorsforthefuture.org.uk/making-space-water-symposium

Anderson, P., Tallis, J.H. and Yalden, D.W. (1997) *Restoring Moorland: Peak District Moorland Management Project: Phase III report*. Peak Park Joint Planning Board, Bakewell, Derbyshire.

Chapman, D.S., Bonn, A., Kunin, W.E. and Cornell, S.J. (2010) Random Forest characterization of upland vegetation and management burning from aerial imagery. *Journal of Biogeography*, **37**, 37–46.

Cole, B., McMorrow, J. and Evans, M. (2014) Empirical Modelling of Vegetation Abundance from Airborne Hyperspectral Data for Upland Peatland Restoration Monitoring. *Remote Sensing*, **6**, 716-739.

Cole, B., McMorrow, J. and Evans, M. (2014) Spectral monitoring of moorland plant phenology to identify a temporal window for hyperspectral remote sensing of peatland. *Journal of Photogrammetry and Remote Sensing*, **90**, 49–58.

Crouch, T. and Walker, J. (2013) *Phytophthora pseudosyringae* on bilberry (*Vaccinium myrtillus*) in the South Pennine Moors SAC: Summary of surveying activities carried out by the Moors for the Future Partnership in 2011-2013. Moors for the Future Partnership, Edale, Derbyshire.

Dean, C., Davison, S., Buckler, M., Walker, J. and Turner, L. (2014) *Moors for the Future Business Plan*. Moors for the Future Partnership, Edale, Derbyshire.

Mackay, A.W. and Tallis, J.H. (1996) Summit-type blanket mire erosion in the Forest of Bowland, Lancashire, UK: Predisposing factors and implications for conservation. *Biological Conservation*, **76**, 31-4.

Maskill, R., Walker, J. and Allott, A. (2012) *Kinder 'Peatlands for the Future' Project Monitoring Report.* Moors for the Future Partnership, Edale, Derbyshire.

McMorrow, J. and Lindley, S. (2006) *Modelling the spatial risk of moorland wildfire*. Final report, Moors for the Future Partnership, Edale, Derbyshire.

Philips, J., Yalden, D.W. and Tallis, J.H. (1981) *Moorland Erosion Project, Phase 1 Report.* Peak Park Joint Planning Board, Bakewell, Derbyshire.

Shuttleworth, E.L., Evans M.G. and Rothwell, J.J. (2010) *Impact of erosion and restoration on sediment flux and pollutant mobilisation in the peatlands of the Peak District National Park.* Moors for the Future Partnership, Edale, Derbyshire.

Tallis, J.H. (1987) Fire and Flood at Holme Moss: Erosion Processes in an Upland Blanket Mire. *Journal of Ecology*, **75**, 1099-1129.

Tallis, J.H., Meade, R. and Hulme, P.D. (1997) *Blanket Mire Degradation: Causes, Consequences and Challenges.* Macaulay Land Use Research Institute, Aberdeen.

Tallis, J.H. (1998) Growth and degradation of British and Irish blanket mires. *Environmental Review*, **6**, 81-122.

United Utilities (2012) *Sustainable Catchment Management Programme, Water Quality Monitoring Results, July 2012*. United Utilities, Warrington.

Worrall, F., Rowson, J.G., Evans, M.G., Pawson, R., Daniels, S. and Bonn, A. (2011) Carbon fluxes from eroding peatlands – the carbon benefit of revegetation following wildfire. *Earth Surface Processes and Landforms*, **36**(11), 1487–1498.

# Chapter 7. Beating the rush: *Juncus effusus* and controversy in bog restoration at Danes Moss, Cheshire and Red Moss, Greater Manchester

**Roger Meade**
Roger Meade Associates

## Summary

Bogs damaged by peat extraction or other activities are important to habitat conservation within the European Union *inter-alia* because of the potential to re-instate peat-forming vegetation within them. This is normally done by raising the water table to saturate the peat with the expectation that plant species typical of intact raised bogs will become established within a few decades. There are examples in which Soft Rush *Juncus effusus* has been an early colonist apparently to the detriment of the bog-building plants and this in turn has cast doubt on the expectations inherent in national and international conservation designations.

Red Moss, a cut-over raised bog in Greater Manchester, half of which had already been lost to landfill, was designated as a long-term waste disposal site in Bolton Metropolitan Borough Council's (MBC) Unitary Development Plan in 1992. This was upheld at a public inquiry in 1993, partly on the grounds that English Nature's expectations for bog restoration on what they had recently designated a Site of Special Scientific Interest were flawed because much of the peat surface was dominated by Soft Rush associated with nutrients from the existing landfill. In addition, Soft Rush was spreading on Danes Moss, rewetted in the 1970s, also close to a landfill site and receiving agricultural run-off. Rush expansion was perceived by the protagonists of landfill as a negative change at Danes Moss, supporting their contention that peat-forming vegetation would not become widely established at Red Moss.

It is now twenty years since the Red Moss Public Inquiry. Studies presented in this chapter show that the spread of Soft

Rush was a temporary phase and that bog-building vegetation represented by *Sphagnum* mosses is developing alongside the rush on both sites.

**Keywords:** restoration, succession, conservation management, designations, landfill, peat formation.

## Introduction

Red Moss was first notified as a Site of Special Scientific Interest (SSSI) in 1993. The notification was quashed following a judicial review of the procedure, but it was notified successfully in 1995 using revised SSSI selection guidelines for bogs (JNCC, 1994). These events were contemporaneous with the inclusion of Red Moss in Bolton Metropolitan Council's Draft Unitary Development Plan (UDP) as a landfill resource, to continue and extend operations that had already created a high mound over half of the peatland (Figure 1). A public inquiry into this UDP policy, precipitated by objections from, for example, English Nature and the Lancashire Wildlife Trust, confirmed the landfill policy. Subsequent events including interventions by Friends of the Earth and the then Secretary of State for the Environment John Gummer coincided with the refusal of the planning application to extend the landfill over the mossland, and this is now managed for bog restoration by the Lancashire Wildlife Trust.

The public inquiry initiated vegetation surveys of Red Moss and some formed part of Bolton MBC's Proof of Evidence in support of the landfill policy (Environmental Research & Advisory Partnership (ER & AP), 1992, 1993). The surveys are used in this paper as a baseline against which to compare an SSSI condition monitoring survey commissioned by Natural England (successor to English Nature) In 2007.

Danes Moss is also formed within the glacial outwash zone close to the south Pennines but lies about twenty-five miles south of Red Moss (Figure 8). The earliest landfill pre-dates its 1967 planning consent and has expanded to now occupy the centre of the original peatland, but some of the mossland, donated by Fisons Horticulture Division to the Cheshire Conservation Trust (now the Cheshire Wildlife Trust) in 1971, remains open peatland. Plant survey carried out between 1973 and 1975 was repeated in 1987 after much of the area had been rewetted in 1974 (Meade, 1992); it was surveyed again for Natural England in 2012.

Soft Rush *Juncus effusus* and Great Reedmace *Typha latifolia* formed dense stands within Red Moss in 1993, linked via drains with the landfill area and other disturbed areas around the periphery. Part of Danes Moss had been rewetted in 1974 and, although there was evidence of the spread of peat-forming species (Meade, 1992), there had been a noticeable spread of Soft Rush by 1993. This was presented by Bolton MBC as an example of how the vegetation of Red Moss would respond to rewetting and it contributed to the failure of English Nature's opinions to carry weight at the public inquiry.

Colonisation of the restoration surface on cutover peat by *Juncus effusus* is a widespread phenomenon and has been studied on, for example, Thorne, Goole & Crowle Moors SSSI on the South Yorkshire-East Riding of Yorkshire-Lincolnshire borders (Dargie, 2001).

## Significant plant species

Only selected species have been included in the plant records contributing to this review, concentrating on those typical of undamaged raised bog and others that suggest unsuitable conditions or other successional trends. This concept is now embodied in the Joint Nature Conservation Committee's (JNCC) Common Standards Guidance for Condition Monitoring on SSSIs (JNCC, 2004), though these post-date the earlier surveys on Red Moss and Danes Moss.

The JNCC's monitoring protocol is based on positive and negative indicator species. Those that are positive for raised bogs include the mosses: *Sphagnum papillosum*, *S. magellanicum*, *S. capillifolium*, *S. tenellum*, and vascular plants such as Andromeda *polifolia*, *Vaccinium oxycoccos*, and *Narthecium ossifragum*. Negative indicators include: *Juncus effusus*, *Urtica dioica*, and *Phragmites australis*. Although not specifically listed for the mire expanse of bogs, *Typha latifolia* is included as a negative indicator for all but the most eutrophic lowland wetlands. Not all *Sphagnum* species are typical of raised bog; several being associated with poor fen. The earliest species maps for both sites do not discriminate between species and show the distribution of the *Sphagnum* genus.

## Plant species and NVC community distribution at Red Moss

Comparison of surveys is made more difficult at Red Moss by changes in the shape and nomenclature of the site compartments used for recording. Nevertheless, best endeavours have been used to match up the compartments so that the point records for species could be collated into diagrams for comparison between surveys on maps and in Table 1.

In the older records for Red Moss (ER & AP, 1993) species presence is displayed as dots, but at unspecified intervals; there is no recorded overlap between species on the single distribution map. The map is supplemented with a description for each compartment (outlines given in Figure 2) in which details are given of the *Sphagnum* species present, and a tabulation of the percentage cover of each species in each compartment. In some instances, a species is included in the tabulation for a particular compartment where there are no mapped dots, and *vice versa*.

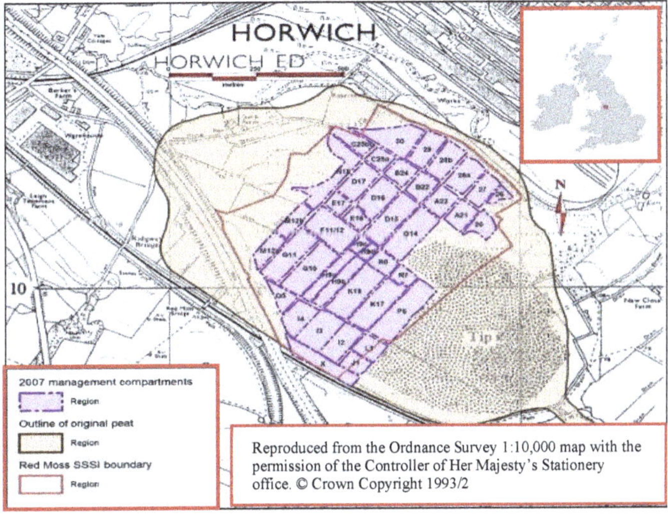


**Figure 1: Red Moss location and land-use.**

The 1993 sketch map compartment outlines have been registered to British National Grid and the species dots given coordinates using MapInfo Professional 8.5. Summary species cover percentages were given (ER & AP, 1993) for each compartment. Comparison is made by tabulating the compartment cover estimates (Table 1) and by displaying the two *Sphagnum* distribution maps side by side (Figure 2).

**Table 1: Comparison of percentage cover estimates for positive and negative indicators.**

| Compartment label equivalents | | Positive Indicators | | | | Negative Indicators | | | | | |
|---|---|---|---|---|---|---|---|---|---|---|---|
| | | Combined *Sphagnum* | | *Eriophorum angustifolium* | | *Juncus effusus* | | *Typha latifolia* | | *Molinia caerulea* | |
| **1993** | **2007** | **1993** | **2007** | **1993** | **2007** | **1993** | **2007** | **1993** | **2007** | **1993** | **2007** |
| 1 | J1 | <1 | 5 | <1 | 2.1 | <1 | 10.7 | <1 | 0 | 95 | 62.9 |
| | L1 | | 5.4 | | 1.4 | | 12.1 | | 0 | | 55.7 |
| 2 | I2 | <1 | 2.9 | <1 | 2.9 | 0 | 3.6 | 0 | 0 | 95 | 57.9 |
| 3 | I3 | <1 | 7.3 | 1 | 8.8 | <1 | 0 | 0 | 0 | 95 | 58.8 |
| 4 | I4 | <1 | 7.2 | <1 | 13.3 | <1 | 20 | 0 | 0 | 95 | 50 |
| 5 | Q5 | <1 | 0.5 | 1 | 10 | <1 | 5 | 0 | 0 | 99 | 59.5 |
| 6 | P6 | <1 | 0 | 2 | 0 | 2 | 5 | 15 | 24 | 70 | 37.5 |
| 7 | K17 | <1 | 36.4 | 2 | 0 | 4 | 37.2 | 2 | 2.8 | 95 | 20.3 |
| 8 | K18 | 1 | 27.4 | 2 | 0 | 2 | 39.6 | 2 | 0 | 90 | 14.1 |
| 9 | H9a | 3 | 20.8 | 6 | 2.4 | <1 | 17 | 0 | 0 | 95 | 31 |
| | H9bcd | | 25.6 | | 2.4 | | 33.9 | | 0 | | 24.7 |
| 10 | G10 | 2 | 39 | 2 | 4.6 | <1 | 0 | 0 | 0 | 95 | 54.5 |
| | (F11/12) | | 9.1 | | 1.9 | | 1.5 | | 0 | | 66 |
| 11 | G11 | 9 | 71.4 | 2 | 4 | 5 | 3.5 | <1 | 0 | 85 | 47 |
| | (F11/12) | | 9.1 | | 1.9 | | 1.5 | | 0 | | 66 |
| 12 | M12a | 10 | 64.3 | <1 | 1.4 | 12 | 11.4 | 0 | 0 | 65 | 56.4 |
| | M12b | | 0 | | 0 | | 0 | | 0 | | 43 |
| 13 | | <1 | | 2 | | 4 | | 8 | | 80 | |
| 14 | O14 | <1 | 6.5 | 4 | 1 | 10 | 19.2 | 40 | 2.8 | 40 | 40.8 |
| 15 | D15 | <1 | 50 | <1 | 0 | 45 | 52.1 | <1 | 0 | 55 | 17.1 |
| 16 | D16 | <1 | 16.8 | <1 | 4.3 | 20 | 27.5 | <1 | 0 | 90 | 13.8 |
| | E16 | | | | | | | | | | |
| 17 | D17 | <1 | 21.4 | 5 | 6.6 | <1 | 0 | 0 | 0 | 90 | 56.6 |
| | E17 | | 11.7 | | 21.7 | | 5 | | 0 | | 30 |
| 18 | N18 | <1 | 16.4 | <1 | 0 | 1 | 5.7 | 1 | 0.3 | 95 | 71.4 |
| 19 | | <1 | | 0 | | <1 | | <1 | | 5 | |

| 20 | 20 | <1 | 14 | 1 | 1.4 | 2 | 0 | 2 | 0 | 70 | 60 |
|---|---|---|---|---|---|---|---|---|---|---|---|
| 21 | A21 | <1 | 0 | <1 | 0 | 2 | 0 | 2 | 0 | 90 | 65 |
| 22 | A22 | <1 | 5 | 1 | 1 | 2 | 10 | 2 | 20 | 95 | 28 |
| 23 | B22 | <1 | 5 | 1 | 0.3 | <1 | 0 | 0 | 0 | 95 | 83.3 |
| 24 | B24 | <1 | 4.3 | 2 | 15.8 | 2 | 0 | 2 | 2.8 | 90 | 45 |
| 25 | C25a | <1 | 0 | 3 | 0 | <1 | 20 | 0 | 0 | 99 | 69 |
| | C25bc | | 2.5 | | 0 | | 0 | | 0 | | 100 |
| 26 | 26 | 0 | 6.3 | 1 | 4.3 | 1 | 0 | 0 | 0 | 65 | 73.8 |
| 27 | 27 | 0 | 14 | <1 | 1 | <1 | 0 | 0 | 0 | 95 | 79 |
| 28 | 28a | <1 | 2.8 | 1 | 2 | <1 | 0 | 0 | 0 | 90 | 85 |
| | 28b | | 4.6 | | 4 | | 0 | | 0 | | 86 |
| 29 | 29 | 0 | | 0 | | 20 | | <1 | | 5 | |
| 30 | 30 | 0 | | 0 | | <1 | | 0 | | 0 | |

Some 1993 compartments have been split following extra bund creation; for example, F11/12 cuts across the 1993 G10 and G11 compartments, and only a few of the original numbers have been retained. The 1993 cover values are assumed to be visual estimates; the 2007 equivalents are the result of dividing the sum of the individual quadrat covers (including zero) by the total number of quadrats recorded in the compartment.

The 2007 condition assessment of Red Moss recorded positive and negative indicator species at a minimum of five points per updated management compartments (shown in Figure 1) and these were used to generate mean frequency and cover values in each compartment for each species.

The 2007 list included twenty-six plant species and some of the 196 quadrats contained only one, as with the dense stands of *Juncus effusus*; others, such as in areas dominated by *Molinia caerulea*, had just three or four associate species. The computer program MATCH (Malloch, 1990) was used as a guide to assigning each 2007 quadrat to a National Vegetation Classification (NVC) community (Rodwell (ed.), 1991-2000). The quadrats were also grouped using TWINSPAN (Hill, 1979) and MATCH was again used to assign the groups to NVC communities. The distribution of these groups is shown in Figure 3.

Groups dominated by *Molinia caerulea* with very few associate species but assigned to different NVC communities by MATCH have been amalgamated in Figure 3 as the M25a *Molinia caerulea-Potentilla erecta* mire, *Erica tetralix* sub-community. When classified individually, the quadrats spanned a wider range of communities including the H2c *Calluna vulgaris-Ulex minor* heath, *Molinia caerulea* sub-community and H9e *Calluna vulgaris-Deschampsia flexuosa* heath, *Molinia caerulea* sub-community, similar to the range found at Danes Moss.

For some groups the highest coefficients were for W4 *Betula pubescens-Molinia caerulea* woodland, especially the W4c, *Sphagnum* sub-community. These have dominant *Molinia caerulea* and moderate to high cover of particularly *Sphagnum fimbriatum*, though other *Sphagnum* species are also included. *Betula pubescens* is almost entirely absent, so its classification as a woodland community is compromised, and the lower scoring open mossland communities such as H9e and M21b were chosen as more appropriate. These communities typically form a mosaic with the M3 *Eriophorum angustifolium* bog-pool community, found along the ditch lines left by peat cutting. The mosaic is widespread, particularly towards the edge of the compartmentalised mossland.

There is a lower cover of *Molinia caerulea* and a concomitant increase in *Sphagnum* species in the M21b *Narthecium ossifragum-Sphagnum papillosum* valley mire, *Vaccinium oxycoccos-Sphagnum recurvum* sub-community. Within this group one quadrat was assigned by MATCH to the M18a *Erica tetralix-Sphagnum papillosum* raised and blanket mire, *Sphagnum magellanicum-Andromeda polifolia* sub-community. This quadrat includes *Sphagnum capillifolium* and one of the two records for *S. magellanicum*. The presence of the M18a would be a strong positive feature in the assessment of the restoration of this damaged raised bog because the community is typical of undamaged bogs (Rodwell (ed.), 1991-2000).

Communities with a significant cover of *Juncus effusus* are split between the almost pure stands and the M6c *Carex echinata-Sphagnum recurvum/auriculatum* mire, *Juncus effusus* sub-community. The latter has a moderate to high cover of *Sphagnum fallax* and occurs furthest away from the landfill area. As a poor-fen community with successional potential for raised bog, the presence of M6c is consistent with the aims of the restoration. The M4 *Carex rostrata-Sphagnum recurvum* mire was given a higher coefficient for the almost pure stands of *Juncus effusus* but these have been defaulted to M6c (darker symbol) because they lack many of the species in the published account of the M4 community.

*Typha latifolia* swamp S12 represents the densest stands but its distribution is far more limited than that of *Typha latifolia* as a species.

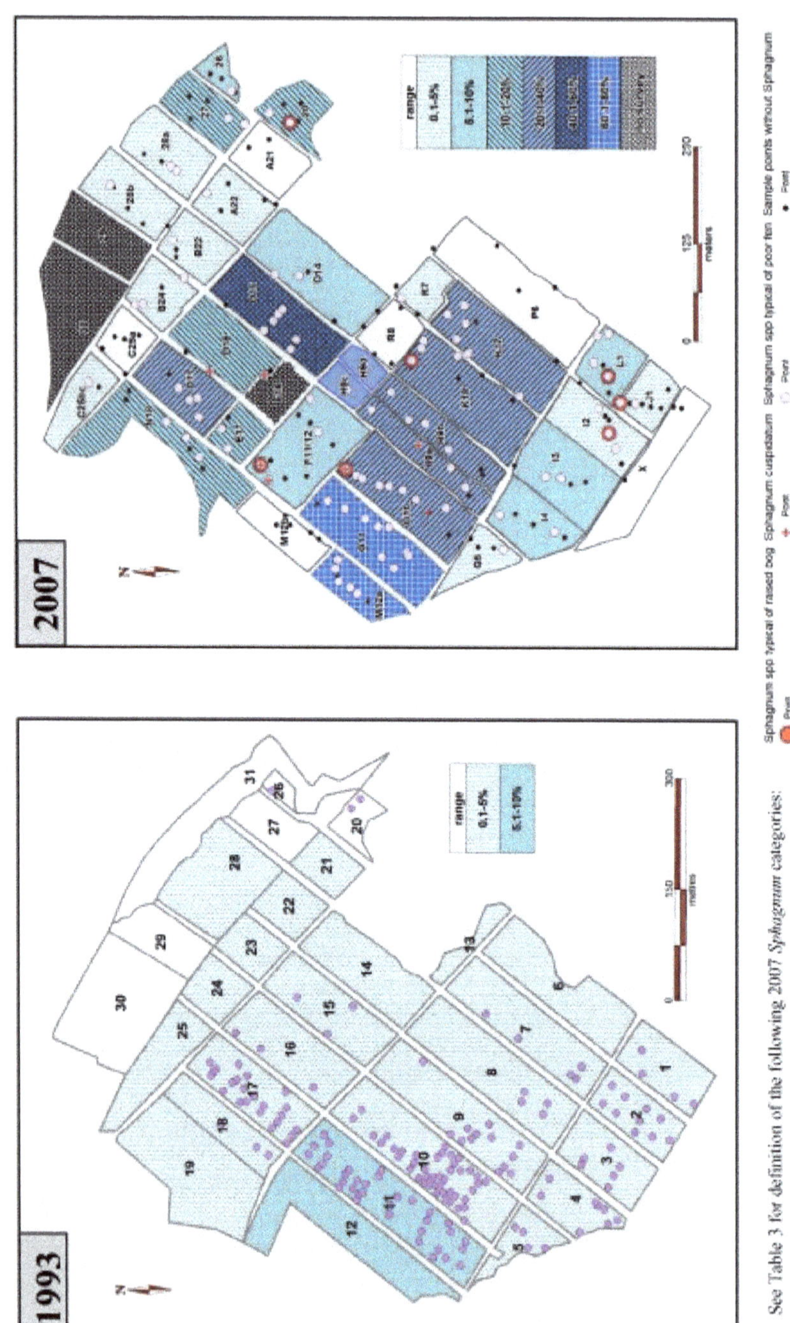


**Figure 2: Positive indicator: Comparison of *Sphagnum* species distribution and mean cover 1993 and 2007**

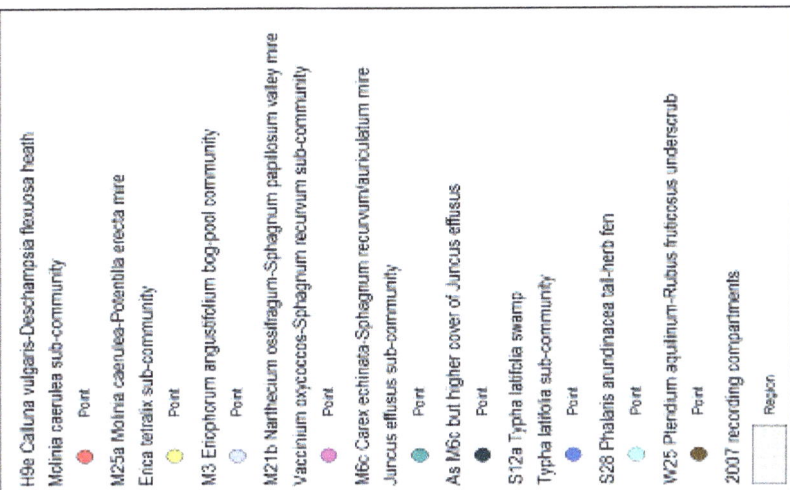


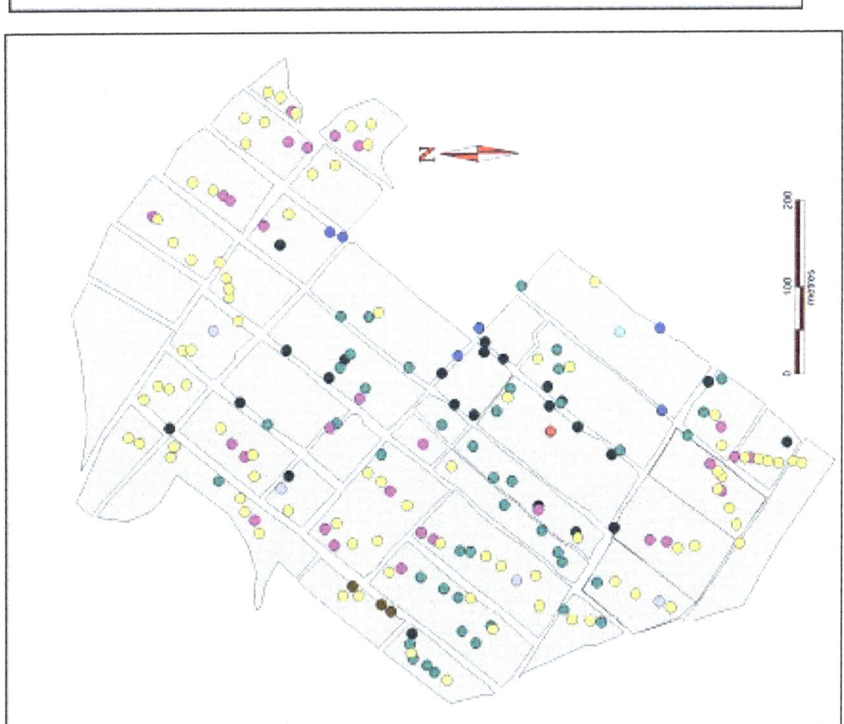


**Figure 3: 2007 NVC communities at Red Moss**

## Changes in species and NVC community distribution at Red Moss

Changes from Table 1 and Figure 2 are summarised in Table 2. The very broad analysis and judgements take account of the difference in methods of assessment for 1992 and 2007.

**Table 2: Summary of changes in positive and negative indicators at Red Moss**

| Plant species | Extent (spread) | % Cover |
|---|---|---|
| **Positive indicators:** | | |
| *Sphagnum* species | Little change, but extended to compartments 26 and 27 in 2007 | Maximum of 5% in any compartment in 1993 to over 60% in 2007 in compartments G11 and M12a |
| *Eriophorum angustifolium* | Lost from seven compartments where present at low cover in 1993 | Measurable increase in three compartments |
| **Negative indicators:** | | |
| *Juncus effusus* | Lost from eleven compartments but has spread to one new compartment | Measurable increase in at least five compartments |
| *Molinia caerulea* | No change | Measurable reduction in eighteen compartments and an increase in one |
| *Typha latifolia* | Lost from seven compartments | Measurable reduction in one and an increase in one. |

'Measurable' is proportionate and equates approximately to a 10% difference, reflecting the limited comparability of the methods used to estimate cover.

There has been an increase between 1993 and 2007 in the cover of the positive indicator *Sphagnum* moss species and a reduction in the cover of the negative indicator species *Molinia caerulea* and *Typha latifolia*. There is a small reduction in the extent of *Eriophorum angustifolium*, though its cover has increased in some compartments. The distribution of *Juncus effusus* is reduced but its cover has increased in compartments closest to the landfill or where influenced by drainage from it or other nutrient sources.

**Table 3 Records of *Sphagnum* moss species at Red Moss**

| Species | Figure 2 group | 1993 | 2007 |
|---|---|---|---|
| *S. capillifolium* | Typical of raised bog | BBS | RMA |
| *S. magellanicum* | | | RMA |
| *S. papillosum* | | EN, BBS | RMA |
| *S. cuspidatum* | *S. cuspidatum* | EN, ER&AP | RMA |
| *S. subnitens* | Typical of fen but also found on raised bog | BBS, EN, ER&AP | RMA |
| *S. fallax* | | BBS, EN, ER&AP | RMA |
| *S. palustre* | | BBS, EN, ER&AP | RMA |
| *S. fimbriatum* | | BBS, EN, ER&AP | RMA |
| *S. auriculatum* | | EN | |
| *S. denticulatum* | | | RMA |
| *S. squarrosum* | | BBS, ER&AP | RMA |

Recorders: British Bryological Society; English Nature; Environmental Research & Advisory Partnership; Roger Meade Associates.

The number of recorded *Sphagnum* species has increased (Table 3), the notable addition being *S. magellanicum*. This record was confirmed by local recorders (Peter Jepson, pers. comm.). Early records for *S. papillosum* were sporadic but it was recorded in five quadrats in 2007, representing a probable increase compared with 1993.

An account of the NVC communities recognised in 1993 (ER & AP, 1993) lists M25 as covering the majority of the site, with M2b and M3 in some of the ditches. No other NVC communities were recorded. While M25 was still widespread in 2007, use of MATCH suggests that blanket use of this label is equivocal, and, based on the classification of individual quadrats, heath communities such as H9e are arguably also present. The apparent absence of M2b may be due to sampling being focused more on the inter-ditch areas, as the M3 community, also in ditches, is less well-represented in the data set than was observed on the ground. The development of community M21b in locations previously described (ER & AP, 1993) as M25 is a positive development towards the restoration of peat-forming vegetation.

## Plant species and NVC community distribution at Danes Moss

The plant survey area (2.6 ha) shown on Figure 4 is small in comparison to the extent of the peat deposit (243ha). It was chosen (the SSSI is 42.5ha) because it was the wettest part of a Cheshire Conservation Trust nature reserve set up in 1971 and its shallow basin topography meant it was possible to raise the water table using just two dams.

Contrary to Red Moss, the Danes Moss study area does not receive surface water from the landfill, and drainage from the tip is routed northwards. The enrichment ditched through the study area prior to its isolation by damming in 1974 was from farmsteads to the south and to a lesser extent from the railway. Silt and dissolved nutrients had entered the study area potentially for decades prior to 1974, encouraging *Juncus effusus* and *Urtica dioica* alongside the deeply-cut ditch. The enrichment and its associated flora were able to spread out beyond the ditch after the outfall had been dammed and the water level raised.

The 1973 and 1987 surveys at Danes Moss recorded the presence of plant species considered to be significant indicators of successful bog restoration, but in 1973 individual *Sphagnum* species were not recorded; *Molinia caerulea* and *Betula* spp were deemed to be ubiquitous and were omitted from the 1973 survey.

Records were made as presence or absence of a species within contiguous 6ft x 6ft quadrats each represented as a square on a graph paper base map in which the width of strips of land lying between series of parallel ditches was approximated to the nearest 6ft and the width of each ditch was assumed to be 6ft; neither assumption was universally true, not least, because ditch width varied along its length. Even so, there was sufficient coincidence between this map and features visible later on an aerial photograph to register it to British National Grid and compile a species list for each of 23,568 virtual contiguous 1987 2m x 2m (approx.) quadrats arising from the digitisation of the individual species maps; the number was reduced to 6,383 by re-grouping the grid references arising from the digitisation and eliminating those with no recorded species. A rationale based on the component species was developed to group the compiled 1987 quadrats so that these and the 2007 datasets could be compared spatially and through the constancy of the component species, and the published NVC constancy tables.

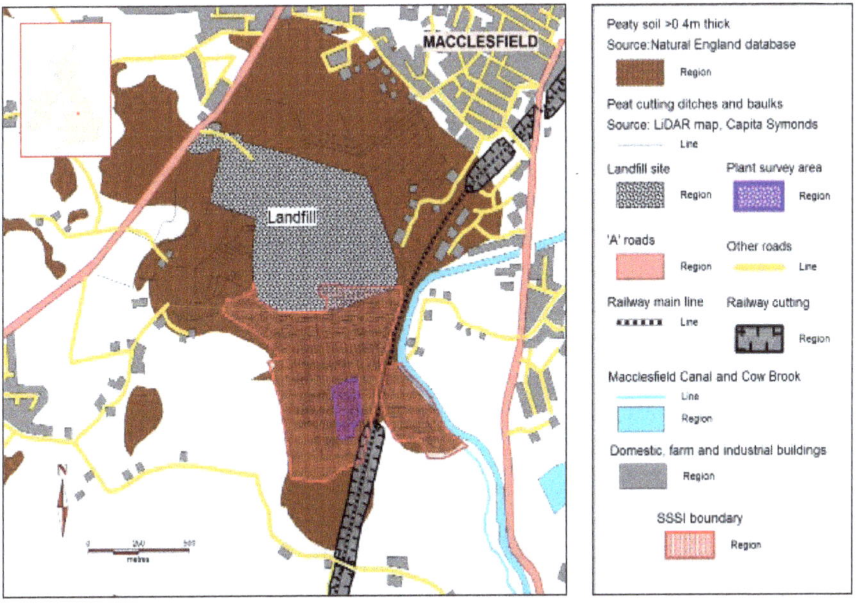


**Figure 4: Danes Moss location and land-use.**

The 2012 survey adopted a stratified-random approach to sampling and the quadrats were later fitted to NVC communities. The stratification was based on field observation because the aerial photograph patterns did not coincide well with the observed variation in the vegetation. Quadrats were given coordinates using a Garmin GPS accurate to approximately five metres.

As at Red Moss, the recorded plant species include positive and negative indicators of raised bog quality (JNCC, 2004). Their distributions are shown as pairs of maps, the first of each pair combining the 1973 and 1987 records, the second showing the 2012 distribution. Although *Typha latifolia* was (and is) present where surface water enters from the railway and old peat processing site in the north east, it has not been included in the mapping due to its very restricted and unchanged distribution. Its 1987 and 2012 distributions are evident from the NVC S12 community points on Figures 9 and 10.

The early and later survey area boundaries are similar but not identical and both are shown on the figures. The surface water was lower and confined to the ditches in 1973 but covered much of the north west of the study area in 1987 after being raised by about 0.5m in 1974. Meade (1992) describes an *ad hoc* division of the study area into three topographic zones as suggested by the distribution of species in 1987. These zones are shown on Figures 9 and 10 to aid comparison and description of the changes. The 2012 base maps also include outlines of shallow pools, remnants of more extensive post-1974 open water, as traced from a 2010 aerial photograph.

Quadrats compiled from the 1987 individual species records were grouped using species combinations and those containing sufficient species were compared to the most likely NVC community (Figure 9), guided by the 2012 groups. The 2012 quadrats, as for the 2007 Red Moss samples, were split into groups of similar stands using TWINSPAN and the groups assigned to NVC communities using MATCH (Figure 10).

The distribution of *Sphagnum* moss (Figure 5) shows it to be closely associated with the ditches in 1973 with additional patches in linear depressions midway between ditches. *Sphagnum* is more strongly associated with the more permanently wet ditches in Zone 1.

The ditch-based distribution changed by 1987, following raising of the water level, to occupy much of the inter-ditch space in Zone 2. The species was mostly *Sphagnum cuspidatum*, but with *S. fimbriatum* away from the ditches and in depressions towards and into Zone 3. Most other *Sphagnum* species were found in Zone 2.

During the interval between 1987 and 2012, much of the open water in Zone 1, created by the earlier raising of the water level, had rafted over (see comments on other species) and *Sphagnum* species eventually increased their range to include the raft, initially formed by *Juncus effusus* and floating peat. The earlier zonation of *S. cuspidatum* and *S. fimbriatum* had changed to *S. cuspidatum* being distributed almost throughout the whole study area, with *S. fimbriatum* typically on the raft in Zone 1 with *Juncus effusus*, and thinly scattered elsewhere within depressions in the drier peat. Greater species diversity, including the typical raised bog species such as *S. papillosum* and *S. capillifolium* were associated with the same ecotone between permanently waterlogged and more fluctuating conditions within this transition zone (Zone 2) in 2012.

A similar pattern of change is seen for *Eriophorum angustifolium* (Figure 6), where confinement in the ditches in 1973 changed to include the inter-ditch areas by 2012. It remains absent from the previously inundated but now rafted over Zone 1 where *Juncus effusus* is still a conspicuous component of the plant communities.

The three surveys record a large expansion in the range of *Juncus effusus* (Figure 7) from confinement within the nutrient-enriched north edge ditch in 1973 to almost half the study area in 2012. The gaps in its distribution for 1987 in the north represent deep inundation and almost permanent open water, though the rush rafted over some of these in the early 1990s. The expansion in distribution and strong growth in the early 1990s may visually support the observation (ER&AP, 1993b) that the aim of restoring peat-forming vegetation had failed, but careful field survey of associated species could have shown it to be an unreliable conclusion.

Changes in *Molinia caerulea* (Figure 8) reveal a loss from the inundated Zone 1 by 1987 and an increased patchiness in distribution elsewhere by 2012. Strongly dominant *Molinia* only survives in 2012 along some of the upstanding inter-ditch areas and on the slightly drier land along the east fringe of Zone 3.

The distribution maps record four important phases:

**Phase 1**

Confinement of *Sphagnum* and *Eriophorum* species to ditch lines away from the wider land drainage system; *Juncus effusus* was only found in or close to the drains passing through the study area carrying nutrients. This is shown in the species maps of 1973-75.

**Phase 2**

Inundation of land in Zone 1 (1974) followed by the loss of all species where constantly under water, with the exception of the moss *Warnstorfia fluitans* and rare strands of *Sphagnum cuspidatum*. The extent of species groups C, H, I and J, composed primarily of *Warnstorfia fluitans* and few other species, show the extent of the open water (Figure 9). *Juncus effusus* formed some associations with other species, and group E, found around the edge of the open water, is analogous to the M4 community described in the 2012 survey. Group G, analogous to NVC community M6c, included *Carex curta* as a constant species.

In Zone 2 bog species increased their range between the ditches, mostly as NVC community M2b but M21b was also represented. There is also a series of groups basically similar to the H9e community that was recorded in 2012, but with a varying number of associates typical of the valley mire M21b community. These are groups L, O, P, R and S, accounting for the driest conditions within which tussocky *Molinia caerulea* was dominant, covering most of Zone 3.

**Phase 3**

When the silt of Zone 1 was exposed in dry summers (Figure 11) there was a massive germination of *Juncus effusus* seedlings. As some parts of the peat surface began to float, more seedlings survived to form a dense stand of rush (Figure 12). These stands occurred close to the public footpath and created the impression that the whole of the study area was dominated by *Juncus effusus*. There was no systematic survey of the vegetation during this phase and the development of the less inundated parts was only recorded with photographs; these suggest that M2b was still widespread in Zone 2.

## Phase 4

While *Juncus effusus* still had a strong visual presence in 2012, systematic survey showed it to occur (mostly) with a carpet of *Sphagnum* mosses, *S. fimbriatum* (community W4c, Figure 13) where formerly covered by *Warnstorfia fluitans*, and *S. cuspidatum* (community M4, Figure 14) towards Zone 2. In both cases the combination of moss and rush formed a floating mat of vegetation able to rise and fall with the water table in Zone 1.

The cut-off point between M4 and M2b on the hydrological gradient is not a clear line because the old pattern of ditches and higher ground between them is still present at right-angles to the gradient. The M4 community extends south-eastwards along the ditch lines into Zone 2 where M2b and M21b are the main communities. While the H9e community with tussocky *Molinia* is still present, it does not form the wide band recorded in 1987 (Figure 9) and the M2b community extends to the edge of the study area in Zone 3.

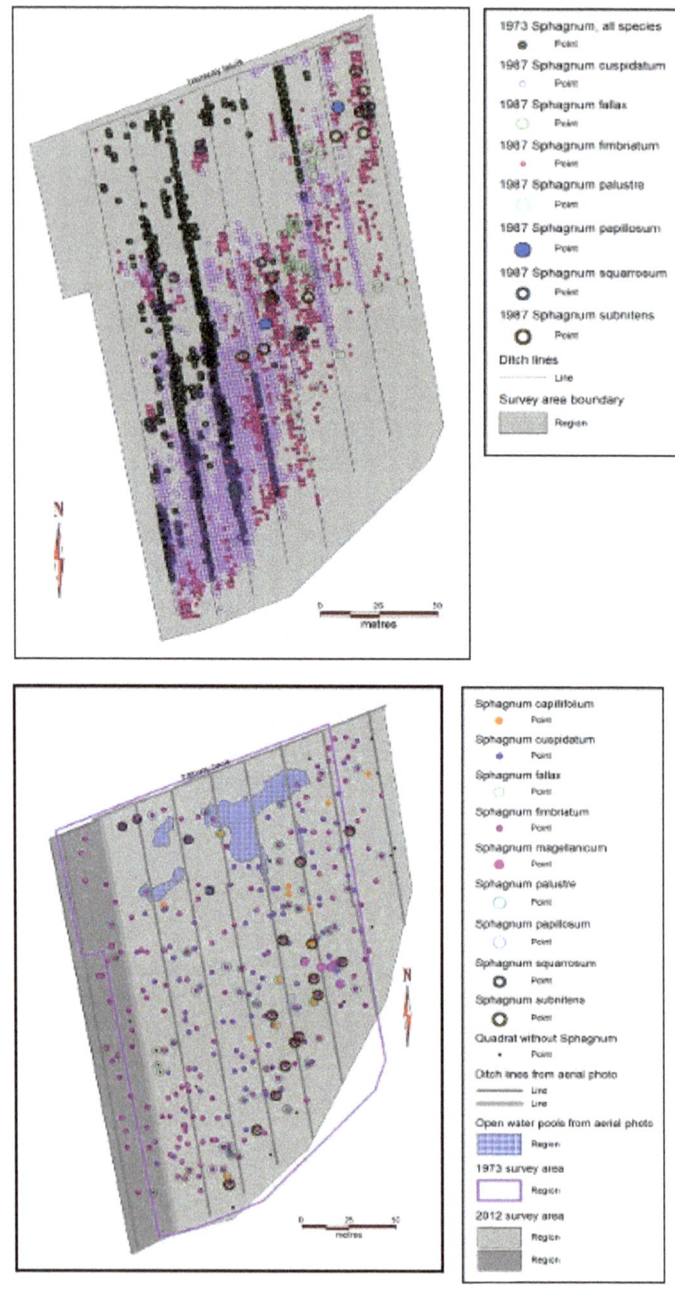


**Figure 5: Distribution of *Sphagnum* moss species at Danes Moss 1973-2012**

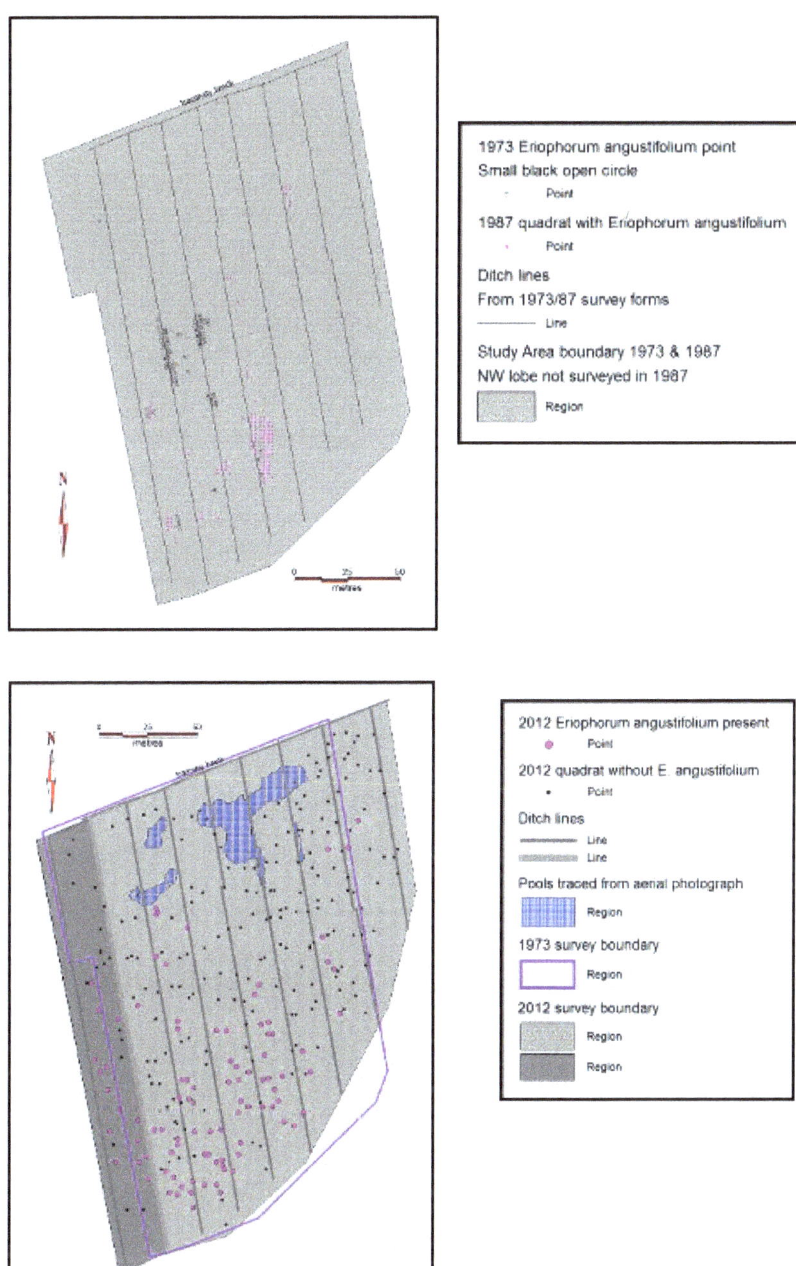


**Figure 6: Distribution of *Eriophorum angustifolium* at Danes Moss 1973-2012**

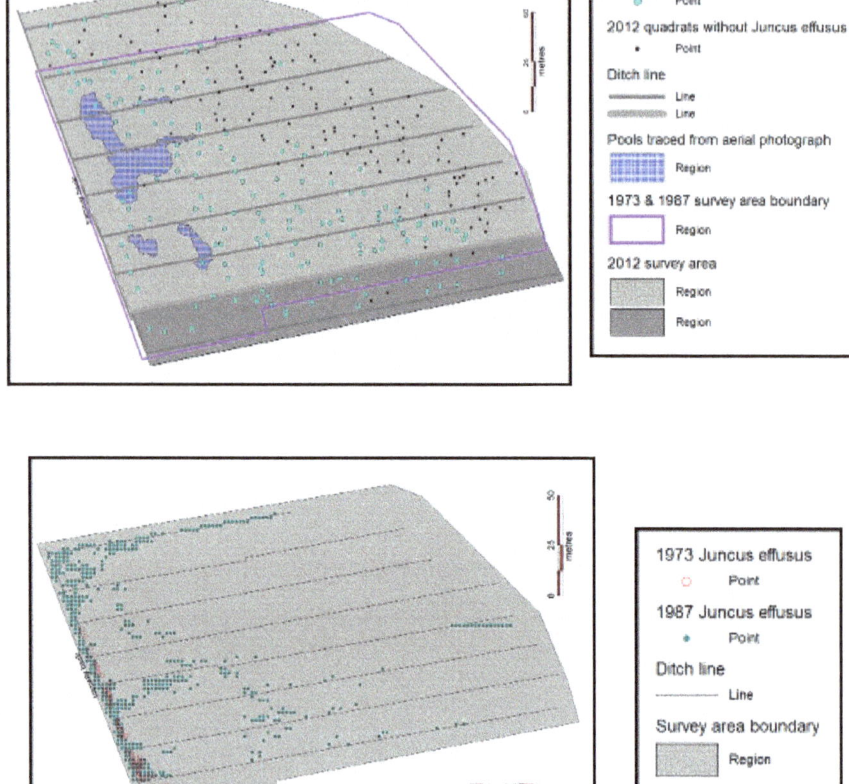


**Figure 7: Distribution of *Juncus effusus* at Danes Moss 1973 – 2012**

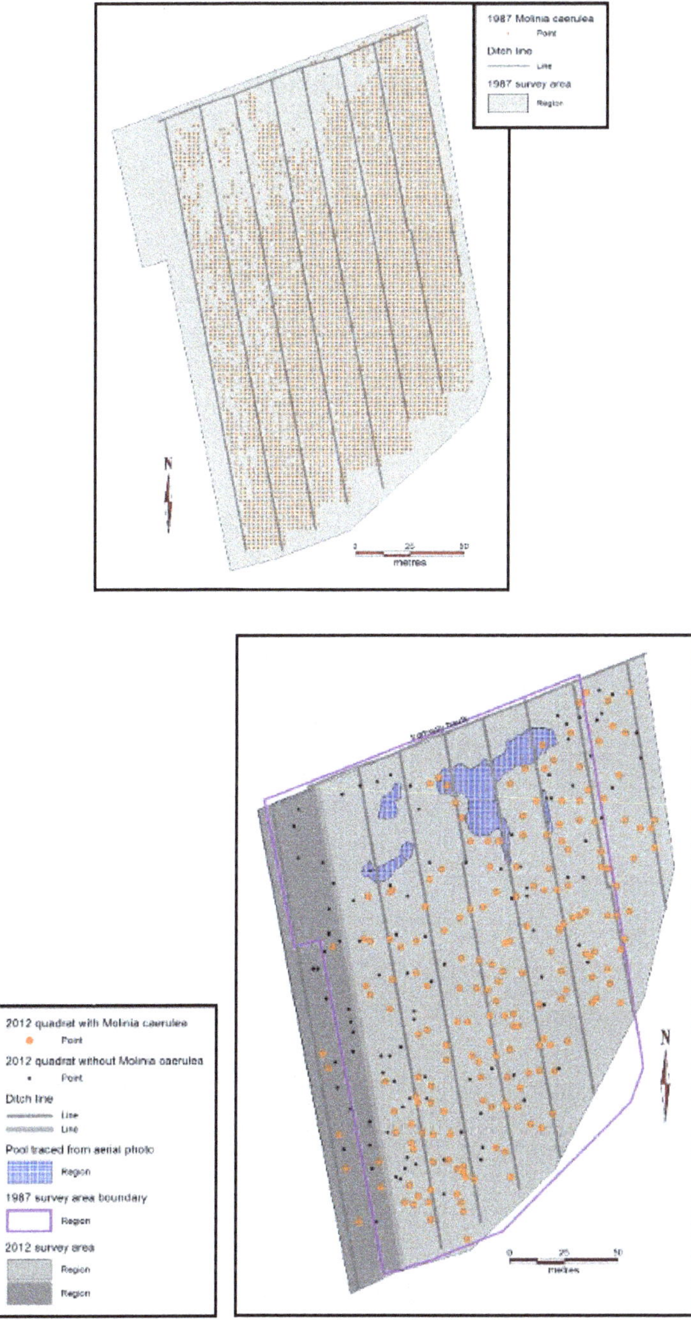


**Figure 8: Distribution of *Molinia caerulea* at Danes Moss 1987 and 2012**

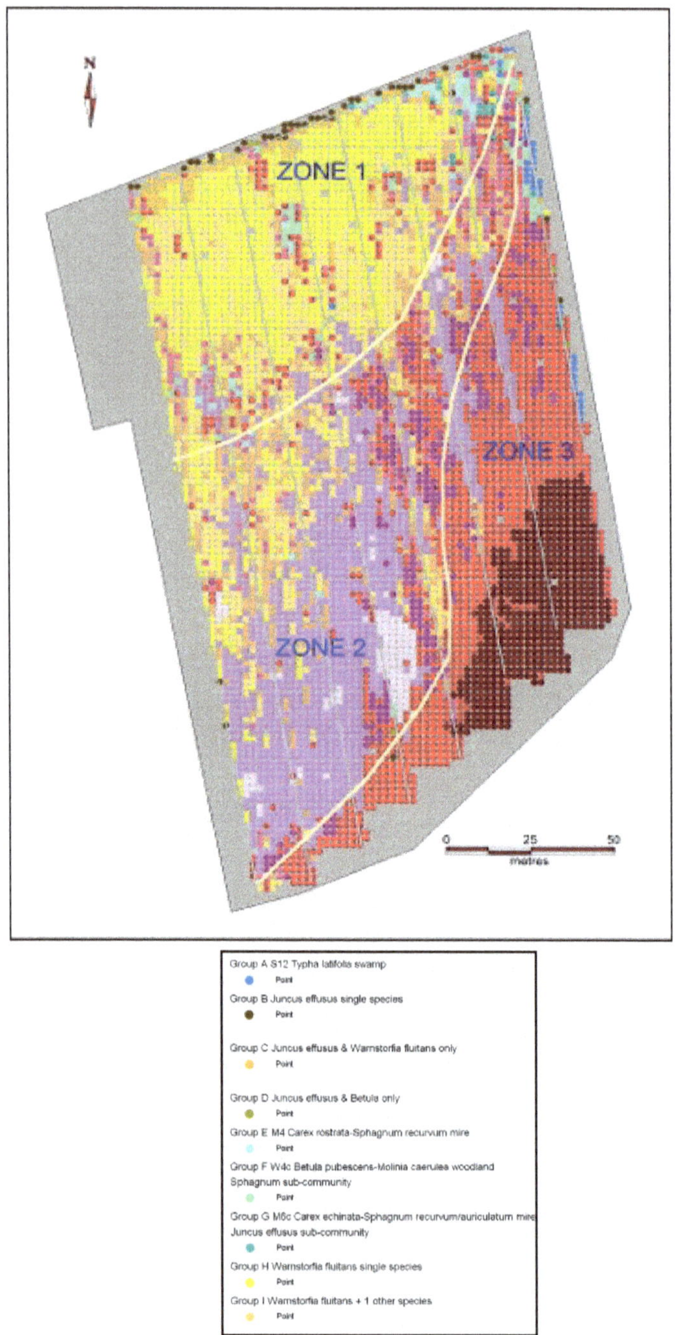


**Figure 9: Distribution of 1987 NVC communities using MATCH classification of TWINSPAN groups of synthesised quadrats**

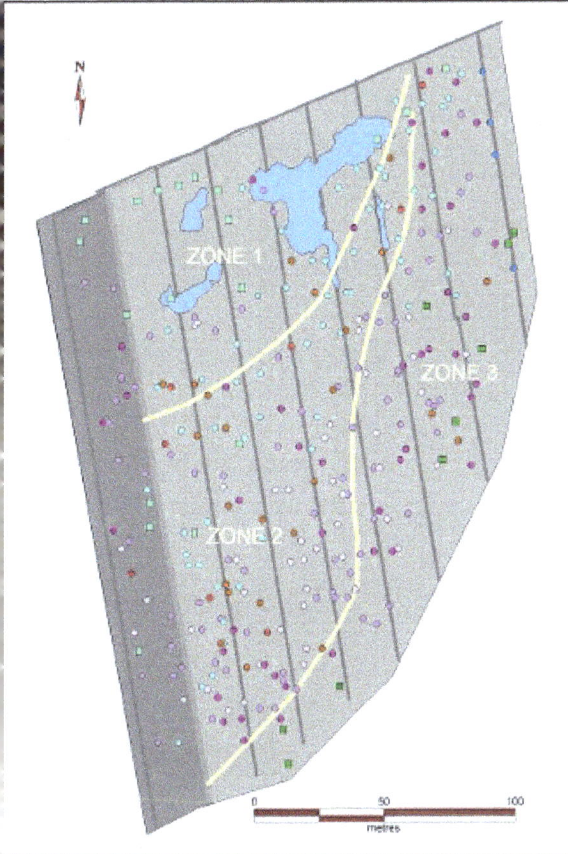


**Figure 10: Distribution of 2012 NVC communities using quadrat locations and a MATCH classification based on TWINSPAN groups**

H9e Calluna vulgaris-Deschampsia flexuosa heath
Molinia caerulea sub-community
Point

M16a Erica tetralix-Sphagnum compactum wet heath
Typical sub-community
Point

M2 Sphagnum cuspidatum/recurvum bog pool community
Inc M2b Sphagnum recurvum sub-community
Point

M3 Eriophorum angustifolium bog pool community
Point

M4 Carex rostrata-Sphagnum recurvum mire
Point

M21b Narthecium ossifragum-Sphagnum papillosum valley mire
Vaccinium oxycoccos-Sphagnum recurvum sub-community
Point

S12 Typha latifolia swamp
Inc S12d Carex rostrata sub-community
Point

W4a Betula pubescens-Molinia caerulea woodland
Dryopteris dilatata-Rubus fruticosus sub-community
Point

W4c Betula pubescens-Molinia caerulea woodland
Sphagnum sub-community
Point

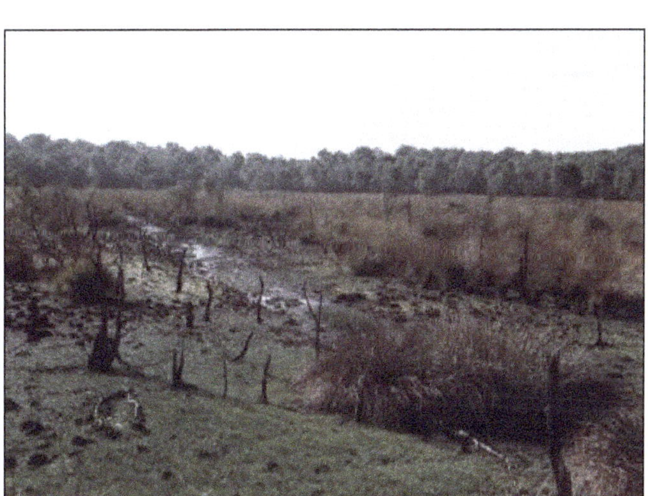

**Figure 11: *Juncus effusus* seedlings on exposed silt September 1989**

**Figure 12: Floating silt and establishment of *Juncus effusus* June 1990**

**Figure 13: W4c vegetation at Danes Moss, November 2012**

**Figure 14: M4 vegetation at Danes Moss**

The vegetation is now a mix of wet heath, bog pool, rush-dominated mire and ostensibly woodland communities following a gentle gradient rising from north west to south east with some reflection of the parallel ditch patterning arising from peat cutting in the 1960s, the higher inter-ditch areas bearing drier heath. The W4c 'woodland' community classification is determined by the ground cover and trees are mostly absent.

There are still shallow pools in Zone 1 but most of those created by raising the water level in 1974 have rafted over with *Juncus effusus* and are now a mix of open rush with a thick carpet of mostly *Sphagnum fimbriatum* (Figure 13). The recognition by this community by MATCH as W4c is clearly erroneous as it is not *Betula pubescens-Molinia caerulea* woodland, lacking birch except for scattered trees and *Molinia*, except as occasional tussocks.

Soft rush is also present at high cover in the M4 community in which the most frequent moss is *Sphagnum cuspidatum* (Figure 14) and this extends south east from the W4c, particularly along old ditch lines. *Eriophorum angustifolium* is frequent within this community and in places forms separate dense stands as the M3 bog pool community.

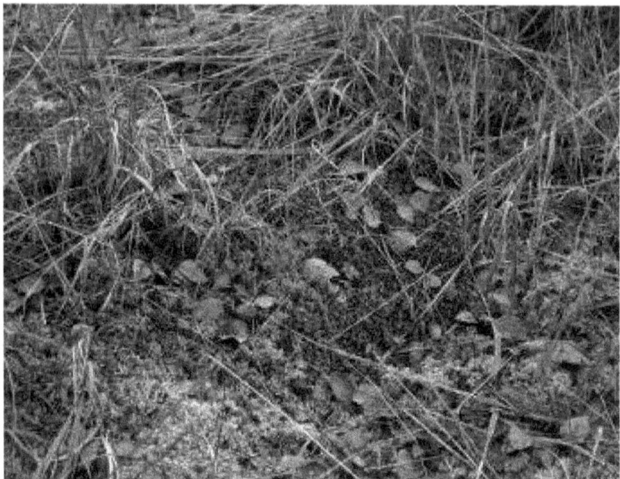

**Figure 15: M21b vegetation at Danes Moss**

Where rush is less frequent and of very low cover there is a transition to the M2b and M3 bog pool communities, along and between the old ditch lines. In turn, this merges with the M21b valley mire community in which there is a greater variety of *Sphagnum* species, including *Sphagnum papillosum* and *S. capillifolium* (Figure 15).

As is evident from Figure 5, *Sphagnum* species are present in nearly all of the quadrats recorded in 2012. With the exception of the drier interface with higher ground in the south east, and in some slightly elevated inter-ditch areas with H9e and M16a heath, there is a continuous carpet of *Sphagnum* over the study area. In the pre-rewetting era of 1973-1975, it was confined to ditch-lines and was absent from many.

## Assessment of changes at Red Moss and Danes Moss

The changes are assessed as increases in species complement, the extent (range) of individual species within each site and the establishment of NVC communities associated with more intact raised bogs. They are tabulated (Table 4) with comments on their strengths and weaknesses as indicators of positive or negative change.

*Sphagnum* is now more widely distributed at both sites but is more extensive at Danes Moss, covering almost the whole 2.6 ha of the study area. The expansion in distribution at Red Moss is more modest but the increase in cover within compartments where it was already established in 1993 is notable. The difference in sampling method between 1993 (whole site cover including ditches) and 2007 (limited number of samples mostly between ditches) makes precise comparison impossible, but suggests that spread and consolidation of *Sphagnum*, as a 'positive' indicator of change has taken place.

Another important consequence of the increased *Sphagnum* cover at Danes Moss has been to provide a spongy and vertically mobile surface, analogous to the acrotelm of a raised bog, through which water can move, and which can adjust to small fluctuations in the water-table. This has developed over Zone 1 and Zone 2 between 1987 and 2012, contrasting with 1973 when it was only found in a few ditches. The change has involved terrestrialisation (Weber, 1902, 1908) of the open water created in Zone 1 and the paludification (Cajander, 1913) of the surface in Zone 2, also extending into Zone 3.

The increase in the number of *Sphagnum* species on each site is modest, but the addition of *S. magellanicum* and *S. capillifolium*, normally associated with raised bog is consistent with the aims of management. The presence of *S. papillosum* at Red Moss was not acknowledged by all contributors to the public inquiry of 1993, but examination of microscopic characters showed it to be present then and it was more widespread in 2007. The increase in distribution and cover of these species marks a positive shift towards the typical flora of a raised bog surface.

Implantation of *Sphagnum papillosum* across a hydrological gradient, either within established *Molinia caerulea* or on bare peat at Danes Moss (Meade, 2003) suggested that the optimum hydrological regime is for the peat to remain damp but to be free from inundation for 80% of the year, and for the water level to not fall more than 30 cm below the peat surface. The experiment also showed that establishment was better within the *Molinia* sward rather than on bare peat, provided the dead leaf litter was periodically removed, as was required to assess the moss growth. Ideal conditions are most likely to be found within Zone 2, where the distribution of *S. papillosum* has increased.

The development of other bog species at Red Moss is modest, with gains and losses of *Eriophorum angustifolium* and little change in the distribution of *E. vaginatum*. *Erica tetralix* remains scarce and *Vaccinium oxycoccos* has not been recorded. At Danes Moss *Eriophorum angustifolium* is much more widespread, forming dense stands of community M3 in pools, and *E. vaginatum* is more densely established within Zone 2. Although *Erica tetralix* remains scarce, *Vaccinium oxycoccos* has spread within Zone 2; *Andromeda polifolia* has not yet been recorded, and *Drosera rotundifolia* was not recorded within the study area. This means that, although a bog-building platform of *Sphagnum* mosses is becoming established at both sites, the diversity of typical bog species remains low.

Dense, tussocky *Molinia caerulea* is found on many cutover and abandoned peatlands in the north west of England, some of which have been designated as SSSIs, including Red Moss and Danes Moss. The surveys of both sites show that raising the water table has been followed by a reduction in the dominance of this grass, and its elimination where permanently inundated. Re-establishment of *Molinia* on the terrestrialising surface is minimal. Moribund or stressed tussocks act as platforms or shelter for the colonisation of other bog plant species, such as *Sphagnum papillosum* (Meade, 2003).

Soft Rush *Juncus effusus* is a common colonist of damp and wet soils (e.g. Meade & Wheeler, 2005), including deep peat. Its locations on Red Moss and Danes Moss are coincident with identifiable nutrient enrichment, in the first case primarily from the landfill, in the second from agricultural holdings. Its apparent reduction in distribution at Red Moss may be in part due to the different survey methods, in that drains may have been included in the 1993 assessment but excluded in 2007, especially as its cover has increased in other compartments. Records of change at Danes Moss are more reliable and can be characterised as four phases in which weakening of the rush cover has eventually occurred, after an initial aggressive expansion. Quadrats recorded at Red Moss in 2007 show that

*Juncus effusus* is accompanied by other species in many cases, though relatively pure stands still exist, and there is currently no evidence to cite Danes Moss as an analogue on which to predict future change.

## Table 4: Summary of changes in positive and negative indicators on Red Moss and Danes Moss

| Criterion | Red Moss | | Danes Moss | |
|---|---|---|---|---|
| | Change | Comment | Change | Comment |
| Extent of Sphagnum species | Found in two additional compartments, main change has been in cover from a maximum of 5% in 1993 to 60% in 2007. | Comparison is between complete survey coverage in 1993 to walkover and sampling in 2007. | From isolation within and around ditches to almost the whole study area (2.6 ha). | While this includes species more typical of poor fen there are also raised bog species; *S. cuspidatum* is very widespread and dominant. |
| Number of Sphagnum species | Increase from nine to ten, the addition being *S. magellanicum.* | Unequivocal. | *Sphagnum capillifolium* and *S. magellanicum* are additions. The extents of *S. papillosum, S. palustre* and *S. subnitens* have increased. | *Sphagnum magellanicum* can be traced to an experimental introduction in the early 1990s (Meade, 2003). |
| Changes in other bog species | *Eriophorum angustifolium* has been lost from some compartments but cover has increased in others. | Present mostly in ditches the species could have been poorly sampled in 2007. | *Eriophorum angustifolium* and *Vaccinium oxycoccos* are more widespread. | Their distributions are no longer limited to the ditches, they are now more widely distributed. |
| Changes in negative indicators | a) *Juncus effusus* is lost from eleven compartments but gained in one. Increase in cover in six compartments.<br><br>b) Cover of *Molinia caerulea* is reduced in sixteen compartments and has increased in | a) Needs to be balanced against the seral importance of the NVC community in which it was found.<br><br>b) Important reduction in competition from *Molinia.* | a) *Juncus effusus* has increased its range to about two-thirds of the area.<br><br>b) *Molinia* is reduced in extent and dominance except where driest. | a) It followed a sequence of aggressive establishment on floating and fixed silt then a reduction in vigour.<br><br>b) Old tussocks are still discernible but are overgrown by e.g. *Sphagnum* and other bog species. |

| | | | | |
|---|---|---|---|---|
| | one, though its extent remains the same.<br><br>c) *Typha latifolia* is lost from seven compartments, increasing in one and decreasing in another of the remainder. | c) The difference in survey methods would mean that very scattered *Typha*, or that confined to drains, would not be recorded in 2007. | c) *Typha latifolia* has not spread significantly. | c) Still associated with the same ditches as in 1973-5. |
| Development of raised bog NVC communities | Development of scattered M21b, more typical of valley fen; M3 bog pool is associated with raised bogs. One quadrat was fitted to M18a by MATCH, a community typical of raised bog. | There is a predominance of *Molinia*-dominated vegetation, much as in 1993, but M21b is likely to have developed since 1993 as it is not mentioned in ER&AP, (1993). | Communities typical of raised bog such as M18 and M19 were not recorded but the bog-pool communities M2 and M3 are now extensive. As at Red Moss, M21b is also recorded. | Distribution follows the hydrological gradient. Raised bog species are most strongly associated with M2 and M21b vegetation, those with *Juncus effusus* fall within the poor fen category. |

The difference in survey methods at Red Moss may also be responsible for the apparent reduction in the distribution of *Typha latifolia*. As for *Juncus effusus*, it may show the species has not spread onto the open peat surface but is still present in the ditches. Unlike *J. effusus*, this species (*Typha*) did not spread at Danes Moss when the water level was raised.

The NVC communities that are useful measures in the management fall into four categories. There is the characterisation of the dry peat vegetation in which *Molinia* is prominent, the bog pools as ditches and expanses of shallow water, development of bog species on non-inundated but damp peat, and those flushed by nutrient-enriched water in which *Juncus effusus* or *Typha latifolia* are dominant. For both sites, relating the communities to the published NVC communities is made less reliable by the small number of species recorded.

Without the use of diagnostic tools such as MATCH the tussocky *Molinia*-dominated vegetation was described as M25 for Red Moss in 1993, and this was also indicated by MATCH as appropriate for some grouped 2007 quadrats. However, applying MATCH to single 2007 Red Moss quadrats gave higher coefficients for H2 and H9 communities in some cases. Of these, the *Molinia caerulea* sub-community of the *Calluna vulgaris-Deschampsia flexuosa* heath (H9e) is analogous to some stands on Red Moss and is even more widespread on Danes Moss. A change from M25 to H9e would be consistent with the development of *Calluna vulgaris* and *Deschampsia flexuosa* as co-dominants with *Molinia*, and this now occurs on both sites.

Bog pool vegetation as either the M2 or M3 community had not become widely established within compartments on Red Moss in 2007, though both are likely to be frequent along ditches that were rarely sampled. However, M2 including the M2b sub-community is widely established on Danes Moss between the ditches to which it was previously confined. It is described (Rodwell (ed.), 1991-2000) as a colonist of shallow workings on peatlands in pool, wet hollow or lawns, but is also typical within hummock-hollow complexes of intact raised bogs.

The development of M21b *Narthecium ossifragum-Sphagnum papillosum, Vaccinium oxycoccos-Sphagnum recurvum* sub-community is a positive change on both sites. Although described (Rodwell, (ed.), 1991-2000) as having a southern focus in the UK and is distinct from the *Scirpus-Eriophorum* or *Erica-Sphagnum* mires, typical of raised bogs, its distribution includes the latitudes encompassing Red Moss and Danes Moss. Although the eponymous *Narthecium ossifragum* is absent the sub-community includes many of the species found on these sites. The situation is similar to that of valley mires in that the ombrotrophic areas of the peat surface are often close to and influenced by groundwater that may be enriched with minerals and plant nutrients, the more intensively flushed areas marking a transition to rush-dominated vegetation and on drier parts to heath vegetation in which *Calluna vulgaris* and *Molinia caerulea* become dominant. It is also significant that the MATCH coefficient for one Red Moss 2007 quadrat was highest for M18a, the *Erica tetralix-Sphagnum papillosum* mire.

The M6c *Carex echinata-Sphagnum recurvum/auriculatum* mire, *Juncus effusus* sub-community is characteristically found in flushes, and so ditches receiving enriched groundwater as found on Red Moss and Danes Moss (1987) are analogous. The use of the NVC community provides an evaluative concept in which the presence of the rush is consistent with a semi-natural habitat, and which can have a successional relationship with the desired end-point of raised bog. Stands in which the rush is dominant and of high total cover are included in the 'type description'.

The rush-dominated communities found on Danes Moss in 2012 are a poor fit with NVC communities, falling between stands with a co-dominance of either *Sphagnum fimbriatum* or *S. cuspidatum*. Although given highest coefficients as W4c and M4 respectively by MATCH, these are arguably local variants of the M6c found on Red Moss. Hydrologically, they occupy a rather different niche in the advanced terrestrialisation of shallow open water having a legacy of nutrient enrichment. The development of the *Sphagnum* carpet may indicate a transition towards M2b or M21b, as small nuclei of additional species such as *S. capillifolium* already occur on the raft where mounds of cut peat blocks or dead *Molinia* tussocks elevate the surface.

Changes in the plant species and vegetation on both sites support the view that those typical of peat formation are becoming more widely established. This vindicates the opinions of those responsible for designating the sites as SSSI, those who put much time and effort into site management, and others whose efforts led to the refusal of the planning application for extension of the landfill at Red Moss. It also shows the sites to be consistent with the European Community's description of degraded raised bog still capable of natural regeneration (European Commission, 1996).

The degree to which the observations apply to the whole sites and are transferable to others must take account of the water supply mechanisms in each case, as far as they are known. For example, the study area at Danes Moss is a shallow depression, isolated from the remainder of the peatland, and more analogous to a basin fen; run-off from the landfill at Red Moss is currently channelled away from the rewetted areas, but presents a technical challenge if rewetting is to be applied to the compartments through which it is cut. Management prescriptions for the SSSIs have been applied to compartmentalised areas and have yet to be seen within plans for the complete mires in which generic concepts such as mire expanse, rand and lagg would be the guiding principle.

## Acknowledgements

Natural England is acknowledged for permission to use data from their condition assessment of Red Moss in 2007 and from a partnership project with Roger Meade Associates to re-survey Danes Moss in 2012. The author is grateful to Dr Bryan Wheeler for assistance with the TWINSPAN and MATCH analyses, and to the Lancashire Wildlife Trust for their consistent input to the management of Red Moss.

## References

Cajander, A.K. (1913) Studien über die Moore Finnlands. *Acta Forestalia Fennica*, **2 (3)**, 1-208.

Dargie, T.D.C. (2001) *The effect of peat depth and quality on primary colonist plants on the Humberhead Peatlands*. Commissioned report, English Nature, Natural England, Sheffield.

Environmental Research Advisory Partnership (ER & AP), (1992) *Red Moss, Horwich, Bolton MB: Objection to SSSI designation presented as evidence at the 1993 public inquiry into objections to Bolton Metropolitan Borough Council's Unitary Development Plan*. Preston.

Environmental Research Advisory Partnership (ER & AP), (1993) *Ecological survey of Red Moss, Bolton, presented as evidence at the 1993 public inquiry into objections to Bolton Metropolitan Borough Council's Unitary Development Plan*. Preston.

European Commission (1996) *Interpretation Manual of the European Union Habitats*. European Commission, DG XI – Environment, Nuclear Safety and Civil Protection.

Hill, M.O. (1979) *TWINSPAN - a FORTRAN program for arranging multivariate data in an ordered two-way table by classification of the individuals and attributes*. Cornell University, New York.

JNCC (Joint Nature Conservation Committee) (1994) *Guidelines for the selection of biological SSSIs: Bogs*. JNCC, Peterborough.

JNCC (Joint Nature Conservation Committee) (2004) *Common Standards Monitoring Guidance for Lowland Wetland*, Version August 2004, ISSN 1743-8160. JNCC, Peterborough.

Malloch, A.J.C. (1990) *MATCH. A computer programme to aid the assignment of vegetation data to the communities and sub-communities of the National Vegetation Classification*. Unit of Vegetation Science, Lancaster University, Lancaster.

Meade, R. (1992) Some early changes following the rewetting of a vegetated cutover peatland surface at Danes Moss, Cheshire, UK, and their relevance to conservation management. *Biological Conservation*, **61**, 31-40.

Meade, R. (2003) *Establishment of peat-forming vegetation on a degraded raised bog: replacing existing plant cover*. In: Meade, R. (ed.) *Proceedings of the Risley Moss Bog Restoration Workshop*. English Nature (now Natural England), Peterborough.

Meade, R. and Wheeler, B.D. (2005) *Raised bogs from gravel pits? Experiences at Hatfield Moors, South Yorkshire*. In: Meade, R. and Humphries, N. (eds) *Minerals Extraction and Wetland Creation*. Proceedings of a workshop held in Doncaster 26-27 September 2005. Natural England, Peterborough.

Rodwell, J.S. (ed.) (1991-2000) *British Plant Communities*. Volumes 1-5. Cambridge University Press, Cambridge.

Weber, C.A. (1902) *Über die Vegetation und Entstehung des Hochmoores von Austumal im Memeldelta*. Berlin.

Weber, C.A. (1908). Aufbau und Vegetation der Moore Norddeutchlands. Engler, *Botanischen Jahrbüchern*, **90**, 19-34.

# Chapter 8. The Delamere's Dragons Project

**Chris Meredith**
Cheshire Wildlife Trust

## The White-faced Darter (*Leucorrhinia dubia*)

The white-faced darter dragonfly (*Leucorrhinia dubia*) was a Local Biodiversity Action Plan species for Cheshire until it became extinct in the region in 2003. This species, Britain's second smallest dragonfly, is a lowland bog specialist named after its white frons (face). As breeding habitat, it requires submerged rafts of *Sphagnum* moss in permanent, low nutrient, acidic bog pools with emergent plants such as cotton grass (*Eriophorum* sp.). For shelter and feeding habitat it requires surrounding low scrub and trees. The white-faced darter is an early species with a synchronous emergence in May-June that marks the beginning of the flight season which ends in mid-July. In the UK, it is found from Scotland to Staffordshire, but this distribution is patchy, and it now has only four English breeding sites; two in Cumbria, one in Staffordshire and one in Shropshire. In Delamere, and indeed nationally, population declines are attributable to loss and fragmentation of habitat through scrub encroachment, drainage, peat cutting, plantation forestry, and water quality changes from water influx from surrounding agricultural land.

**Figure 1: A male White-faced Darter Dragonfly (*Leucorrhinia dubia*)** ©Vicky Nall 2013

## Reintroduction to Cheshire

In 2011, a steering group was set up and commissioned a feasibility study to investigate whether a white-faced darter reintroduction programme had potential in Delamere. The study followed on from a report produced in 2003 which identified over 100 wetland hollows hidden within Delamere Forest and created management plans for them. After each basin was assessed using criteria based on known white-faced darter habitat requirements, a basin named Doolittle was selected as the most suitable site and could be made ready for a pilot reintroduction with minimal work. Further basins that were identified as likely to be suitable but needing more work were identified and made a focus of the 'Delamere's Lost Mosses' project, to be run in conjunction with the white-faced darter reintroduction.

After a successful pilot year in 2013 that saw individuals emerging, ovipositing, and defending territories in Delamere, 'Delamere's Dragons' project funded by Heritage Lottery Fund in partnership with the Forestry Commission, continued to reintroduce the white-faced darter dragonfly into a newly-restored peat basin in Delamere Forest in Cheshire throughout 2014, 2015 and 2016. To reintroduce this species, a two-stage translocation is required from a donor population (a population deemed strong enough to sustain loss of some individuals in a breeding season). This project is unique in that it has two donor populations: Fenns and Whixall Moss NNR in Shropshire and Chartley Moss NNR in Staffordshire (both managed by Natural England). Stage one involves moving final instar larvae just prior to the flight season so that these will emerge the following month. This thereby confirms that the new habitat is indeed suitable for the species and allows the second stage to proceed. The larvae are easily identifiable due to three ventral stripes on the underside and migrate closer to the water surface before emergence, making the task of finding and collecting them much easier. The second stage of translocation takes place just after flight season in July/August and involves the moving of *Sphagnum* moss containing white-faced darter dragonfly eggs laid throughout the season at the donor sites to boost numbers at the recipient site.

©Tom Marshall 2013

**Figure 2: White-faced darter (*Leucorrhinia dubia*) larvae**

By 2016, numbers should be sufficiently high, and it is hoped that the white-faced darter dragonfly will naturally disperse to other sites within Delamere Forest that are currently being restored by the 'Delamere's Lost Mosses' project. Dispersal success will help to inform and direct management of the habitat with regards to habitat connectivity and buffer zones within the forest. The ongoing population dynamics and dispersal success will be measured and monitored by a team of volunteer surveyors trained and ready to keep watch of this new population.

## A unique research opportunity

The two donor sites make this project (only the third odonata reintroduction project in the UK) unique and Cheshire Wildlife Trust is working with Manchester Metropolitan University (MMU) to fully embrace the potential for important conservation genetics research. By working in partnership with MMU, a genetic baseline will be established from the populations at both sites to then detect the relative success of the individuals from each donor site in Delamere as well as the mainland Europe origin(s) of the existing British populations. This information will begin to answer the question "does source matter?" and further inform the IUCN guidelines on invertebrate reintroduction. It will also begin to reveal the genetic diversity and speciation rates of the long-isolated populations in Britain which will help to understand the security of their future in Britain.

The emergence conditions of the white-faced darter will also be carefully assessed in the large populations present at both donor sites. Information on emergence preferences at these sites will be used to tailor management of the new site for the species as well as further important research on this declining species to put a halt to its decline and see the species colonising new sites throughout Britain.

## Science and communities

Peat bogs are a tough habitat to 'sell' to the general public, especially when their restoration often involves the removal of trees. The Delamere's Dragons project is using the white-faced darter as a flagship species to raise awareness of the importance of peatland habitats and the restoration works happening in Delamere Forest. It aims to give local people ownership of something very special and unique to them. So far, the project has a mailing list of over 120 people who are interested in dragonflies and the importance of the bog habitats in Delamere to them. These people are beginning to understand and appreciate the importance and beauty of bogs and will help to spread a new attitude to the 'wet, swampy bits' of Delamere Forest and are helping collect the valuable field data needed for this research project. It is hoped that by the end of the project, this interesting and challenging mix of new science and community involvement will have helped secure the long term future of peat habitats and their species in the Delamere area, protected and appreciated by the local community, Cheshire Wildlife Trust and the Forestry Commission.

## Bibliography

Bentley-Fox, H. (2000) *A study to determine the habitat requirements of the White-faced darter (*Leucorrhinia dubia *(Vander Linden)) at Fenn's, Whixall and Bettisfield Mosses National Nature Reserve (NNR)*. Unpublished MSc. dissertation, Farnborough College of Technology School of Environmental Management, Farnborough.

Cheeseborough, I. and Uff, C. (2000) *An Investigation into the Importance of Scrub on the Breeding Dragonflies of Whixall Moss*. English Nature internal report, Peterborough.

Hayes, C. (2011) *Assessment of Basin Mire Sites in the Delamere Forest Area: Potential for the re-introduction of White-faced Darter dragonfly (WFD)* Leucorrhinia dubia. Internal report prepared for Natural England, Forestry Commission and Cheshire Wildlife Trust, Peterborough.

Hayes, C., Bentley, D., Drake, M. and Bennettt, S. (2003) The *Lost Meres and Mosses of Delamere Forest Project*. Internal report prepared for English Nature, Forestry Commission, Cheshire Wildlife Trust and Cheshire County Council.

Joy, J. (1992) *A Survey of the Odonata of Fenn's, Whixall and Bettisfield Mosses in 1992 with particular emphasis on the White-faced Dragonfly* Leucorrhinia dubia. English Nature internal report, Peterborough.

# Chapter 9. The Delamere's lost mosses project

**Katie Piercy**
Cheshire Wildlife Trust

## A glacial beginning

The origin of the rare and valuable Delamere mosslands goes back to the end of the last glacial period. Around 15,000 years ago Delamere, along with most of Northern Britain, was covered in a thick glacial ice sheet. When the ice began to retreat around 10,000-15,000 years ago, it left behind a landscape layered with glacial till and peppered in hollows known as kettle-holes. It is these kettle-holes that today form the bogs scattered throughout Delamere forest, and the same process which formed the wetland complex now highlighted as nationally important in the Meres and Mosses Natural Area.

Having been formed in a dramatic and devastating fashion, these kettle-holes now developed slowly over the next few thousand years, filling with peat forming vegetation. By the medieval period most had developed their own lowland raised bog ecosystems, schwingmoor or remained as meres. In time, the Delamere mosses became part of the Norman hunting forest of Mara. Together with the adjoining hunting forest of Mondrem, it covered over sixty square miles, protecting this area against agricultural use by forest law. A mosaic of heathland, mossland and woodland habitats, this landscape was inhabited by wild boar, red and roe deer, all long gone today. However, in 1812, when forest law was finally removed, agricultural practice began to infiltrate into these precious ecosystems.

Mosses, viewed as dangerous and unproductive areas of land, were drained whenever possible. During the Napoleonic era, Delamere's mosses were particularly targeted for drainage, in order to use the area to produce oak timber for the Napoleonic wars. These drainage attempts were often only partly successful, but in time attempts were more effective, and today Delamere is more known for its woodland than its bogs.

## Seeing the Moss for the Trees

Hidden between Delamere's conifer plantations and ancient woodland, remnants from the hunting forest of Mara, lies a series of peat basins.

Around two decades ago these basins, mostly drained and forested, would barely have been distinguished from the rest of the forest, but for a few specialist bog species, clinging on in the dampest ditches, and amongst the forest clearings. Sphagnum species, cotton grasses, bilberries and heathers could be found scattered between pines, spruces and sweet chestnuts. However, in the 1990s the Forestry Commission decided to deforest one of Delamere's largest basins, Great Blakemere (Figure 1), and block the outflow to allow the basin to refill with water.

Due to the sloping nature of the site the eastern end of the basin became flooded, whilst the western end became damp enough to encourage revival of some of the mossland species within the area. Within a few years the basin had been transformed from conifer woodland to transition mire habitat, with specialist species such as round-leaved sundew (*Drosera rotunifolia*), and even county rarities such as royal fern (*Osmunda regalis*) reappearing. This flagship project demonstrated how effective mossland restoration could be within Delamere forest, and to what level the mosses could recover. Over the next 15 years the Forestry Commission worked with partners to begin the restoration of further peat basins.

In 2011, the Delamere white-faced darter steering group was established to assess the feasibility of reintroducing the dragonfly into the acidic pools of the restoring mosses. The potential of a reintroduction catalysed the need to boost and continue the restoration work to date. With this in mind plans for the Delamere's Lost Mosses project began.

## Delamere's Lost Mosses Project

In November 2013, a four year project began aiming to restore damaged peat basins in and around Delamere forest. Funded by WREN, Cheshire Wildlife Trust, Forestry Commission,

Cheshire West and Chester Council and Natural England the project focuses on ten sites within the landscape, one of these sites being Delamere Forest itself. Each of the areas for restoration are Local Wildlife Sites or hold SSSI or RAMSAR status. The aim within the four years is to restore 120ha of transition mire and quaking bog habitat across these ten sites, through use of contractors and local volunteers coordinated by a Project Officer.

Since the project began over 80 volunteers have been recruited from the local area. Meeting twice a month these volunteers are helping to clear some of the regenerating birch which has taken over many of the drier sites, where conifer clearance has allowed pioneer woodland to take over the peat basins.

Ditch blocking is also a key aspect of the restoration of the bogs, with several different methods, including sluices, plastic piling and peat dams having been used across the sites in the past. Water levels must be raised and maintained at the correct levels in order to keep the basins from converting to woodland. With 'unparalleled' potential for transition mire and quaking bog restoration across Delamere (Natural England) it is also vital that some basins are flooded and left to develop over years to come. Due to their past management and current condition, not all basins can, or will, develop into the same habitats. However, in time a mosaic of mossland, fen and wet heath habitats can be created.

## Delamere Living Landscape Scheme

Working in partnership, the Delamere's Lost Mosses project initiates Cheshire Wildlife Trust's Delamere 'Living Landscape Scheme'. The scheme aims to deliver the vision of a coherent and healthy ecological network of peatland habitats that people enjoy and value. As well as the restoration of the peat basins within and around the forest the Lost Mosses Project is looking at the Delamere landscape as a whole and will identify where and how to make the landscape more permeable to mossland species. One species of particular interest is the white-faced darter dragonfly (*Leucorrhinia dubia*) (Figure 2). The species became locally extinct in Delamere in 2003 due to a change in pH levels in its only remaining breeding pool.

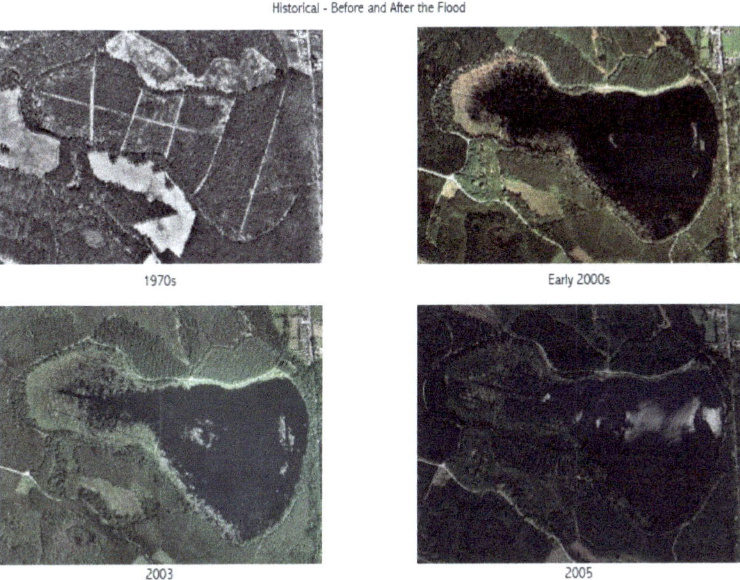


**Figure 1. Restoring Blakemere Moss.**

**Figure 2. White-faced darter dragonfly.**

A reintroduction project began in 2013, and it is hoped that in time the dragonfly will begin to disperse itself throughout the forest to other suitable pools, from its current reintroduction site. Other important species, such as *Sitticus floricola* (colloquially known as the Delamere jumping spider) are currently confined to isolated pockets of habitat, and unable to bridge the gaps between other potential breeding sites. By connecting these habitats with suitable corridors and stepping-stones it is hoped that these specialists will be able to thrive throughout the Delamere landscape.

Already some species have begun to take advantage of newly restored habitats. The green hairstreak butterfly (*Callophrys rubri*), resident at Flaxmere SSSI on the edge of Delamere forest, has this year been recorded on a restored area of heathland on the edge of the forest. Hopefully, this is the first step in its journey through the Delamere landscape.

## Bibliography

Bennett, S. (2013) *Meres and Mosses - Delamere Landscape Project*. Cheshire Wildlife Trust, Cheshire.

Hayes, C. (2004) *The Lost Meres and Mosses of Delamere, An ecological appraisal and wetland enhancement project*. Ecology First, Cheshire.

Hayes, C. (2011) *Great Blakemere, Delamere Forest, Cheshire, Ecological Appraisal and Outline Management Plan*. Ecology First, Cheshire.

# Chapter 9. Diversity of Estonian mires and mire forests

**Jaanus Paal**
University of Tartu, Estonia.

## Summary

Estonia is situated between 57°30′34″ – 59°49′12″ N and 21°45′49″ – 28°12′44″ E. The total area of the country is 4,522,726 ha, of which 9.2% is made up of the more than 1,500 islands and islets. Mires and paludified areas occur all over the country.

Minerotrophic fens are the most widespread, occupying 515,000 ha or 57% of the total mire area. Mixotrophic (transitional) mires are represented on 114,000 ha (12%) and bogs on 278,000 ha (31%). More than 16,500 of the Estonian peatlands cover an area bigger than 1 ha and 143 peatlands expand over more than 1,000 ha. The average thickness of the peat deposit of the mires is 3.2 m, while the maximum depth recorded is up to 18 m.

**Figure 1. Typical fen (minerotrophic mire).**

**Figure 2. Transitional bog (Mixotrophic mire).**

Species-rich fens are mainly found on the calcareous sub-surface on Saaremaa Island and in the western coastal part of the mainland. Poor fens are more common in the eastern part of the country. Characteristic are the communities dominated by sedges such as *Carex elata*, *C. lasiocarpa*, *C. appropinquata*, *C. vesicaria*, *C. rostrata*, *C. nigra*, and *C. panicea*. Spring fens are distributed rather sparsely over the country, mostly located on the marginal slopes of the Pandivere and Sakala Upland and on Saaremaa Island. The water of the rare soligenous or spring fens is usually calcium-rich and supports communities such as *Schoenetum nigricantis*, *Scorpidio–Schoenetum*, and *Juncetum subnodulosae* (on Saaremaa Island).

**Figure 3. Quaking fen (Minerotrophic quagmire).**

**Figure 4. Soligenous or spring fen.**

Two regional types of ombrotrophic bog complexes are distinguished in Estonia – a "western" type and an "eastern" type. The marginal slopes of the western type have a steep rise. The bog expanse is even and relatively flat with an irregular pattern of compound microsites. *Trichophorum caespitosum* and *Drosera intermedia, Sphagnum rubellum, S. imbricatum*, and *S. magellanicum* grow mainly in the bogs of the western type. The bogs of the eastern type are convex, with a well-developed concentric pattern and no distinct steep slope. Eastern bogs have favourable conditions for *Chamaedaphne calyculata* and *S. fuscum*.

**Figure 5. Treed ridge-hollow-pool bog subtype.**

# Chapter 10. Monitoring vegetation changes at Johnny's Flush exclosure Moor House NNR

**Rob Rose[1], John O' Reilly[2].**
Centre for Ecology & Hydrology[1], Ptyxis Ecology[2]

## Summary

Upland calcareous flushes have a distinctive and diverse vegetation composition which includes a number of rare and unusual plant species such as the Marsh Saxifrage (*Saxifraga hirculus)*. Until the early 1970s, the sheep numbers on the Moor House Reserve were unregulated and there was concern that the habitat was being degraded by over-grazing by sheep. A number of grazing exclosures in various vegetation types were set up for long-term monitoring and in 1972 a grazing exclosure was set up at Johnny's Flush to monitor the effects of grazing in a flush with a known Marsh Saxifrage population. Fixed transect points were established and the vegetation in the paired grazed and ungrazed plots was monitored. The Johnny's Flush exclosure has remained in place and repeat surveys of these plots have been done at irregular intervals, the most recent being in 2013. This chapter describes the changes that have occurred in the vegetation and seeks to relate these changes to the removal of grazing, changes in grazing intensity and wider environmental change spanning over forty years.

**Keywords:** long term monitoring, upland, grazing, environmental change, conservation management.

## Background

Moor House is an upland, moorland site situated in the north Pennines. The vegetation is predominantly blanket bog and upland grassland with smaller areas of other vegetation types, including both acid and calcareous flushes. Originally a grouse-shooting estate it extends across an area of 3,500 ha. It was purchased by the Nature Conservancy as a National Nature Reserve and research station in 1952 to provide facilities for the ecological research on upland habitats. Part of the remit was, *'to use the Reserve for monitoring and research to determine optimum vegetation management prescription'* and *'to protect and enhance the conservation value of the Reserve'*. To this end a number of long-term experimental plots were set up to monitor the effects of different types of upland land use and management. These values are continued today with the site being owned and managed by Natural England for conservation but with a range of research being done by universities and research centres.

## Site description

Johnny's Flush is a large, flushed area situated on the north facing side of Knock Fell within the Moor House NNR. It is at an altitude of about 640m at the point where spring lines give rise to the Moss Burn. The spring lines emerge from a layer of limestone that overlays impervious shale and sandstone. The water that has percolated through the limestone is base-rich and as it is ground-water fed is relatively constant throughout the year. Beneath the peat layer of the flushed area is a layer of clay that prevents seepage to the subsoil maintaining a high water-table at all times. The stratigraphy and hydrology of the site in relation to the vegetation has been described by J.A. Adcock (unpublished report) in 1954 and a copy of his diagram of the section of geological strata underlying the flush is given below (Figure 1). From the same year, a full species list with abundance scores for the site is given in an unpublished report by C.D. Pigott (some details of Pigott's report were published in Pigott (1956) but the site was not referred to by name). Further work by Eddy, Welch & Rawes (1968) at this site and other similar sites at Moor House were recorded by the random quadrat method. From these studies flushes such as this one at Moor House were noted as interesting and unusual vegetation assemblages by Ratcliffe, (*A Nature Conservation Review*, 1977) and a combination of information from these early datasets and similar sites in the central Scottish Highlands provided the basis for the M38 *Cratoneuron commutatum-Carex nigra* spring vegetation type described by Rodwell (1991).

## Grazing and management

In the early part of the last century, the number of sheep grazed by local farmers (commoners) on commonland was unregulated other than by the numbers of sheep that their low-altitude winter grazing could support. Improved farming methods such as moving animals to lower lying farms and more reliable sources of winter feed was reflected by the steady increase in the numbers of sheep that farmers could stock. This in turn led to concerns of over-grazing of moorlands (Pearsall, 1950). Locally, the annual Ministry for Agriculture returns for sheep numbers in the three parishes with common rights at Moor House support the view that at this time grazing intensity was increasing. During the mid-1960s, Moor House was the main British moorland site for the International Biological Programme (IBP) research and a major part of the programme was to quantify grazing intensity at the site. Detailed studies by Rawes and Welch (1969) estimated that there were 15,400 sheep on the Reserve in the summer months, an average of 4.4 sheep/ha across all vegetation types. The formalization of grazing rights under the Commons Registration Act (1965) was completed for Moor House in 1972 and grazing was restricted to a total of 2.0 sheep/ha. This stocking rate was maintained until 2001 when, after the foot-and-mouth disease outbreak, some grazing rights were extinguished, and a new overall stocking density of 0.5 sheep/ha was established.

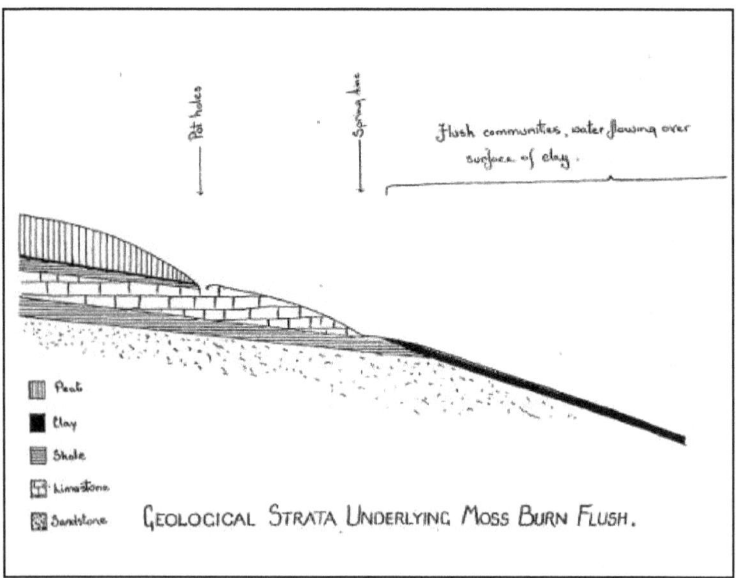


**Figure 1. The stratigraphy of Johnny's flush (also known as Moss Burn flush) from J.A. Adcock (unpublished report) 1954.**

It is thought that Moor House and the surrounding area have been grazed by shepherded flocks of sheep for centuries (Welch & Rawes, 1966). However, in modern times the sheep have not been shepherded and have roamed freely across a wide area of moorland. Due to the remote nature of the site and the severity of the winters, grazing has been restricted to the summer months with the animals (mostly ewes with single lambs) driven on to the site in May and removed in early November for tupping and over-wintering. However, during the grazing season they are gathered twice (for shearing in July and again in September when the lambs are removed for fattening). This pattern of grazing use continues to this day.

## Methods

## The experimental plot recording

The plots were set up in 1972 to monitor the effects of grazing (and the absence of grazing) as part of a series of similar paired plots in a range of vegetation types. The recording was done to monitor both species frequency and vegetation structure by using pin quadrat method.

The study plots (6m x 10m) were selected (by eye) to be representative of the flush area and were established close together using permanent markers. A fence was erected around one plot with 1m internal and 2m external 'buffer strips' along the fence line and between the fence and the un-fenced plot. At the time of each survey, transects were located at 1m intervals and at 1 m intervals along each transect a frame with five fixed-pin positions was placed. Each pin was divided into four height strata 0-10 cm, 10-20 cm, 20-30 cm and >30 cm.

All vascular plant species were recorded as the number of 'hits' within each strata giving a stratified cover and abundance score. Non-vascular plants were recorded on a presence only basis for each pin. These details were recorded by Marrs *et al.* (1986). The initial pin quadrat survey was done in 1972 at the time of fencing and repeated in 1974. Further surveys using the same method were then carried out in 1983, 1996 and most recently in 2013.

## Data

The pin quadrat data (species and strata information) from each of the surveys were combined into a common database. For each species Ellenberg values (from Plantatt, 2004; Bryoatt, 2007) and Grime plant functional type C-S-R radii were applied (Grime scores to vascular plants only). The individual pin data were combined for each 1m quadrat, in each plot, in each survey giving sixty replicate quadrats that were recorded in each survey year. Analyses were done using simple t-tests on the numbers of species recorded or the averaged Ellenberg or Grime scores calculated for each quadrat.

## Results

To compare the average species number across the two sites, the data from each 1m quadrat were averaged and the mean number of species recorded. This is shown in Figure 2. These data show that at the time the exclosure was set up and in the survey two years later the species numbers in both plots was similar. Subsequent re-surveys in 1983 and 1996 show a decline in species diversity with a slight recovery by 2013. After the initial surveys in the 1970s, the subsequent surveys show that the enclosed plot consistently has significantly fewer species within it.

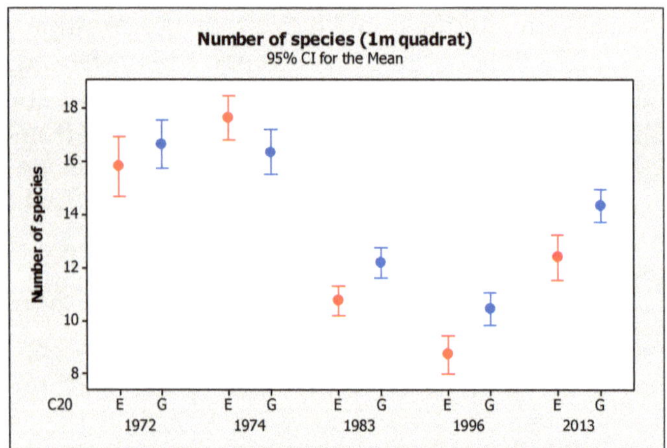


**Figure 2. The average number of species recorded in a 1m quadrat in each survey. The values for the Enclosed (ungrazed) plot are in red and the values for the Grazed plot in blue. Error bars are 95% confidence intervals.**

Overall numbers of vascular plant and bryophyte species losses and gains recorded over the total period were counted. Note that losses and gains refer to the chance of being recorded by the pin quadrat method rather than the presence or absence from the plot as a whole. Increases and decreases (for those species with a total of ten or more records), were estimated for both the grazed and enclosed plots. Species were deemed to have increased or decreased by referring to the slope of a simple linear regression line of number of pin hits against date of survey.

**Table 1. Losses and gains of both vascular plants and bryophyte species between 1972 and 2013.**

| | Vascular plants | | Bryophytes | |
|---|---|---|---|---|
| | Enclosed | Grazed | Enclosed | Grazed |
| 'New' | 3 | 6 | 1 | 3 |
| 'Lost' | 13 | 8 | 10 | 5 |
| Increasing | 17 | 18 | 7 | 8 |
| Decreasing | 17 | 16 | 10 | 11 |
| Total | 50 | 48 | 28 | 27 |

Table 1 shows that there has been both vascular plant and bryophyte species change in both the grazed and ungrazed plots and that vascular plant and bryophyte changes observe similar numerical patterns. In the grazed plots, more new species have been recorded and fewer species that were originally found have been lost. There are similar proportions of both vascular plants and bryophytes increasing and decreasing in both plots.

Figure 3 shows the changes in the cover of vascular plants. This has been divided into a ground layer (the 0 to 10cm strata) and a cover layer (the combined 10cm to 20cm, 20cm to 30cm and over 30cm layers). All pin touches for vascular plants are recorded.

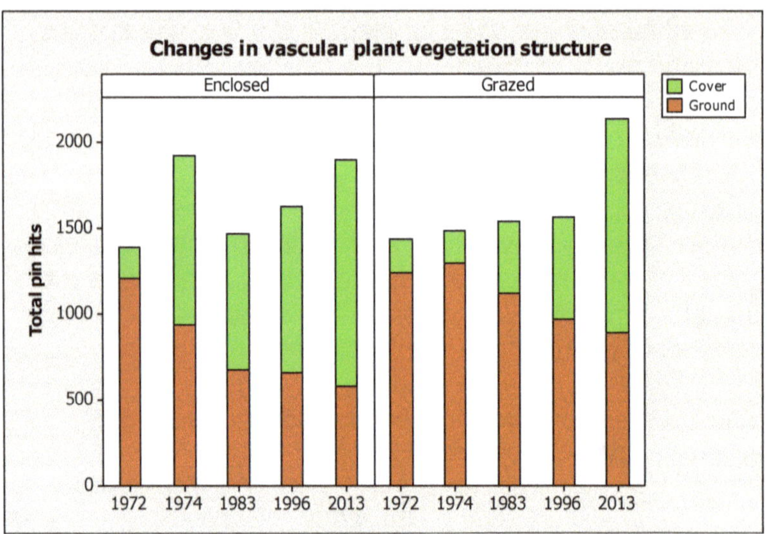


**Figure 3. Vascular plant structure. A stacked histogram of the total number of pin hits in each survey and treatment at ground and canopy levels.**

These histograms show that the original vascular plant structure consisted of predominantly low growing (<10cm) vascular plants. The enclosure resulted in a far greater proportion of taller vegetation in 1974 onwards with a decline in the density of pin touches at the ground level. The grazed plot shows consistent results between 1972 and 1974 but increased proportions of cover i.e. more taller plants in 1983 and 1996 with a further increase in the 2013 data. The results for the grazed plot reflect the changes in grazing intensity at the site and in all cases as the cover value increased the number of pin hits at the ground level decreased. In addition to the changes in vascular plant height and density in both the ground and cover layers (above) the relative proportions of forbs and graminoids was investigated (see Table 2). The results are displayed as the percentage of forb cover.

**Table 2. Percentage forb cover as measured by the proportion of forbs in the total number of vascular plants recorded.**

| | Enclosed | | Grazed | |
|---|---|---|---|---|
| | Ground | Cover | Ground | Cover |
| 1972 | 13.3% | 1.3% | 13.7% | 0.9% |
| 1974 | 16.1% | 1.4% | 10.6% | 2.7% |
| 1983 | 39.0% | 21.3% | 11.5% | 1.9% |
| 1996 | 38.5% | 46.3% | 10.2% | 1.1% |
| 2013 | 49.6% | 45.0% | 11.0% | 4.3% |

These data show that whilst in the grazed plot the relative proportions of graminoids and forbs has remained stable at ground level throughout the forty-year period with a small increase in cover, the proportion of forbs in the enclosed plot has steadily increased at both levels.

Differences between the bryophyte diversity of the grazed and enclosed plots have also been analysed. Two sample t-tests on the bryophyte diversity of the quadrat data showed no significant differences between the grazed and enclosed plots in 1972 or 1974 but significant differences thereafter. Changes over time within the plots also show a number of significant differences (see Table 3) with a small early increasing effect of exclosure only between 1972 and 1974, reductions in species number between 1974 and 1983 and between 1983 and 1996 in both grazed and enclosed plots but a significant increase in both treatments between 1996 and 2013.

**Table 3. Bryophyte diversity changes between surveys.**

| Time period | Enclosed | Grazed |
|---|---|---|
| 1972-1974 | *+ve | ns |
| 1974-1983 | *** -ve | *** -ve |
| 1983-1996 | ** -ve | *** -ve |
| 1996-2013 | *** +ve | *** +ve |

(ns = not significant, * $p<0.05$, ** $p<0.01$ and *** $p<0.001$) increases and decreases indicated by +ve and –ve.

Ellenberg indicator values for light, moisture, reaction (pH) and nitrogen were calculated for all species occurring in each 1m quadrat. These values were averaged for each quadrat and the averaged quadrat data are presented in Figures 4 to 7.

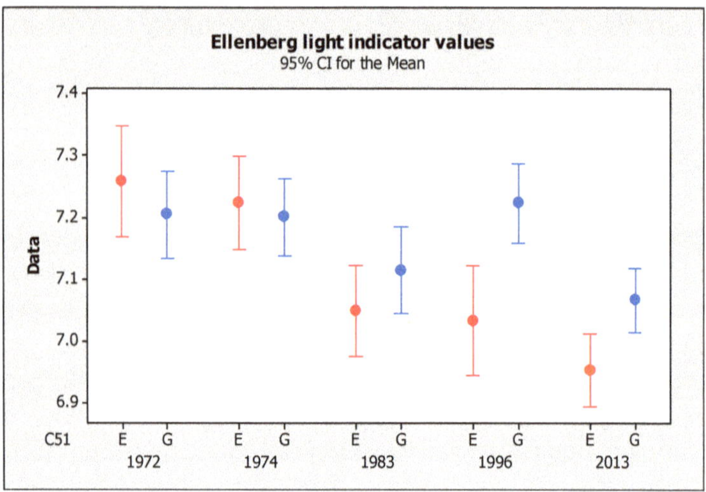


**Figure 4. Ellenberg light indicator values. The values for the Enclosed (ungrazed) plot are in red and the values for the Grazed plot in blue. Error bars are 95% confidence intervals.**

The Ellenberg light indicator values given in Figure 4 show a small trend towards a less well-illuminated plant community. The trend is slightly greater in the ungrazed plot where there has been a greater increase in cover vegetation.

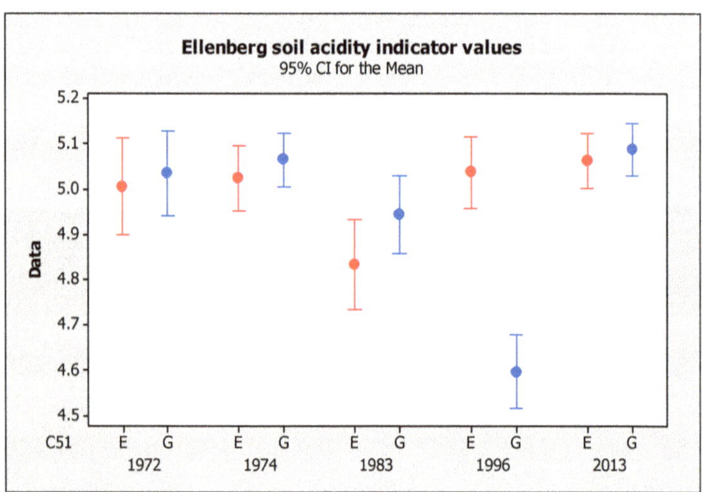


**Figure 5. Ellenberg soil acidity indicator values. The values for the Enclosed (ungrazed) plot are in red and the values for the Grazed plot in blue. Error bars are 95% confidence intervals.**

With the exception of the outlying point in 1996 for the grazed plot there is no indication of changes in the soil acidity requirements of the plant communities either between treatments or over time.

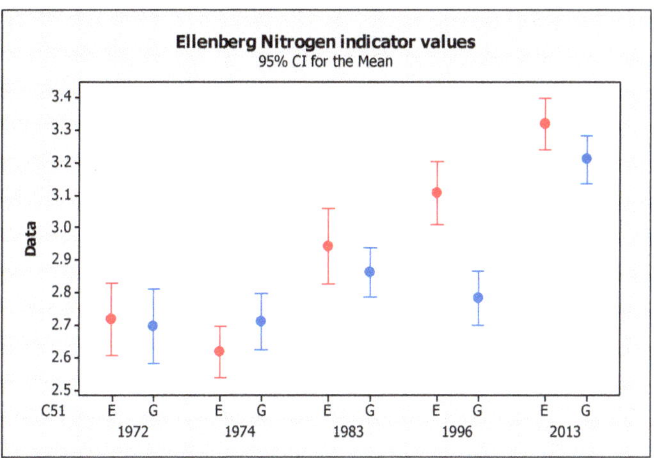


**Figure 6. Ellenberg Nitrogen indicator values. The values for the Enclosed (ungrazed) plot are in red and the values for the Grazed plot in blue. Error bars are 95% confidence intervals.**

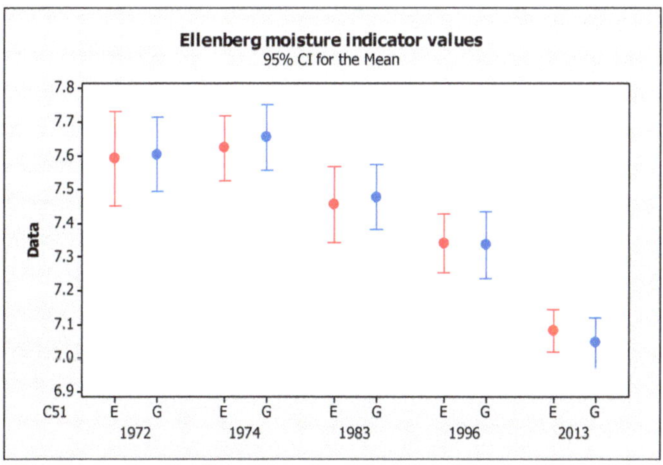


**Figure 7: Ellenberg soil moisture indicator values. The values for the Enclosed (ungrazed) plot are in red and the values for the Grazed plot in blue. Error bars are 95% confidence intervals.**

The indicator values for Nitrogen show a trend towards an increasing Nitrogen requirement of both grazed and ungrazed plant communities over time. The changes in Ellenberg Nitrogen indicator values for the ungrazed community are consistently less than those for the grazed community.

The Ellenberg value for salt tolerance was not calculated because the measure covers saline environments and changes in salinity in terms of the magnitude described by Ellenberg values are not expected at the site. The majority of species present were deemed to have zero salt tolerance.

A similar analysis was done using Grime CSR scores (for Competitor, Stress tolerator and Ruderal species) but no obvious differences between the grazed and ungrazed plots or temporal changes were identified. This was probably due to the relatively small variability of the CSR plant scores exhibited by the plant community and the few species for which data were available (only vascular plants).

## Discussion

Prior to the establishment of Moor House as a NNR the vegetation would have been managed by burning of the heather moorlands to provide optimal grouse rearing habitat with sheep grazing predominantly on the grassland areas. The change of land use from grouse shooting moorland to nature conservation changed the habitat management primarily by reducing burning from being a frequent occurrence across all heather dominated areas to being used only for research purposes at selected sites. Whilst the reduction of heather burning would not have a direct effect on the grassland and flush vegetation, the decrease in area of recent re-growth of the burnt moorland has greater grazing potential than more mature stands of heather. Therefore, this may have had the impact of increasing the grazing intensity on the grasslands and flushes. This combined with the farming improvements of the time that allowed individual farmers to manage larger flocks of sheep led to the realization that high intensity grazing of moorlands was not sustainable and that controls needed to be put in place.

From the comparative work on these plots, it seems clear that the reduction in grazing at Johnny's Flush has resulted in changes in both plant species composition and vegetation structure. There are also indications that the major overall grazing changes on the Reserve, the formalization of sheep stocking densities in 1972 and the further reduction in sheep numbers following the foot and mouth outbreak in 2001 have led to some of the changes at Johnny's Flush. The most obvious change has been the increase in vegetation height, along with the increased forb abundance. The mean Ellenberg values for light correspond to generally well-lit conditions expected in grazed grassland environments. The slight trend towards some semi-shade tolerance in the plant community is consistent with the increased density of cover of plants between 10cm and 30cm in height. Due to the harshness of the climate increased herb height or shrub or tree growth that would result in an increasingly shaded environment is unlikely to develop. However, many of the plant species that were originally abundant were predominantly small vascular plants or bryophytes. These have declined presumably due to the shading effect.

In addition, some of the wider environmental factors appear to have had an effect. Nitrogen is an indicator of soil fertility and moorlands being low nutrient systems are likely to be sensitive to changes in nitrogen input. The management of the Moor House site does not include any nitrogen additions and the changes in nitrogen status due to grazing animals, in this habitat, are more likely to result in a depletion of nitrogen both due to the off-take of lambs and that dunging tends to occur when sheep are at rest in drier habitats. Therefore, the most likely reason for the trend towards species with slightly higher soil fertility Ellenberg indicator preferences is due to atmospheric inputs which although these vary locally, they have generally remained at a similar level for most of the period of this study.

Other environmental factors such as acid deposition appear to have had little effect. There are no signs that the significant reductions in atmospheric acid deposition (Evans *et al.*, 2011) have influenced the elements of the plant community that favour soils of a more basic nature. The mean Ellenberg soil acidity preferences of both the enclosed and grazed plant communities have remained similar throughout the time period. Despite being surrounded by acidic peat soils the flush maintains a more calcareous nature because the main water source is from a ground water spring that originates from limestone rocks. The spring feeds the flush with water that is of higher pH that maintains these conditions. Other changes such as those in the Ellenberg soil moisture values are not easily explained. The results suggest that the site is moving towards a drier plant community type. As the site is ground water spring fed the water supply should be relatively well protected from fluctuations in soil moisture. Average annual rainfall records show no major trends although it is possible that there is an increasing frequency of extreme periods of drought and flood which may account for the small shift in wetness tolerance.

## Conclusions

This work has shown that the changes in grazing regimes (on both the grazed and enclosed plots) have had an effect and that they have exhibited similar overall trends. The mechanisms of the changes are not completely clear cut but some indications of vegetation change being related to environmental changes are suggested by the trends in Ellenberg values. Ellenberg values for light and moisture tend to show trends towards plant communities that favour slightly more shaded and drier habitat preferences. Reaction (soil acidity) showed no trend over time, but nitrogen showed an increase at each survey. Although the trends exhibited are small (less than half of an Ellenberg value point) and probably not on their own significant in terms of individual species presence or absence, the combined effects along with the cessation or reduction in grazing have resulted in a considerable change in the species composition and relative abundance on the site and its vegetation structure.

The method of data collection used above is not directly comparable to the methods used in the original surveys or the quadrat data used to describe National Vegetation Classification plant communities. However, it is apparent from the dominance of bryophytes (in particular *Palustriella* species) and the overall species richness of this flush recorded in the 1950s and 1960s and in the 1970s, when the experiment was set up, that the vegetation could have been described as NVC community, M38

*Cratoneuron commutatum-Carex nigra* spring vegetation. Over time, species diversity decreased and became more grass and sedge dominated the M37 *Cratoneuron commutatum-Festuca rubra* spring community is a more appropriate approximation of the vegetation type. The most recent survey suggests that Johnny's flush is now more like a variant of M10 *Carex dioica-Pinguicula vulgaris* mire community, as the vegetation is much taller and no longer dominated by *Palustriella* species although other bryophytes are still common. Also, the vascular plant component is much more developed as in M10 whereas in typical M37 or M38 they are much more sparse. Indeed, one of us, (J. O'Reilly), has studied a large number of *Palustriella* flushes in the North Pennines and failed to find any examples of true M38 suggesting that the changes noted at Johnny's Flush are somewhat typical of vegetation change in the area since the 1970s.

## Acknowledgements

We wish to thank the scientists and botanical surveyors who have recorded the data at intervals throughout the period, the Environmental Change Network (ECN) for the maintenance and curation of the historical data, and Natural England staff at Widdybank Farm for initially setting up and maintaining the plots.

## References

Eddy, A., Welch, D., and Rawes, M. (1969) The vegetation of Moor House National Nature Reserve in the North Pennines, England. *Vegetatio,* **16**, 239–284.

Evans, C.D., Monteith, D.T., Fowler, D., Cape, J.N. and Brayshaw, S. (2011) Hydrochloric Acid: An Overlooked Driver of Environmental Change. *Environ. Sci. Technol.*, **45**, 1887–1894.

Hill, M.O., Preston, C.D. and Roy, D.B. (2004) *PLANTATT - Attributes of British and Irish Plants: Status, Size, Life History, Geography and Habitats* ISBN 1870393740

Hill, M.O., Preston, C.D., Bosanquet, S.D.S. and Roy, D.B (2007) *BRYOATT - Attributes of British and Irish Mosses, Liverworts and Hornworts. With Information on Native Status,*

*Size, Life Form, Life History, Geography and Habitat.* NERC Centre for Ecology and Hydrology and Countryside Council for Wales, Centre for Ecology and Hydrology, Monks Wood, Abbots Ripton, Huntingdon, 88pp.

Marrs, R.H., Rawes, M., Robinson, J.S. and Poppitt, S.D. (1986) *Long-term studies of vegetation change at Moor House NNR: Guide to recording methods and the database.* Merlewood Research and Development Paper, No 109. ISSN 0308-3675.

Pearsall, W.H. (1950) *Mountains and Moorlands.* Collins, London.

Pigott, C.D. (1956) The vegetation of Upper Teesdale in the North Pennines. *Journal of Ecology*, **44**, 545-586.

Ratcliffe, D. (1977) *A Nature Conservation Review.* Cambridge University Press, Cambridge.

Rodwell, J.S. (1991) *British Plant Communities Volume 2 Mires and Heaths.* Cambridge University press.

Welch, D. and Rawes, M. (1966) The intensity of sheep grazing on high-level blanket bog in upper teesdale. *Irish Journal Of Agricultural Research*, **5** (2), 185-196.

# Chapter 11. Blackland: Dynamics of an anthropic, organic soil system in the Outer Hebrides

**M.N. Scherbatskoy[1], B.C. Ball[2], A.C. Edwards[3] and R.M. Rees[2]**

[1] Blackland Centre, Grimsay, North Uist, Western Isles, Scotland; [2] S.R.U.C. Edinburgh, Scotland; [3] S.R.U.C. Aberdeen, Scotland

## Summary

This chapter introduces the term 'blackland' to describe a type of wet, acidic, highly organic, anthropic agricultural soil system common in the Hebrides and west of Scotland. Over many generations, blackland crofting created small-scale, mixed-use, agricultural mosaics on some of the most marginal land in Europe. Until the mid-twentieth century, blackland supported substantial crofting communities, producing oats, barley and hay through soil development with seaweed, shell sand and manure. The paper provides an initial description of the blackland system and the social and environmental factors which created and maintained it.

In an effort to integrate anthropic and natural factors in an understanding of blackland systems and their recent decline, the paper discusses factors operating on multiple levels from Context (large-scale, technological, policy and climate factors) downwards through Landscape, Field, Surface, and Subsurface levels. Each level affects those below; the changes which cascade through the system are noted and discussed. Novel and unusual methods were used to arrive at a preliminary classification of blackland soils into five groups. Field observations found strong similarities to the concept of 'moorsh forming process' (MFP) developed in research in Poland; examples of soil building and decline in blackland are noted. The value of traditional agricultural systems such as blackland is discussed in the context of climate change.

**Keywords:** agricultural, anthropic, blackland, crofting, Hebrides, soil system

## Introduction

Thousands of hectares of land which supported families and livestock in the islands and west of Scotland until the 1960s are now derelict. Today they are overgrown or overgrazed with their unique character and management techniques overlooked - even disparaged - by agriculture and science alike. Both living memory and ubiquitous cultivation marks attest to former productivity: attention to soil building and biodiversity once enabled such land to support large populations. The present research examines the problem of the marginalisation of such formerly useful land, and asks the question*: What happened?*

Much is known about some aspects of the land, soils and systems under study, but no previous attempt can be found to join them together into a coherent whole. This has impeded understanding of the problem - or even recognition that there is a problem. The potential contribution of such land to contemporary issues of climate and food has been overlooked. If we accept that there is an urgent global need to provide production systems that are able to sustain growing demands for foods, feeds and fuels without exacerbating climate change, then an understanding of systems which were stable over generations is fundamental and essential.

A new study on regeneration of this historic system is underway in North Uist (western Scotland) which addresses its unique character while building on past understanding of traditional agriculture, natural peatlands and climate effects. A new term 'blackland' has been introduced to identify a distinct anthropic, organic soil system; this term is derived from the Gaelic words *talamh dubh* which originally described the narrow belt of blacker soil bordering the sandy *machair*. The term blackland has been expanded to include the highly organic agricultural soils stretching across the islands and onto the western Scottish mainland which share similar characteristics. (It is worth noting that most of the literature on peatland has been concerned with undisturbed areas, therefore the term 'peaty soils' is often used to refer to highly organic soils.)

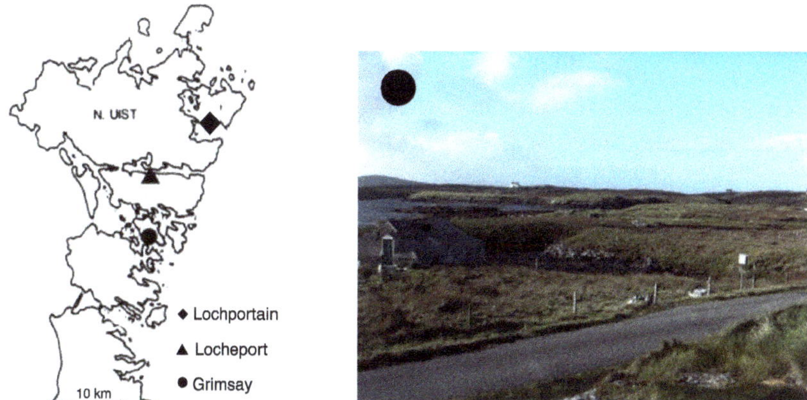


**Figure 1: Location of blackland research sites in North Uist and Grimsay, Outer Hebrides.**

This new research contends that while the parent material of blackland may often be sphagnum peat, it is no longer peat (defined as a range of dead plant material from partly decomposed fibre to burnable black colloidal solid). Blackland is anthropic, meaning it has been modified in essential aspects by long human interaction. Such land has been managed, grazed or cultivated for hundreds if not thousands of years, and unique management systems have evolved, which in turn have produced enduring structural and other changes to the soil itself. While blackland shares many characteristics with peatlands such as very high organic matter content, it also differs in important ways including acidity, hydraulic conductivity, nutrient cycling and physical structure; it is also better able to support plant growth.

## Background

Soils modified by humans are described as anthropogenic or anthropic. In Northern Europe plaggen soil is usually described as a man-made layer over a less fertile sand or glacial till. Conry (1972) described heavy peaty soils in the Dingle Peninsula which had been amended through use of shell sand and seaweed. The concept of anthropic soils, whether technically plaggen or not, is relevant to blackland areas, because Hebridean crofters routinely refer to their soils as 'built' (Norton, 2009). This process was referred to over the centuries by writers such as MacDonald (1811) and Carmichael (1883).

Three further aspects of the blackland system contribute to an understanding of its dynamics.

## Crofting

Blackland is a product of crofting, which has been the defining factor in the history and use of the Hebrides for at least 200 years. Crofting was a form of small-scale, mixed-use, low-external-input agriculture which originated in the Gaelic communities of the north and west of Scotland, continuing a pattern of cultivation dating to the Neolithic. Today, over 700,000 ha (Jones, 2011) are held in this form of heritable tenancy in crofts ranging from 1 - 15 ha; the term croft refers to an individual holding.

Until the mid-twentieth century, crofting included a mix of arable rotation with improved hay- and grassland, gardening, and rough grazing. The usual crops were oats, kale, barley and potatoes. Most crofts carried one or two cattle plus followers, and sometimes a horse. Dairy was an important dietary component; cattle were sold for export to the mainland for slaughter or finishing. Almost all feed was grown on the croft.

A crofter was defined by the Napier Commission (the body charged by H.M. Government in1883 with investigating conditions in the Highlands and Islands of Scotland) as 'a small tenant of land with or without a lease, who finds in the cultivation of his holding a material part of his occupation, earnings and sustenance, and who pays rent directly to the proprietor'.

## Soils

*The West Highland Survey* (Fraser Darling, 1955) estimated that one sixth of all crofting land was on predominately peaty soils; calculation thus suggests that >100,000 ha might be considered blackland. Crofts usually have a diverse range of physical attributes; Fraser Darling noted *'earlier generations (aimed) that crofts should as far as possible have a variety of soil types'*.

However, the extent and distribution of anthropic soils in Scotland is unknown, as '*the former Soil Survey of Scotland, when mapping soils from the 1950s to 1980s, considered soils as 'natural entities' so there was little consideration given to anthropogenic influences*' (Scottish Government, 2006). This suggests that normal methods of soil description and analysis techniques often either do not apply or need to be changed to be meaningful for blackland soils. Local variations in moisture status, drainage and topography result in variable vegetation composition and subsequent soil development. Heterogeneity in soil type is great: areas containing similar soil can be smaller than 100m$^2$, so it is important to be able to describe the soil resource at small scales. Thus, soils and their agronomic capabilities are best described using local 'on-the-ground' methods rather than using large scale land use capability classifications.

Most agricultural production occurs on mineral soils where mineral particles make up ~45% of the soil, and organic matter (living and dead) ~3-10%. Particles and organic matter combine to form structures called aggregates and crumbs. These give the soil its strength and contain pores that conduct and store water, air and living organisms in the soil. Peats, in contrast to mineral soils, contain <20% of mineral particles, making many properties and behaviour very different from mineral soils. Depending on geology, there may also be little contribution of minerals for plant nutrition. The nutrient status of peaty soils is generally poorer than in mineral soils, with high acidity, very low P status, low N availability and variable K. Normal methods of soil analysis are adequate to specify the status of these minerals but may have to be interpreted in terms of land character and management.

Soil structure is an important property used in the description of the capability and function of soils. Methods using 'normal' structural terms for describing aggregates (Ball *et al.*, 2007) usually do not apply on highly organic soils as these are often replaced by the compacted remnants of degraded mosses and moor plants. Nevertheless, dark well-structured soils with stable crumbs were found in drier parts of the research area, formerly improved by addition of shell sand and seaweed.

In general, peaty soils are fragile and need careful description, restoration, usage and monitoring that respects their high variability.

## Carbon

As soils with very high organic matter content - from 30% to >80% by weight in previously cultivated areas, blackland is a reservoir of carbon compounds. As such it needs careful consideration to be managed sustainably and loss of carbon as $CO_2$ kept to a minimum.

The amount of carbon stored in any soil is a consequence of the balance between the inputs of organic material (from plant and animal activity) on the one hand, and decomposition leading to carbon dioxide release on the other (Rees *et al.*, 2005). Where there is a balance of inputs and outputs, it can be expected that under constant climatic conditions an equilibrium would eventually be reached where no further changes in soil carbon stocks would occur. Although inputs of carbon from plant growth and animal activity in the west of Scotland are often not particularly high, decomposition tends to be slow as a consequence of soil and climatic conditions. The area receives high annual rainfall ( >1,250 mm) and so the soil profile often has a very high seasonal water table. In addition, low soil pH will limit microbial/fungal activity reducing decomposition rates.

Disturbance by ploughing and drainage tends to dry the soil which encourages microbial activity and respiration of the peaty component. Over a long period of time, this returns carbon dioxide to the atmosphere and diminishes the resource. Raising soil fertility increases nitrogen availability which may be transformed by the microbial processes of nitrification and denitrification into nitrous oxide. However, preliminary findings showed surprisingly low emissions of both nitrous oxide and carbon dioxide from old blackland agricultural soils freshly turned for planting (Knox, 2013). This effect may be associated with efficient recycling of nutrients and carbon within the system.

Management of these soils can be used to enhance soil productivity without necessarily causing a decline in organic carbon content. Although drainage and liming contribute to an increase in decomposition rate of soil organic matter, management activities such as the addition of manures, seaweed and crop residues can be used to offset any net losses. Archaeological studies have shown that the long-term management of organic soils using these practices can be sustainable, allowing increases in soil fertility to occur alongside maintenance of or an increase in the soil organic carbon content of the soil (Guttmann *et al.*, 2006). The challenge for blackland soils therefore is to achieve this twin objective of maintaining organic carbon whilst increasing soil fertility through appropriate management interventions.

Predicted benefits of management are often equivocal, as uptake in one pathway may lead to losses in another (Worral, 2010). Bringing back land formerly abandoned from agriculture was suggested by Powlson *et al.* (2011) as a suitable strategy. The small-scale mosaic of blackland areas makes them suitable for carbon sequestration techniques such as tree planting (desirable as a wind break for arable areas and for stock). The most important climate effect in reuse of derelict land may lie in reducing 'carbon footprint' through a return to local food/feed production. In the 1960s, almost all food and feed in the crofting areas of Scotland was grown locally; in 2010, almost all is purchased, with the majority grown under high input regimes on distant farms.

Research on fen peats in Poland noted the loss of carbon on drainage, but the resulting 'muck soils' became stable and supported vegetable and root crops (Okruzko, 1968). The term moorsh or 'moorsh forming process' (MFP) was proposed by Okruzko in 1993. Brandyk *et al.* (2003) state '*the moorshing of organic soils comprises biological, chemical, and physical changes driven by a decrease in water content and an increase in air content*'.

Okruzko and Ilnicki (2003) distinguished two processes taking place in organic soils: paludification (peat accumulating) and decession (peat mineralisation) with moorsh forming. Their research in Poland appears to have taken place primarily in fen ecosystems; however, the concept of MFP may begin to explain some observable processes in blackland soils. Decession, which the Polish studies viewed as an agricultural problem, in the case of blackland may explain positive soil processes through which very highly organic soils develop structure and crumble and become more workable.

## Methods

Analysis of blackland soils was linked to socio-economic drivers, culture and management in an attempt to *'explore the complex 'feedback loops' between anthropogenic and natural processes'* (Mercer & Tipping, 1994). The principal author's situation as tenant of a large, derelict, blackland croft in North Uist (Outer Hebrides) and involvement in the west coast crofting community over the past five years was useful. Local knowledge suggested that the historic system of blackland could not be understood through single topics as crop rotation or soil structure: the interdependence of people, livestock, wildlife and land was essential.

## Site description

The main research site was a 15-ha croft *Kenary* at 5 Scotvein, Grimsay, North Uist in the Western Isles of Scotland, which aerial / satellite photography and living memory record as being heavily worked.

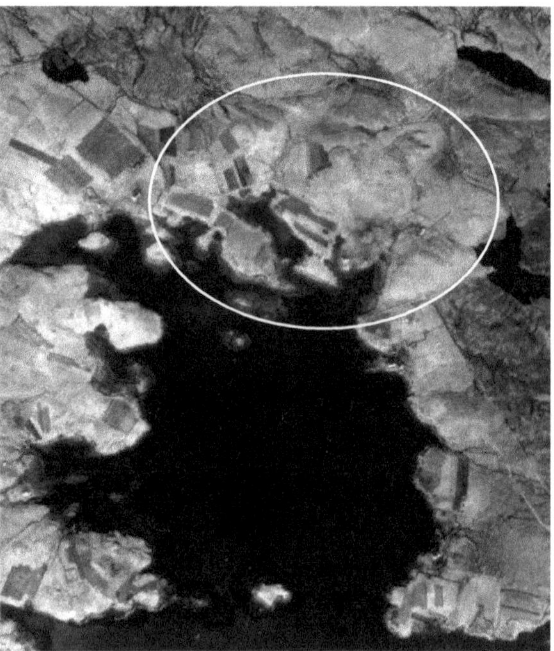

**Figure 2. Blackland agriculture in 1956, Scotvein Bay, Grimsay circled: the Grimsay research site (*Kenary*)**

However, as with many other crofts, it had been left unmanaged except for casual grazing by sheep for over fifty years; virtually all traces of use disappeared, and substantial changes occurred in the plough layer. Two other blackland crofts in North Uist at 24/25 Locheport and 5 Lochportain were also investigated through a set of samples from each. These three crofts had very similar management histories; all arable cropping ended in the 1960s, with no fertiliser use or mowing of the fields since then. The area is entirely in crofting tenure, with crofts held by the same families for over a century, giving a long-term, stable management history. Data from the above sites were supplemented by observations and photographic records of cultivation traces in blackland areas throughout the Hebrides and in the west of Scotland.

## Sampling Framework

Blackland is very variable over short distances, variable in the way it was worked over time, and variable in its response to cessation of working. The main challenge of the blackland research was to arrive at suitable means of sampling, and to develop a method of evaluation applicable to complex small-scale agriculture. The research concentrated on creating baseline data and developing appropriate descriptive methods, leading to an appreciation of system dynamics and preliminary classification.

A novel sampling framework with two datasets - one random and one selective - was developed:

- transect data, sampled every 60m along four transects to give an overview of land character and terrain, but these often missed areas of past use; and
- target data described areas known or thought to have been productive in the past.

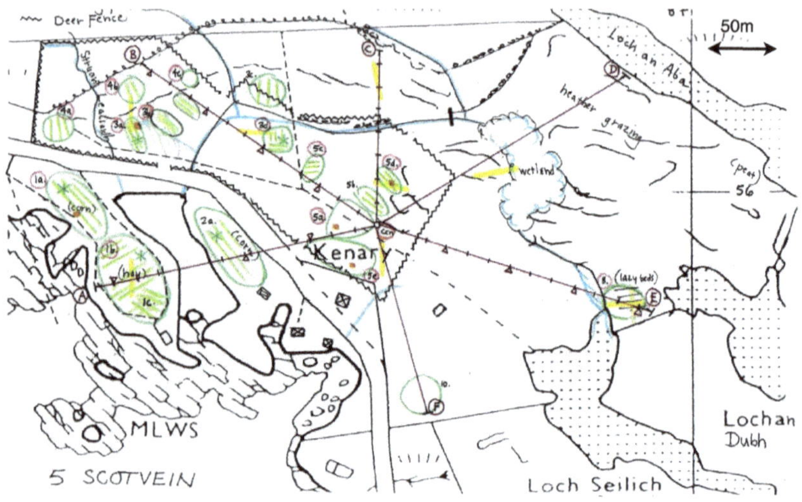


**Figure 3. Sampling framework at Kenary. O target areas ▲ transect points.**

Data were collected through six parameters (selected during an evaluation period in 2010) using identical methods in both transect and target sets, over the course of one year. Measurements were made either at the sampling point or within a 2m radius of it, depending on data type. The two data sets totalled twenty-three measurements at thirty-seven sites and were considered to give a fair representation of blackland crofts.

**Table 1. Parameters and measurements used in evaluation of blackland**

| Parameters & Measurements | Units | Comment |
|---|---|---|
| Past Use | | |
| 1. cultivation | B / P / M / N | beds, plough, managed, no sign |
| Topography | | |
| 2. soil depth | mm. | 1600 maximum |
| 3. slope | degrees | by estimation |
| 4. relief | cv / cx / f | convex, concave, flat |
| 5. aspect | degrees | from North |
| Soil Structure | | |
| 6. acrotelm | mm. | 0 - 100 |
| 7. catotelm | mm. | 0 - 200 |
| 8. O2 layers | no. of layers below catotelm | |
| 9. presence of worms | Y / N | |
| 10. presence of sand | Y / N | |
| 11. rooting to 200mm. | Y / N | |
| 12. colour | Y / Br / Blk | yellow, brown, dark to black |
| 13. decomposition | von Post units | 1-10 |
| 14. porosity | % | |
| Hydrology | | |
| 15. character | R / G / O | rainfed, groundfed, runoff |
| 16. water table: range | mm. | 0 - 400 |
| 17. water table: median | mm. | |
| Soil Chemistry | | |
| 18. pH | log H+ | |
| 19. P | mg/l | |
| 20. K | mg/l | |
| 21. Ash | % | |
| 22. Smell | -1 / 0 / 1 | pleasant/good, questionable, bad |
| Vegetation | | |
| 23. Soil functionality | Blackland Vegetation score | |

No data on microbiota were collected; no laboratory work was done beyond simple agricultural analysis.

## Descriptive Methods

Three classic and novel tools were employed to describe the blackland system.

- The classic von Post Humification Scale, developed during the Soil Survey of Sweden (von Post, 1926) provided a rapid, sensitive and multi-variate method for characterisation of blackland soils. It accurately delineated characteristics such as fibre integrity, colour and viscosity of exudate, and presence of colloidal particles. The von Post scale proved essential to the structural description of blackland soils which display a continuum from sponge-like with nearly unlimited hydraulic conductivity to impermeable black peat.

- Blackland Vegetation Scoring (BVS) was devised during the research to quantify soil functionality based on the existing vegetation. Plant species distribution and abundance is a precise indicator of underlying soil conditions because plants must grow in the same spot for their lifetimes and each species is adapted to (and limited by) the conditions and available nutrients in the soil. BVS was based on the Ellenberg Indicator Variables (Ellenberg, 1974; Hill, 1993), and a grazing value system found in the MLURI Land Capability Classification (1991). BVS enabled the vegetation of a site to be represented by a single number which could then be easily incorporated into whole system analysis of a given area. This may be a novel solution to the problem of integrating botanical description of an ecological unit with other statistical data.

- The Blackland Index was developed as an initial analysis of derelict croft land, as a means of observation and comparison by land managers.

## Analysis

Data were collected through a range of parameters including nominal, discontinuous, and continuous. Data were analysed through bi-variate methods including box- and scatterplots, and through multi-variate methods including Principal Component Analysis and hierarchical dendrograms.

## Results

Analysis revealed unexpected relationships and processes in the dynamics of formerly productive anthropic organic soils.

### Phosphorus availability

Phosphorus (P) is considered the limiting factor in blackland areas; for example, >80% of recent SRUC advisory soil samples fell into the low or very low P category (Edwards, unpublished). Contrary to predictions from the literature, it was very low in formerly cultivated areas, usually <3mg/l (available); recent measurements on Barra found P levels in heavily grazed fields to be similar. Deeper soils had higher P levels. There was a slight negative relationship between higher BVS and P availability and between pH and P, suggesting unforeseen processes in the blackland system.

### Soil depth and cultivation

Data showed a strong correlation between soil depth and cultivation method. The deeper areas >800 mm were more likely to have been cultivated in beds, whereas shallower areas were ploughed or otherwise managed. Soil depth also showed a slight inverse correlation with BVS.

### Decomposition

Von Post decomposition scores showed statistical relationships with soil depth, colour, K, pH, ash, hydrology, and smell, revealing its predictive value as a multi-variate indicator for field analysis.

## Principal Component Analysis

Principal Component Analysis (PCA) showed that component 1 (ash, decomposition, soil depth) explained the largest share of variation (33%). The sixteen numerical variables used in PCA explained a total of 65% of the variation among the sampling points i.e. 35% of the variation was not explained.

## Clustering: the Power of Gower

The hierarchical dendrogram generated using the Gower distribution provided a powerful summary of the characteristics of blackland in the study area. It grouped the sampling points into four branches which corresponded well to initial observation, i.e. sampling points that appeared to present distinct similarities in the field also tended to group according to the dendrogram. Group C (noted through ecological observation and scatterplot anomalies) did not cluster due to internal and possibly unmeasured dissimilarities. The Gower dendrogram was then interpreted using results from all other statistical methods.

The Gower dendrogram provided a clear overview of the character of blackland, enabling definition of five possible types. Vegetation scores were not included in the dendrogram but were integrated into the Summary (Table 4) as an independent comparison.

## Discussion

Description and classification of blackland soils was undertaken, then interpreted through a framework at five levels. This framework includes the anthropic and natural factors which affect soil performance and functionality, to reveal the dynamics of change within the soil system. Changes at higher levels cascade through the system, resulting in effects at lower levels.

Table 2 displays factors leading to change within the blackland system over two time periods and five levels, with one pathway leading to soil improvement (decession) and the other to declining functionality (paludification). The Early Period (1860 to World War I) covers the peak of traditional crofting, with maximum land use corresponding with maximum population and maximum soil development. The Modern Period (1960 to 2010) was a time of significant decline in land use, population and soil health.

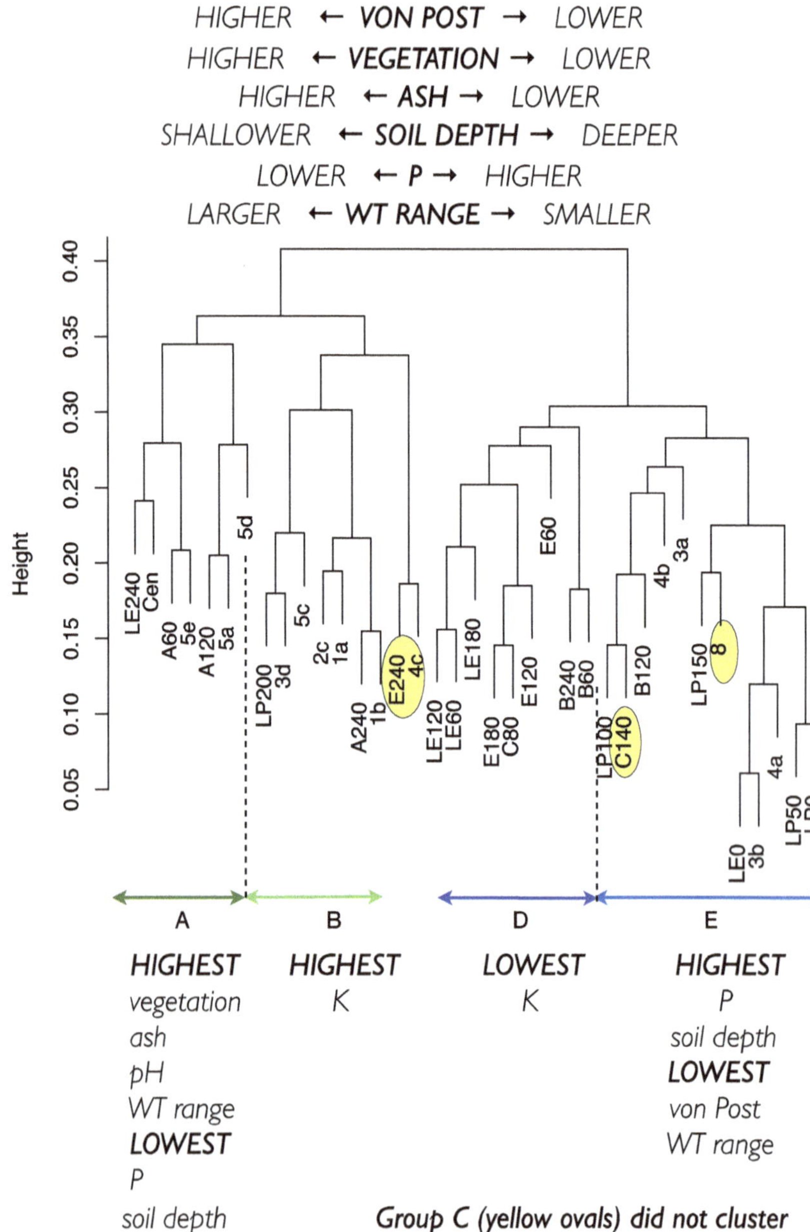


**Figure 4. Gower dendrogram showing groupings and trends.**

The following sections discuss system dynamics as shown in Table 2.

**Table 2. Blackland systems framework**

BLACKLAND SYSTEM FRAMEWORK
Cascade of Effects on Soils

| EARLY PERIOD<br>1860s + 50 years | Levels & Factors | MODERN PERIOD<br>1960s + 50 years |
|---|---|---|
| | Context | |
| highest population 1863 | = climate stable * | population/labour reduced |
| subsistence + cash income | population changes = | by WWI & II & birth control |
| | technology changes = | transport & fossil fuel use increase |
| | policy changes = | change in agricultural payments |
| | Landscape | |
| arable rotation/lazybeds + grazing | = mosaic = | rough grazing |
| cattle: home & export | | sheep: export |
| labour on croft + PT employment | | paid FT employment |
| nutrients recycled | | nutrient loss |
| | Field | |
| drainage extended & maintained | = family circumstances/preference = | cultivation ceases; drainage not maintained |
| cultivation & ploughing | | milk cow unnecessary |
| knowledge accumulation | | loss of skills |
| | Surface | |
| increase in aeration | = highly organic = | waterlogging |
| no excess vegetation | | moss/litter build up |
| | Subsurface | |
| *decession* | = dynamic = | *paludification* |
| becomes more friable, increased microbial | | becomes colder, wetter, more acidic |
| von Post 7 - 8 | | von Post 1 - 6 |

*KEY: = direction of effect * atmospheric $CO_2$ exceeds 350 ppm in 1988*

## Context

*Context* refers to those factors beyond the control of any individual or small community; it includes climate and natural disaster, but also changes in law, policy and technology. From this level, large-scale effects cascade downwards.

Climate was apparently stable during the Early Period. Manley (1979) noted *'There is little to support the view that climate was significantly better early last century, or indeed for many centuries previously'*. Rather the drivers were technological and policy changes during the Modern Period, causing the traditional high-labour low-external-input system to collapse. Depleted by two World Wars (to which the islands sent the highest proportion of their men of any part of Britain), and with smaller families now preferred, labour was less and less available. Simultaneously, technological change brought agricultural machinery powered by fossil fuels, which required cash that a croft could not produce. Topography dictated very small (0.1 - 0.5 ha) field size which could neither accommodate nor justify modern machinery.

The 1960s began a period of major change in the blackland soil system. The Uist road network was completed in 1963, liming and cropping subsidies were withdrawn in 1976 and 1981 respectively (Hunter, 1976); sheep headage payments were introduced from the early 1980s (Thomson, 2011). These major modifications at *context* level initiated changes that cascaded down the system, ultimately damaging the soil's productive capacity.

## Landscape

*Landscape* is the overall organising principle of land use in a specific area. It is governed by land form - hills, plains, mosaic - and by the overall style of agriculture adopted by the communities within that ecological unit (see Figure 2).

Long-established communal practice created a distinctive pattern of land use in the west of Scotland as an efficient means of utilising the mosaic of small fields and varied habitats through a cattle/grazing/arable system. The hill was used for rough grazing during the summer months, the in-bye (managed fields closer to the house and byre) for hay and winter grazing, and arable to produce cereals and roots; a fourth component, proximity to the shore, had dictated settlement patterns before the road network, and continued as an important resource for soil amendments. This method both produced family food and cash income, and stabilised the landscape. Cattle were sold for cash; since at least the eighteenth century, the islands were a source of young stock for mainland markets and farms (Cregeen, 2004). Their indiscriminate grazing habits tended to prevent invasion of rush or bracken; their stabling provided fertiliser. An arable rotation with sophisticated water management provided winter feed. Unusable bits of the mosaic acted as reservoirs for wildlife, plant species and invertebrates (Firbank *et al.*, 2008). Fenton (1992) emphasised that the persistence of local techniques was not a sign of backwardness, but of adaptation to difficult circumstances.

Maintaining the nutrient balance across these four land-use components was essential for long-term viability of the community and had a direct impact upon the area and productivity of the arable component (Dodgson, 1992). Re-cycling of nutrients (nitrogen and phosphorus) in traditional systems on marginal land such as blackland is essential, and ultimately determines the structural stability and productivity of the system.

The Atlantic climate, in which precipitation routinely exceeds transpiration (Schulte, 2012), produced a distinctive adaptation to the arable component. A hand-turned, raised bed or ridge often known in English as 'lazybed' was used throughout the blackland areas; *'Ridges are almost always aligned... up and down the slope, and were presumably created with the two-fold purpose of draining the soil and elevating the tilth so as to catch the maximum strike of the sun'* (Mercer & Tipping, 1994). Fenton (1994) commented that '*it is important to stress the quite sophisticated nature of lazy-beds*'. A bed structure also enables the gain of a few critical cm on the water-table and helps insulate the growing area from the underlying reservoir of permanently wet peat.

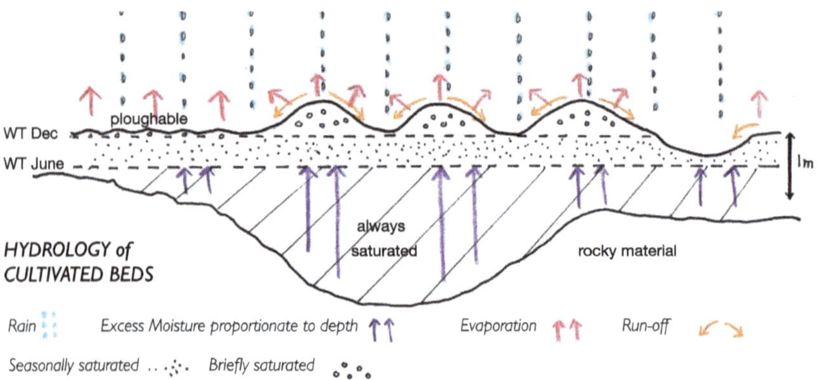


**Figure 5. Hydrology of cultivated beds.**

This virtuous circle of land management was broken by effects from the *context* level beginning in the 1960s, which made the cattle/nutrient re-cycling/arable system untenable. Headage payments encouraged the overstocking of sheep, which did not require stabling and used less manpower. As better transport meant that milk could now be bought in shops, the family cow and her calves disappeared, and with them the growing of winter feed. People sought paid employment wherever they could find it, as the combination of subsidies and low lamb prices were insufficient to participate in the growing cash economy. Full-time employment meant less time for the land, which began to deteriorate rapidly due to lack of maintenance. The traditional landscape of hill, in-bye and arable disappeared in the blackland areas.

## Field

*Field* is the level of family decision-making, based on preferences for crops and livestock, and on family resources, and varied from croft to croft. Achieving maximum returns through nutrient balance consumed both time and energy and was complicated by the lack of a formal knowledge structure to calculate their quantity.

**Figure 6. Field level: Traces of past management, Ardroil, Lewis**

Efficient use of resources is essential to maintain equilibrium in the agricultural systems of marginal areas such as blackland. Potential limitations are imposed by resource availability. In the earlier period, regular incorporation of the available amendments would have included some combination of the re-use of the household midden (organic wastes and ash), together with local materials such as marl/ shell sand, manure/bedding and seaweed (Smith, 1994). P in significant quantities is provided only by manures, composts and the household midden; precipitation and manure/urine supply N and K. Seaweed was a major amender, and contains nitrogen, potassium, sulphur and many trace elements; it also appears to have important effects as a soil conditioner (Knox *et al.*, 2013). Uist shell sand contains liming value of up to 42% $CaCO_3$ equivalent. Since the actual nutrient value of amendments was unknown, patterns could develop not only of insufficiency but of over-supply. Calculation of nutrient balance on five traditional mainland farms revealed a surplus of both N and P in the arable component (Dodgson & Olsson, 1988), showing that labour was not always used most effectively.

Agricultural soils in general can be 'improved' as a result of some combination of management factors interacting over time to improve the physical (e.g. drainage, soil depth), chemical (liming, fertiliser additions) and biological (organic matter and plant traits). Anthropically modified soil profiles can retain attributes and landscape features that inform on cumulative past management. The memory effects of improvements can vary considerably.

**Table 3: Soil properties grouped quantitatively according to rate of response to anthropogenic forcings (after Richter, 2007)**

| *Dynamic <10 years* | *Slowly dynamic <100 years* | *Persistent >1000 years* |
|---|---|---|
| Labile Organic Carbon | Clay mineralogy (Fe/Al oxides) | Inorganic texture |
| Acidity and salinity | Stabilised humic substances | Rock volume |
| Cation exchange capacity | Occluded fractions of C, N and P | Horizons |
| Bulk density, aggregation and porosity | | Clay mineralogy |
| Rooting depth | | |
| Plant available nutrients | | |

The long-term structural effects (MFP) within organic soils as described by Illniki (2003) and discussed below (subsurface) appear to be slowly dynamic; in the research areas they have persisted for more than fifty years.

Beginning in the 1960s, families were no longer able to keep up the physically taxing routine of applying heavy, bulky amenders such as shell sand and seaweed. Cheap industrial slag, a good source of P, no longer existed. While in many lowland areas physical issues associated with cultivation had been 'overcome' through the tremendous increase in mechanical power available, these had very limited applicability for small-scale systems such as blackland. With the cattle gone and sheep now on the land, there was no reason to. Since management ceased in the 1960s, the blackland fields deteriorated rapidly.

## Surface

*Surface* is the usual realm of agricultural research, including vegetation and the plough layer, and can be explored by the naked eye and hand tools. Changes at *context*, *landscape* and *field* levels affect soil structure and functioning. The FAO (2011) noted the rapidity of change in organic soils; OM in the research areas ranged from 40% - 87%.

The most noticeable effect of cessation of management was the buildup of a thick layer (<10mm - 200mm) of moss and litter above former agricultural soils in the short space of 50 years.

**Figure 7. Surface level build-up of moss above former agricultural soil.**

A diplotelmic system of growing sphagnum above and a semi-decomposed catotelm below (von Post 3 - 5) developed, depending on site hydrology, above reasonably well-structured, friable black soil. Sphagnum is well known as an "*ecological engineer', producing decay-resistant litter, increasing the peat accumulation rate, withdrawing nitrogen and phosphorus, and determining the carbon balance of the system*' (Peatscapes, 2008). Sphagnum also acidifies its surroundings through its very high cation exchange ability, binding mineral ions and releasing hydrogen ions into the surrounding water. Formerly cultivated soil became more acid, covered by a permanently wet blanket which drowned the roots of vascular plants, and which made it slow to warm in the spring.

This effect can be seen in varying degrees across the landscape and reflected in the blackland groupings. Table 4 shows the preliminary classification of blackland into five groups, interpreted by statistical results and by representative photographs of each type. The coalescing of analytical data, past management and present vegetation into clear groupings was striking.

**Group A** is composed of shallow fields <300mm, the most recently cultivated (1960s), with the highest ash, pH and BVS; the median von Post score was 7. Group A is the easiest to regenerate, usually requiring nothing more than mowing to produce usable grass. The plough layer is black, friable and sweet-smelling, and considered a Score I soil of very good structural quality (Ball *et al.*, 2007). There is almost no build-up of moss and litter.

## Table 4. Summary of blackland soil groupings and characteristics

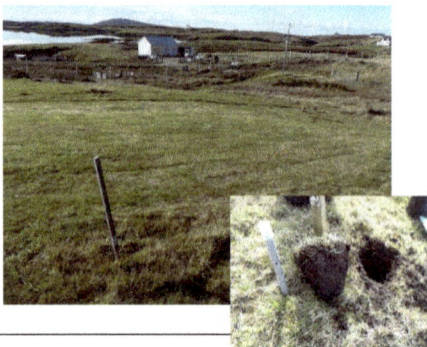

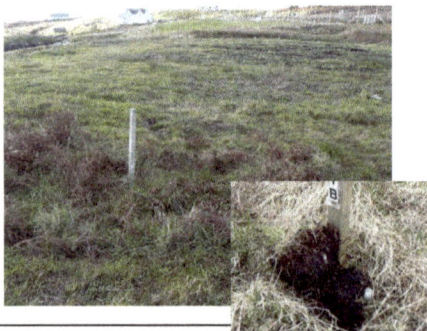

| GROUP | VARIABLE | MEDIAN | RANK | No. in GROUP |
|---|---|---|---|---|
| **A** | *Modern agriculture (1960s), best grasses, shallow* | | | **7** |
| | vegetation | 55 | **highest** | |
| | ash % | 57.9 | **highest** | |
| | von Post | 7 | | |
| | depth | 300 | **shallowest** | |
| | cultivation | P/M/N/B | | |
| | pH | 4.9 | **highest** | |
| | P | 1.9 | **lowest** | |
| | slope ° | 10 | | |
| | hydrology | RGO/RO/R | | |
| | WT range | 200 | **largest** | |
| | K | 96 | | |
| **B** | *Modern agriculture (1960s), deeper, all possibly CF in 1960s* | | | **7** |
| | vegetation | 52 | | |
| | ash % | 30.5 | | |
| | von Post | 8 | | |
| | depth | 630 | | |
| | cultivation | P/B/N/M | | |
| | pH | 4.9 | | |
| | P | 7.1 | | |
| | slope ° | 5 | | |
| | hydrology | R | | |
| | WT range | 190 | | |
| | K | 127 | **highest** | |
| **C** | *Constructed group of outliers based on initial observation: poor vegetation, no rush, free-draining* | | | **4** |
| | vegetation | 17 | **lowest** | |
| | ash % | 13 | **lowest** | |
| | von Post | 9 | **highest** | |
| | depth | 740 | | |
| | cultivation | N/B | | |
| | pH | 4.2 | **lowest** | |
| | P | 5.0 | | |
| | slope ° | 5 | | |
| | hydrology | R | | |
| | WT range | 190 | | |
| | K | 85.8 | | |

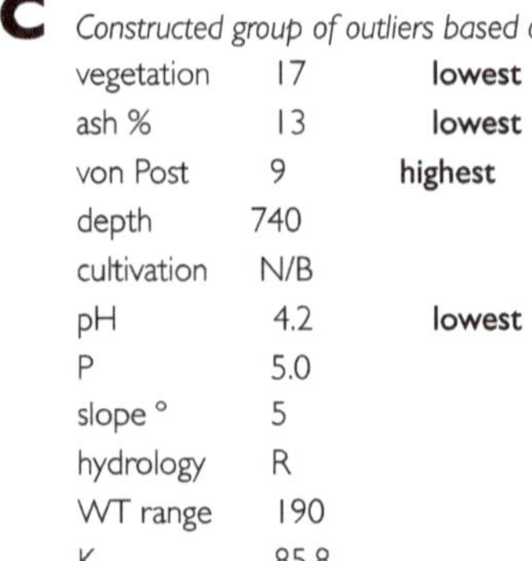

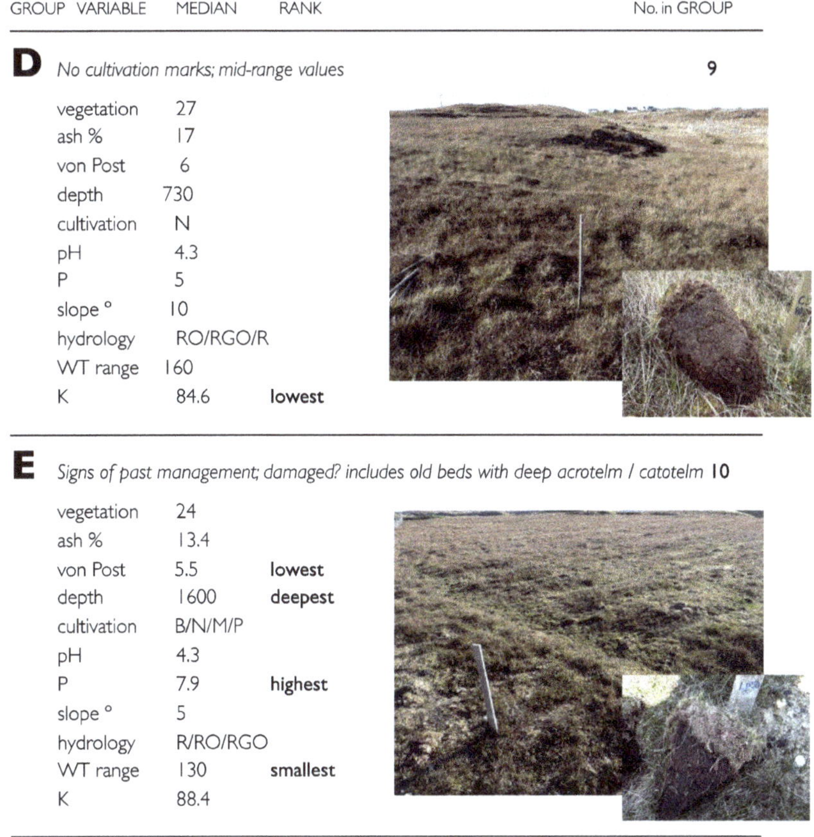

| GROUP | VARIABLE | MEDIAN | RANK | No. in GROUP |
|---|---|---|---|---|
| **D** | *No cultivation marks; mid-range values* | | | 9 |
| | vegetation | 27 | | |
| | ash % | 17 | | |
| | von Post | 6 | | |
| | depth | 730 | | |
| | cultivation | N | | |
| | pH | 4.3 | | |
| | P | 5 | | |
| | slope ° | 10 | | |
| | hydrology | RO/RGO/R | | |
| | WT range | 160 | | |
| | K | 84.6 | **lowest** | |
| **E** | *Signs of past management; damaged? includes old beds with deep acrotelm / catotelm* | | | 10 |
| | vegetation | 24 | | |
| | ash % | 13.4 | | |
| | von Post | 5.5 | **lowest** | |
| | depth | 1600 | **deepest** | |
| | cultivation | B/N/M/P | | |
| | pH | 4.3 | | |
| | P | 7.9 | **highest** | |
| | slope ° | 5 | | |
| | hydrology | R/RO/RGO | | |
| | WT range | 130 | **smallest** | |
| | K | 88.4 | | |

**Group B** includes deeper fields with similar soil, also cultivated in the 1960s. Ash, pH and BVS were slightly lower than Group A; the von Post score was 8. There was slightly more build-up of moss/litter.

**Group C** contains four sites which often clustered strongly and as anomalies in regression analysis, but not in the Gower dendrogram. Their visual appearance was similar and striking with vegetation mainly of sedges and bryophytes but no build-up. The soil was brown and compact with a von Post score of 9.

**Group D** may represent the background condition of the landscape, with mid-range values and no sign of any past management, beyond use as rough grazing for hundreds of years.

**Group E** appears to include the oldest agricultural workings on the deepest soils, usually cultivated in beds. It shows the thickest build-up of litter and moss, up to 200mm, with a fully diplotelmic sphagnum system on top of previously worked soils. When management ceases, drains become overgrown and beds become waterlogged.

These five groupings form the basis of a classification system for blackland soils and also point to past use and future potential. Only 50 years of disuse converted formerly productive agricultural soils into unidentifiable waterlogged, acidic and overgrown plots. A blanket of partially decomposed litter and sphagnum is a formidable agricultural challenge. Practical trials to regenerate blackland fields are ongoing in the research areas.

## Subsurface

*Subsurface* includes soil chemistry, microbiology and interactions requiring laboratory analysis. The cumulative impact of decisions at higher levels is manifest most strongly here, initiating processes which either improve or reduce soil function. In the Modern Period, the cultivated horizons were buried but not obliterated by changes at *field* and *surface* levels.

Hints as to how a structured agricultural soil evolved from peat may perhaps be found in the concept of moorsh forming process (MFP); descriptions from the literature correspond to conditions observed in the field:

*'The moorshing of organic soils comprises biological, chemical and physical changes driven by a decrease in water content and an increase in air content...The basic feature differentiating the moorsh from the peat layer is soil structure: the moorsh is usually grainy, while the peat ranges from fibrous to amorphous depending on the degree of humification.'* (Brandyk *et al*., 2003)

*'Swelling - shrinkage processes resulting in moorshing and cracking increase water and air conductivity....with peat transforming into grains and aggregates; coke-like peat materials made of small, hard and irreversibly dried particles' may appear.* (Okruzko & Illnicki, 2003)

Although considered a problem in Poland, we believe that MFP exists as a positive force in the Atlantic climate of the Hebrides. Over time these 'grains and aggregates' enable the highly organic soil to develop a structure similar to that of mineral soils, increasing aeration and decreasing moisture retention, and becoming more favourable to agriculture. The dynamic of the Early Period may have resulted in the favourable field conditions of Groups A and B with well-structured yet highly organic soils and may be the end result of the decession process over centuries.

By contrast, the dramatically different condition of Group E in the Modern Period may be viewed as an example of paludification with peat beginning to form. The research suggests that the single most important determinant of direction - towards decession or paludification - is soil depth. Shallower areas can dry during the summers and resist build-up at *surface* level, whereas cultivated areas deeper than *c.*1m tend to deteriorate rapidly, presumably due to the inexhaustible reservoir of moisture in the peat below. These formerly worked soils could gradually disappear and become a horizon in the archaeological record.

Changes at *context* level imposed modifications on *landscape* and *field*, with rapid effects at *surface* level leading to impacts on soil, and on *subsurface* chemical and microbial processes sufficient to obliterate centuries of functioning agriculture. The concept of MFP may explain how the blackland soil system either moves upward through human intervention towards decession and agricultural productivity, or downwards towards paludification.

## Conclusions

The anthropic, organic soil system which is blackland presents an example of the rapid collapse of a traditional system. However, once understood, it may usefully provide lessons in historical resilience and a way forward. The initial classification of blackland as developed during the current research may prove useful for re-evaluation of other abandoned agricultural land on organic soils. Sometimes indistinguishable to the naked eye, the five groups from A to E have very different potential for re-use, and present very different levels of difficulty in restoration.

Systems such as blackland may be an example of a 'third way' between the twentieth century absolutes of conservation and production by drawing attention to overlooked and forgotten methods. Given that world climate is likely to become more unstable, an evaluation of the traditional agricultural strategies which enabled small populations to continue for generations on some of the most marginal agricultural land in Europe might be valuable (Scherbatskoy *et al.*, 2015):

- Firstly, land exists in significant quantity, well-suited to the grazing animals which alone on rough terrain can turn sunlight into food. Small-scale, neglected agricultural systems can be found world-wide: from the blacklands of the west of Scotland, throughout Europe (MacDonald *et al.*, 2000) to the American hill farms of Kentucky, Vermont and Virginia (Berry, 2006; Salatin, 2010) and beyond, formerly productive land is plentiful.

- Secondly, the flexibility of a diverse landscape mosaic engenders system resilience: in a dry year, one area is productive, in a wet year, another. Unique landraces of crops develop in various climates and soils to take advantage of local conditions - in contrast to the cultivars of industrial agriculture which often require that the land adapt to them.

- Thirdly, the habit of care, thrift and adaptation ingrained in populations on the edge to ensure their survival may have lessons for us all in an age of uncertainty.

Generations of management created useful soils in ecosystems throughout the world, and several decades of neglect saw their decline. The paradox of underused land and vanishing skills at a time of increasing demand for food, growing climate instability and rising fuel prices cannot be easily dismissed.

## References

Bradley, R.I., Milne, R., Bell, J., Lilly, A., Jordan, C. and Higgins, A. (2005) A soil carbon and land use database for the United Kingdom. *Soil Use and Management,* **21**, 363-369.

Ball, B.C., Batey, T. and Munkholm, L. (2007) Field Assessment of soil structural quality - a development of the Peerlkamp test. *Soil Use and Management,* **23**, 329-337.

Berry, W. (2006) An Introduction to Soils and Health. *Hudson Review*, **29**(2).

Bibby, J.S. (1982) (ed.) *Land Capability Classification for Agriculture.* Macaulay Institute for Soil Research, Aberdeen.

Brandyk, T., Szatylowitcz, J., Oleszczuk, R. and Gnatowski, T. (2003) *Water-related Physical Attributes of Organic Soils.* In: Parent L.E. and Illnicki P. (eds) *Organic Soils and Peat Materials for Sustainable Agriculture.*: CRC Press, Florida, USA.

Carmichael A. (1883) *Grazing and Agrestic Customs of the Outer Hebrides.* In: *Napier Commission on Crofting.* Edinburgh, the Crown, 451-482.

Conry, M.J. (1972) Pedological Evidence of Man's Role in Soil Profile Modification in Ireland. *Geoderma*, **8**, 139-146.

Cregeen, E.R. (2004) *Recollections of an Argyllshire Drover.* John Donald, Edinburgh.

Dodgshon, R.A. (1994) *Rethinking Highland Field Systems.* In: Foster, S. and Smout, T.C. (eds) *The History of Soils and Field Systems.* Scottish Cultural Press, Aberdeen.

Ellenberg, H. (1974) Zeigerwerte der Gefässpflanzen Mitteleuropas. *Scripta geobotanica*, Göttingen, **9**.

FAO (2011) Classification of Organic Soils. www.fao.org/docrep/x5872e/x5872e07.htm

Fenton, A. (1994) *Field Systems and Cultivating Implements.* In: Foster, S. and Smout, T.C. (eds) *The History of Soils and Field Systems.* Scottish Cultural Press, Aberdeen.

Firbank, L.G., Petit, S., Smart, S., Blain, S. and Fuller, R.J. (2008) Assessing the impacts of agricultural intensification on biodiversity: a British perspective. *Phil. Trans. R. Soc. B*, **363**, 777 - 787.

Fraser Darling, F. (1955) (ed.) *West Highland Survey.* Oxford University Press, London.

Fraser Darling, F. (1945) *Crofting Agriculture.* Oliver and Boyd, Edinburgh.

Guttmann, E.B., Simpson, I.A., Davidson, D.A. and Dockrill, S.J. (2006) The management of arable land from prehistory to the present: Case studies from the northern isles of Scotland. *Geoarchaeology-An International Journal*, **21**, 61-92.

Hill, M.O., Mountford, J.O, Roy, D.B. and Bunce, R.G.H. (1993) *Ellenberg's indicator values for British plants. ECOFACT Countryside Survey*, Vol.2.

Hunter, J. (1976, rev. 1992) *The Making of the Crofting Community.* John Donald, Edinburgh.

Jones, G. (2011) *Trends in Common Grazing.* European Forum on Nature Conservation and Pastoralism, Lampeter, Wales.

Knox, O.G.G., Marsden, T.J., Warnick, S., Scherbatskoy, M.N., Wilson, D. and Harvie, B. (2013) *Seaweed and the reworking of old agricultural production systems to provide improved sustainability and ecosystem services.* SRUC Crop and Soil Systems Research Group, Edinburgh.

MacDonald, J. (1811) *General View of the Agriculture of the Hebrides.* Edinburgh.

MacDonald, D., Crabtree, J.R., Wiesinger, G., Dax, T., Stamou, N., Fleury, P., Guttierez Lazpita, J. and Gibon, A. (2000) Agricultural abandonment in mountain areas of Europe. *Journal of Environmental Management*, **59** (1), May 2000.

Manley, G. (1979) *The climatic environment of the Outer Hebrides. Proceedings of the Royal Society of Edinburgh*, Section B, **77**, 47-59.

Mercer, R. and Tipping, R. (1994) *The Prehistory of Soil Erosion in the Northern and Eastern Cheviot Hills, Anglo-Scottish Borders.* In: Foster, S. and Smout, T.C. (eds) *The History of Soils and Field Systems*. Scottish Cultural Press, Aberdeen.

Norton, M. (2009) *The Crofting Year.* Isle of Lewis: Western Isles Council, Stornoway.

Okruzko, H. and Illnicki, P. (2003) *The Moorsh Horizons as Quality Indicators of Reclaimed Organic Soils.* In: Parent L.E. and Illnicki P. (eds) *Organic Soils and Peat Materials for Sustainable Agriculture.* CRC Press, Florida, USA.

Okruzko, H. (1968) Soil-forming process in drained peatland. *Transactions of the Second International Peat Congress,* **1**, 189–198. HMSO, Edinburgh.

Peatscapes Project (2008) *Sphagna as Management Indicators*. www.ptyxis.com.

Powlson, D.S., Whitmore, A.P. and Goulding, K.W.T. (2011) Soil carbon sequestration to mitigate climate change: a critical examination to identify the true and the false. *European Journal of Soil Science*, **62**, 42-55.

Rees, R.M., Bingham, I.J., Baddeley, J.A. and Watson, C.A. (2005) The role of plants and land management in sequestering soil carbon in temperate arable and grassland ecosystems. *Geoderma*, **128**, 130-154.

Richter, D.D. (2007) Humanity's transformation of Earth's soil: Pedology's new frontier. *Soil Science*, **172** (12), 957-967.

Salatin, J. (2010) *The Sheer Ecstasy of Being a Lunatic Farmer.* Self-published, USA.

Scherbatskoy, M.N., Edwards, A.C. and Williams, B.L. (2015) *Assessing an organic, anthropic soil system in the Outer*

*Hebrides: Blackland.* In: *Visual Soil Evaluation: Realising Potential Crop Production with Minimum Environmental Impact.* CABI, Wallingford, UK.

Scottish Government (2006) *Scotland's Soil Resource: Current State and Threats.* www.scotland.gov.uk/Publications/2006/09/21115639/12.

Thomson, S. (2011) *Response from the hills: Business as usual or a turning point?* (http://www.sruc.ac.uk/info/120484/support_to_agriculture_archive/81/2011_response_from_the_hills.

von Post, L. and Granlund, L.E. (1926) Södra Sveriges Torvtillgånger, I. *Sver. Geo. Unders.* C35, **19** (2).

Worral, F., Bell, M.J. and Bhogal, A. (2010) Assessing the probability of carbon and greenhouse gas benefit from the management of peat soils. *Science of the Total Environment,* **408**, 2657-2666.

# Chapter 12. The Thorney Problem of Water Management

**Kieran A Sheehan**
JBA Ecology

## Introduction

This chapter looks at the Thorne, Crowle and Goole Moors Water Level Management Plan (WLMP) and how this is being implemented by the internal drainage boards (IDBs) responsible for it and the problems encountered along the way in dealing with the public and interested parties in and around Thorne Moors.

## Humberhead Levels

Thorne Moors is situated in the Humberhead Levels, a large, low-lying area of England bounded by the Yorkshire Wolds and the Lincoln Edge to the east, the Magnesian Limestone Escarpment to the west and by glacial moraines to the north and south (in the Vale of York and the Trent Vale respectively). The Levels cover an area of approximately 167,000 ha with much of the area below 10m AOD (ERYC, 2006). Today most of the land-use is agricultural as much of the fenland in the Levels has been drained and turned into high quality arable farmland (Defra, 2011). In places in and around the confluence of the rivers Ouse and Trent, this has been augmented by a process known as warping (Figure ), where land is allowed to flood at high tide after which the water is impounded and allowed to drain down. This deposits a layer of silt which is added to layer by layer at each tide. Over a period of typically a year, this practice can raise land levels by a metre or more and dramatically improve the land quality in the process (Gaunt, 2014 p.16).

Within the Levels there are large areas of peat that were laid down in a peri-glacial environment, however, much of these have now been lost as a result of land drainage activities, excessive ploughing, warping and direct extraction. The two largest areas of remaining peat are Thorne and Hatfield Moors: lowland raised mires that were formed where the distributaries of the Don met the rivers Trent and Ouse. As with the rest of the Levels, these mires have suffered from drainage, peat extraction and warping over the centuries and are now but shadows of their former selves. However, they still represent the largest area of lowland peat mire in England (Natural England, no date) with Thorne Moors being the largest terrestrial SSSI in the country.

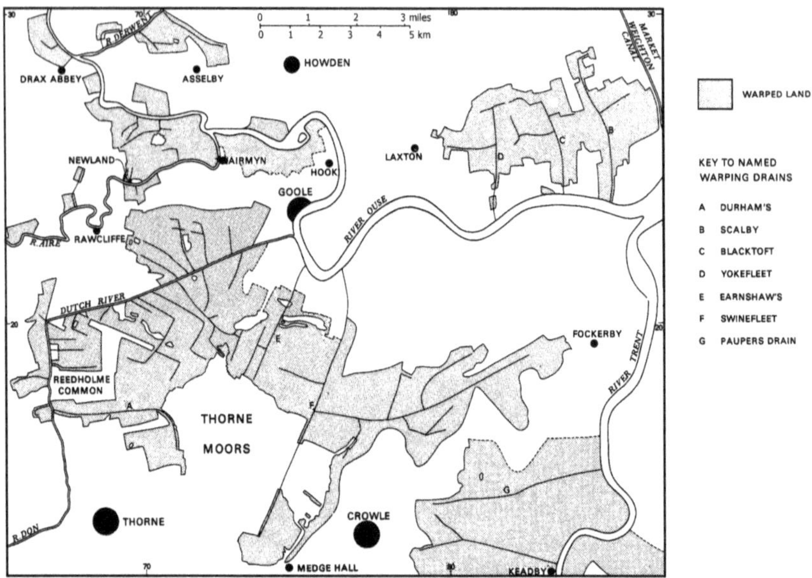


**Figure 1. Warping in and around Thorne Moors (after Gaunt and Buckland)**

## Hatfield Moors

Hatfield Moors is situated some two miles south of Thorne Moors and is a large remnant raised mire that developed over a sandy substrate (Figure 2). As with Thorne Moors, they are situated within a pumped drainage catchment, all of which is now managed by the Doncaster East Internal Drainage Board, following the amalgamation of a number of smaller IDBs in 2012. The site itself is managed by Natural England and all the water that is discharged enters the DEIDB system and is eventually pumped into the River Trent.

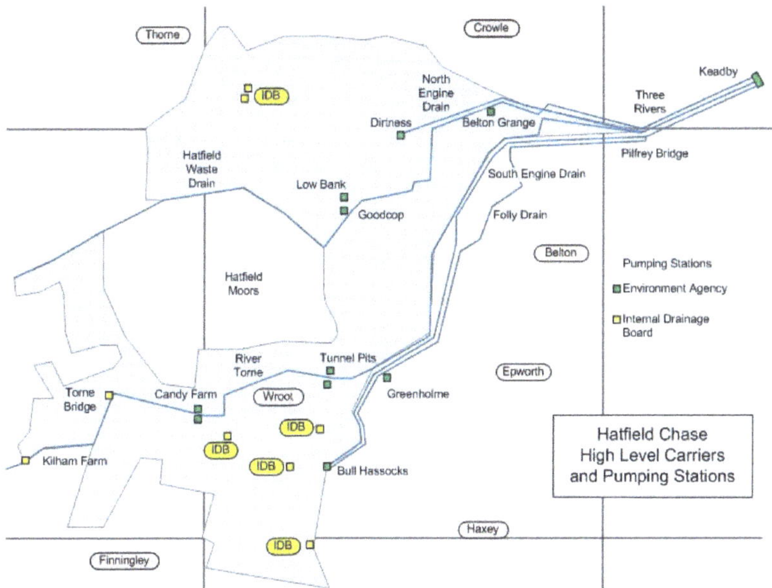


**Figure 2. Simplified Drainage Map of Hatfield Chase Showing High Level Carriers and Pumping Stations (Evens 2010)**

## Thorne Moors

This moor is the main subject of the chapter and is composed of a series of intergrading peat domes that coalesced into a large lowland raised mire *c.*4,500 years ago (Smith, 2002). The mire lies on clay which forms an aquitard (Gaunt, 2014 p.12) and grew from a series of pools and fens that existed on the land surface at that time (P. Buckland pers. comm.). The bog at that time lay within the distributaries of the River Don, although the drainage was modified heavily in the 17th Century and the River Don now flows northwards to the west of the mire (Ibid, p.14; Taylor, 1987 p.37): a course that is entirely artificial (Gaunt, 1987 p.42). The mire today is a degraded raised bog that has been extensively cut and milled for peat, leaving a matrix of habitats *in situ.* However, in the main the northern half of the mire (Goole Moors) is composed of a flat, milled surface whilst the southern half (Thorne Moors) is higher, more undulating and covered with Birch (*Betula pendula* and *B. pubescens*) scrub (Figure ).

The eastern portion is separated from the rest of the mire by the Swinefleet Warping Drain, a clay-lined high-level carrier that was put across the mire in 1821. As a result, the drainage of the bog has been modified dramatically (Figure 4) with all the water leaving the mire entering pump-drained catchments.

**Figure 3. Thorne Moors Main Vegetation Types and their Locations (Jones and Sheehan, 2010)**

## Rainfall

The rainfall in the Thorne Moors area is very low, typically 600mm per year (Buckland and Sheehan, 2013). This means that for a bog to grow here at all is challenging yet we have England's largest raised mire in one of the driest parts of the country. This bog is now heavily modified with large drains cut into it to facilitate the extraction of peat. In view of this, any rainfall landing on the bog has a hard time staying on the bog (a prerequisite for raised mire growth) so, at present, the bog is at risk from drying out and oxidation, should the water level management regime be allowed to remain as it is.

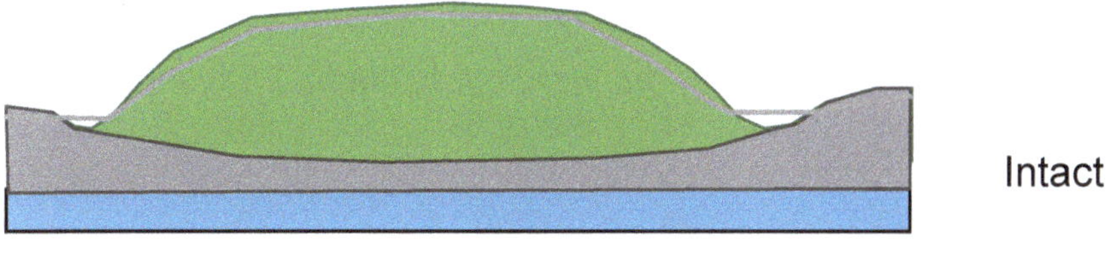


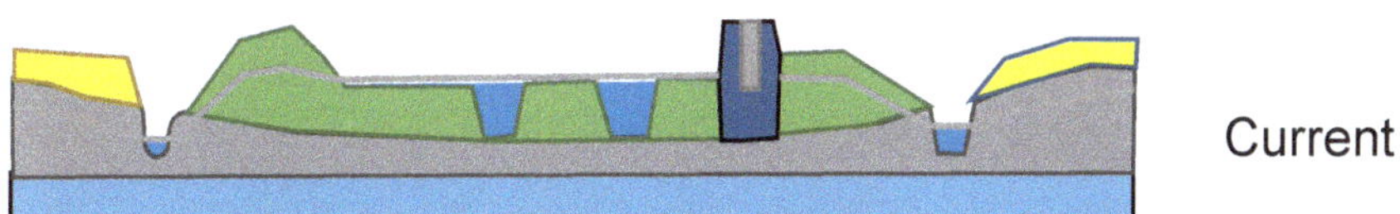


**Figure 4. Cross Sections of an Intact Raised Mire (above) and Thorne Moors (below)**

## Draining a Bog

In order to be able to extract peat from a raised bog it is essential that the water table be lowered to allow access to the peat above the water level, so that it can be cut or milled. In order to facilitate this, large trapezoidal drains are dug that will permit any water falling on the mire to be conveyed rapidly off-site (Figure 5). The same approach is taken to the draining of land: large drains are dug in a criss-crossing network across the land that allows water to flow away rapidly.

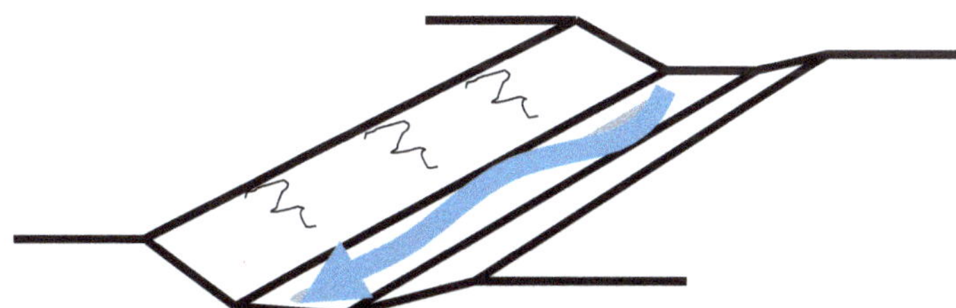

**Figure 5. Trapezoidal Drain in Cross-Section**

This was what was done in the 17th Century to allow peat to be cut from the mire to fuel local houses and industry. However, by doing this on Thorne you are discharging the water as fast as possible onto the surrounding flat land that is pumped-drained: in other words, you are contributing to flooding problems in the drainage district by increasing the height of the flood spike on the hydrograph and potentially overloading the pumps.

In order to reduce the height of the flood spike, and release the water from the bog more slowly, it would seem sensible to try and hold more water on the mire, i.e. encourage it to act like a flood storage reservoir. This is essentially what the aims of the WLMP are – to manage water levels on the moors to allow the moors to reach favourable conservation status and, at the same time, reduce the risk of flooding on the surrounding land. There are obvious synergies here that should allow this to happen, however, in reality, things were not that simple.

## Drainage Districts

Thorne, Crowle and Goole Moors are surrounded by six drainage districts, each of which is controlled by an Internal Drainage Board (Figure 6). The six boards surrounding the moors are shown in Table 1.

**Table 1. Thorne Moors IDB Partnership Members**

| Drainage Boards |
|---|
| Black Drain IDB |
| Dempster IDB |
| Doncaster East IDB |
| Goole Fields IDB |
| Reedness and Swinefleet IDB |
| Thorntree IDB |

Due to the funding regime imposed by the Environment Agency (EA), only one IDB was able to draw down the funding for the plan and, for historical reasons, the responsibility to implement the WLMP was placed upon Tween Bridge Internal Drainage Board. In 2012, this board amalgamated with a number of other boards in the Doncaster Area to become the Doncaster East IDB and it is this board that is currently funding the WLMP, via grant-in-aid from the Environment Agency.

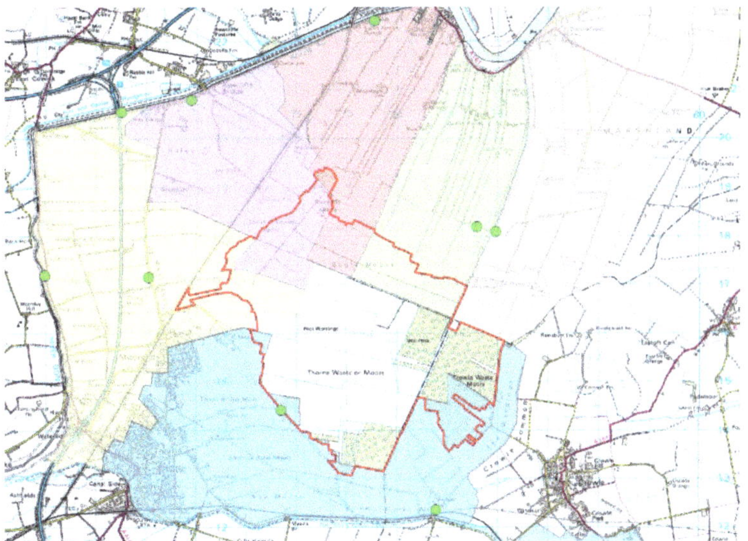

**Figure 6. Drainage Districts Surrounding Thorne Moors (Crown Copyright 2014. All rights reserved. Licence no: 100018880 2014. Used with Permission)**

Under the Land Drainage Act 1992, IDBs have a duty *to further the conservation and enhancement of natural beauty and the conservation of flora* [and], *fauna*, however, this duty has not always been recognised by IDBs, many of whom still believe that the function of an Internal Drainage Board is land drainage: nothing more, nothing less. To date, the two major problems facing the plan have revolved around the funding for the project and the perceived conflict between the land drainage and conservation functions of IDBs.

In such catchments, water is typically controlled by two different drainage systems: the low level drainage network and high level carriers. The former is the network of drains that receive water from the (under) field drains, roads and, in some cases, urban areas. These drains then convey the water to a pumping station where the water is pumped up to a higher level from whence it typically flows to another pumping station and so on. Eventually after one or more of these steps, the water is pumped into a high-level carrier where it discharges into the sea or a main river (Figure ).

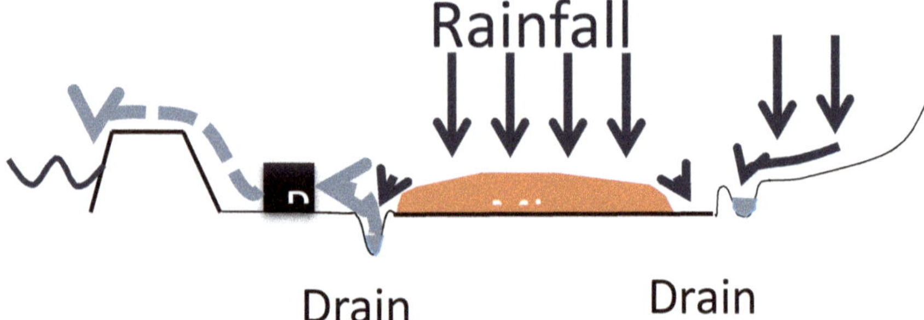


**Figure 7. Pumped Drainage Catchment and Raised Mire**

The high level carriers receive water from the low level system but also intercept streams and rivers from higher up the catchment and carry the water in trapezoidal (usually straight) drains to the main river, in other words keeping excess water away from low-lying land, keeping the latter dry and reducing the need for pumping (see Figure ). In some cases, the main rivers themselves have become high level carriers, and they are often perched and disconnected from their floodplains. Good examples would be the Rivers Hull and Ancholme: the latter having been straightened whilst the former has retained its meanders, but not its connection with its floodplain.

## Perceptions

In implementing the WLMP for Thorne Moors, one of the key requirements was to get the agreement of the six IDBS in the partnership to implement the WLMP. This was relatively easy initially, however, once the plan reached the implementation phase, the perceptions that people had about the plan began to interfere with its success and nearly resulted in the cancellation of the plan altogether. How did this happen?

In order to understand this, it needs to be appreciated that Internal Drainage Boards have been around for a very long time in the Humberhead Levels, and they are effectively run by the landowners who farm in the drainage district and who have a vested interest in keeping their land free from flooding. Indeed, this was the original function of drainage boards when they were set up in the Levels in the 17th century. These boards are now public bodies (not clubs or co-operatives) and those that sit on them are elected. However, the electoral process is an archaic one in that those with the largest land holdings within the drainage district, have more votes than those with smaller landholdings. This means that, in effect, the largest landowners or their representatives usually sit on the governing bodies of IDBs which means that board positions are inherently patrimonial in nature (Sheehan, 2013). There is a caveat here though and this concerns drainage districts where there are large urban centres. In these cases, a Special Levy is paid by the local council to the drainage board to reimburse it for the benefit the urban area receives in terms of reduced flooding, and, in return, the council has the right to appoint a number of members to the IDB equal to the number of rate-payers (landowners) plus one: in other words, a simple majority. In practice this rarely happens (Rhead et. al., no date; JBA, 2006 p. 84) and IDBs in the main continue to be run by large landowners who, because land is a heritable asset, have in effect an inherited position on a public body. It was a poor understanding (perception) of this system of governance at the outset that was to lead to a near failure of the WLMP in December 2012.

The other difficulty that arose as the plan progressed was the perception of many IDB board members of what a raised bog was and how this related to the role of the board in land drainage. In some ways this was the 'shock of the new' but, in combination with the poor understanding of the governance and vested interests of those who sit on Internal Drainage Boards by the project team, this created a perfect storm that led to the crisis of December 2012.

## Reality

## Political Interference

In advance of the proposed amalgamation of a number of IDBs into the new Doncaster East IDB in April 2012, there was a power struggle between a number of rate-payers, who saw their power potentially diminished by the creation of the new, larger board and another group (which included council appointees) who wanted the amalgamation to go ahead. Mud was slung and, in the course of this, a complaint was made to the Environment Minister regarding the WLMP and its governance along with a request that the amalgamation be put on hold until the allegations in the letter could be investigated.

In the event, the allegations were withdrawn within 24 hours and the amalgamation Statutory Instrument (SI 2012:1027) went through in April 2012. However, this use of the WLMP as a punch-bag was to continue as those who lost the amalgamation fight continued to criticise the plan and point out that, as it was a Tween Bridge IDB plan, it had to be formally adopted by the new Doncaster East board. Eventually this came to a head in December 2012 when an Extraordinary General Meeting of the board was called to vote on whether the plan should continue or not. At this meeting the main arguments given for not continuing with the plan were:

1. Drainage Boards are concerned with land drainage, not conservation.
2. The plan is a waste of money.
3. The works will raise water levels on the moors and therefore flood the surrounding land.
4. The works will increase the future flood risk on the surrounding land.

## What is the reality?

Point 1 is inaccurate as, under the Land Drainage Act 1991, IDBs have a duty *to further the conservation and enhancement of natural beauty and the conservation of flora* [and], *fauna* (LDA 1991 as amended).

Point 2 is a value judgement but the plan is an expression of Government policy and has been fully-funded by the Environment Agency so no residual cost will fall on the ratepayers of the IDB district: the UK Government risks being fined by the EU for non-compliance with the Habitats Directive and bringing this site (and others) into favourable (recovering) condition will prevent these financial penalties.

Point 3 is incorrect as in order to extract peat a series of trapezoidal drains were installed on Thorne Moors to remove water as quickly as possible to drain the moors and allow machinery on site. Since the land surrounding the moors is generally at a lower level than the remaining peat mass, the water will pool here unless pumped away, i.e. on the agricultural land. Intuitively then, if water is retained on the moors, it will discharge water more slowly or it will be lost by evapotranspiration into the atmosphere reducing the flood risk to the surrounding catchments as well as reducing their pumping requirements.

Point 4 assumes that the water that falls on the moors will be held on the moors by dams etc. and this will increase in depth until it flows over the top onto the surrounding land. This is patently absurd, however, at a meeting on the 7th of December 2012, a request was made that the IDB provide a guarantee to landowners that the land around the moors would never flood: something that would never be asked of the Environment Agency.

Once these arguments had been defeated, the plan was voted through, with the help of local council appointees. However, objections to the plan were still being made by the other IDBs in the partnership. These revolved around the fact that the plan had obtained £3m in funding and that it was not right that Doncaster East should control all these funds. It was felt by many boards that these funds should be split six ways and that each of the drainage boards in the partnership should be able to implement the plan as they saw fit and that this could be done much cheaper this way. In parallel with this was a claim that the plan had become too big and that this was not what was intended when the partnership was formed. The latter point may or may not be the case but the perception by many of the smaller boards in the partnership is that this plan was being foisted upon them without their agreement in their drainage districts, i.e. areas that they control. This has created bad feeling and has resulted in many of the drainage boards still claiming that Argument 1 is valid. This in effect is a diversionary tactic as the real difficulty many boards have with the plan is a perceived loss of control (Sheehan, 2013). However, if expressed publicly, this argument is not likely to gain much traction with the wider public, and hence the continuous reversion to Argument 1.

## Moving On

### Work

In view of these problems, it was essential from the outset that everything that was done to control water levels on Thorne Moors was backed up by robust research as, if it were not, it would be open to challenge, either through bad publicity or via legal avenues. Because of this a monitoring network was installed on Thorne Moors in 2009 to supplement that already installed by Natural England and, over the three years of the plan to date this has been supplemented where it has been assessed there are data gaps. This network consists of rain gauges, dipwells, stilling wells and boreholes containing dataloggers (Figure ).

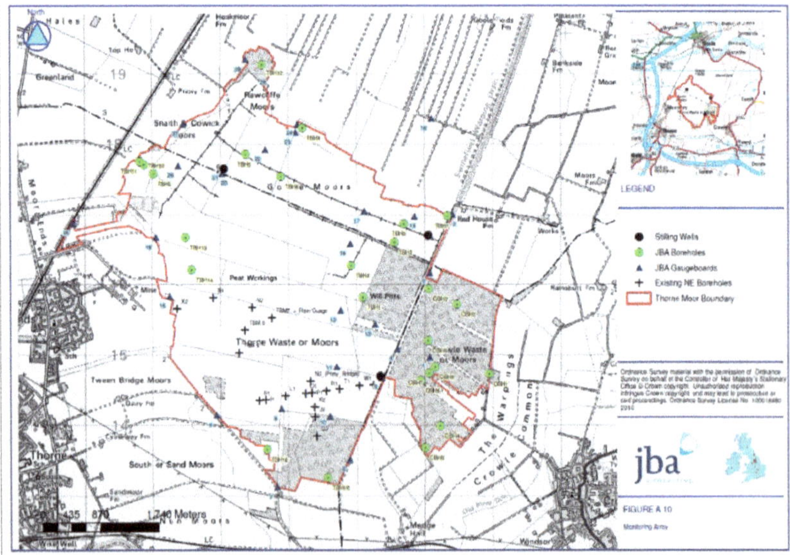


**Figure 8. Thorne Moors Monitoring Network in 2010 (Jones and Sheehan, 2010)**

Through installing this network, we have gained a unique understanding of the ways in water travels through and across the mire to the existing pumping station on the Swinefleet Warping Drain. This programme of 'Investigative Studies' led to the production of a plan (Jones and Sheehan, 2010) by which the desired water levels set out in the WLMP (TMIDBP, 2010) were to be achieved. This plan showed how water levels on the moors could be optimised without causing additional flood risk within the IDB catchments and demonstrated that any changes resulting from works would be gradual and monitored so, if anything unplanned were to occur, remedial action could be taken in good time. In order to achieve this the monitoring network is now being enhanced through the use of telemetry which will link it in to the systems operated by the Doncaster East IDB and Reedness and Swinefleet Drainage Board. This will ensure that, when there are flood events, water is held back on the moors to ensure that the current drainage infrastructure is not overwhelmed, protecting properties near Crowle and in Swinefleet. It will also eliminate the need for anticipatory pumping, whereby the existing pumping station is turned on in anticipation of expected rainfall, lowering water levels on the mire. This, east of the Pennines, can cause excessive drying of the moors as rainfall in inherently unreliable in duration and amount due to rain shadow and Föhn effects.

This plan gained the approval of the Environment Agency in February 2011 and funding of £2.9m was granted under the Flood and Coastal Erosion Risk Management budget: the same budget stream that funds coastal and river flood defences, demonstrating the robustness of the plan in terms of flood risk.

## Publicity

At this point the key was to increase publicity for the plan, to gain public buy-in amongst the communities surrounding the mire. However, getting through to the target audience has not proved easy, nor is the target audience necessarily that easy to identify. In terms of decision makers, all of the relevant individuals and organisations are aware of the plan and its aims. This does not of course mean that they all support it. In terms of getting the message out to local residents about what we are doing and why, we have been much less successful. In spite of two full-scale public consultations on the plan, most people in the area are unaware that any such plan has been written or indeed, is being implemented and, of those that do, many are under the impression that the works are being carried out by Natural England. Why is this? The general consensus on this is that:

- People do not always read the print media.
- They know of the existence of the project website.

- Even if they do read the print media, do they read the public notices.
- If they did read such notice, would they attend public events to make their opinions known?

Sadly, to date it would appear that in general they have not.

## Media

Formal advertising of notices has not worked in raising awareness and nor has the provision of a website with a section for comments: this has only been used twice in the last three years, by one individual with a particular issue. Informal article writing has been effective in the case of a partner organisation. However, these articles do not have 'official' approval. Article writing takes time and this means money. Is it acceptable to devote time (and spending money) to writing articles for local press outlets when there is no guarantee of them being published? To date we have not adopted this approach. We have also considered sponsored publications or sections within the local press, but this requires a substantial financial commitment in terms of printing and publishing costs as well as in time. To offset this, partner organisations have been asked for help but, as these all have slightly different *raison d'êtres*, this has proved difficult to put into practice.

## Working with others

This is a key component of any project of this type, where there are multiple beneficiaries and stakeholders. However, there is a problem in that projects tend to work with the same partners all the time: the wildlife trusts, local volunteer groups and similar. There is a cosy relationship here and it is difficult to break out of this. How do you involve industry and working families, those who may view the bog as a wasteland on the one hand or somewhere you take the kids and dogs for a walk on the weekend? How do you engage these groups who are often monetarily rich but time poor?

## Openness

This is something we value in the implementation of the WLMP and have championed from the very beginning. This, it turns out, has been a sea-change in the way that things were done in the past. However, criticism is still received by those who have not asked for information or looked for it, that it is not available. Others, who are used to working in a different way, are uncomfortable with working in an open environment where minutes of meetings (warts and all!) are uploaded onto the World Wide Web for all to see.

## Give and take

Maybe this title should be 'give a little, take a lot!' This would be an ideal world, however, in order to make progress, there is a need to compromise. This is essential and may at times mean you have to swallow your pride and give up on cherished ideas no-one else supports or work with people you would prefer not to.

## Lessons Learned

There is a need to tackle perceptions head-on: yours and others. These can be a threat to a project but can also offer opportunities to understand the positions of others and challenge pre-conceived ideas. In order to do this, it is essential that you have a good understanding of the sensitivities of others. This may take time to do but it is time well-spent. It may very well be that what may appear at first glance to be a potential stumbling block is in fact not and the real reason behind it lies somewhere else, i.e. the project is perceived as a threat to something you may not have considered.

Cultural sensitivities are also important and can be overt, in the case of not wanting a cherished view spoiled by wind turbines, or more subtle, for instance a change to the way an organisation works. Many third sector (and even public) bodies have an internal culture and way of working that, in some cases can be centuries old and change is often resented: *if it ain't broke, don't fix it*. However, it may need to be explained that change is inevitable, and the institution's ways of working are archaic and may need updating. This is by necessity a longer-term task and change needs to be incremental in order to gain support, i.e. evolutionary not revolutionary. By taking such an approach, you will gain allies and make far fewer enemies. It will also allow time for the project team to gain a deeper understanding of the organisations with whom they have to work and the key individuals within these.

## References

Buckland, P. C. and Sheehan, K. A. (2013) *Thorne and Hatfield Moors BES Field Day*. [Online available at: http://www.ukeconet.org/wp-content/uploads/2013/09/BES-Thorne-and-Hatfield-Moors-Handout.pdf [Accessed 30 August 2014].

Defra (2011) *English Nature Natural Areas _ an Introduction 22. Humberhead Levels*. [Online available at: http://adlib.everysite.co.uk/adlib/defra/content.aspx?id=000IL3890W.16NTBYVUMEY20M [Accessed 30 August 2014].

ERYC (East Riding of Yorkshire Council) (2006) *Landscape Character Assessment*. [Online available at: http://www.eastriding.gov.uk/corp-docs/forwardplanning/docs/lca/final/type7.pdf [Accessed 30 August 2014].

Evens, R. (2010) *Hatfield Chase High Level Carriers and Pumping Stations*. [Online] Available at: http://en.wikipedia.org/wiki/Hatfield_Chase#mediaviewer/File:Hatfield_Chase_map.jpg [Accessed 30 August 2014].

Gaunt, G.D. (1987) *The Geology of the Thorne Area*. In: Taylor, M., *Thorne Mere and Old River Don*. Ebor Press, York.

Gaunt, G.D. (2014) *Geology of the Area around Thorne Moors: A Summary and Update*. In: McDonald, I. and Wall, C., *Thorne Moors A Botanical Survey.* Thorne and Hatfield Moors Conservation Forum, Thorne.

JBA (JBA Consulting) (2006) *Internal Drainage Board Review Final Report February 2006* [Online available at: http://archive.defra.gov.uk/environment/flooding/documents/who/idb/jbareport.pdf [Accessed 3 September 2013].

Jones, A.J. and Sheehan, K.A. (2010) *Thorne, Crowle and Goole Moors Water Level Management Plan Final Report.* [Online available at: http://www.thornepeatland.org.uk/media/515/2008s3746_thorne_wlmp_hydrogeology_report_20final_figs.pdf [Accessed 4 September 2013].

Natural England (no date) *Humberhead Peatlands NNR.* [Online available at: http://www.naturalengland.org.uk/ourwork/conservation/designations/nnr/1006766.aspx [Accessed 30 August 2014].

Rhead, B., Vickers, T. and Moodie, S. (no date) *Internal Drainage Board Membership And Representation Survey Analysis*. [Online available at: http://www.ada.org.uk/downloads/other/downloads_page/IDB_Membership_and_Representation_Survey_Analysis.pdf [Accessed 3 September 2013].

Sheehan, K.A. (2013) *Peat, Politics and Patrimonialism*. In: Rotherham, I.D. and Handley, C. (eds) *War and Peat.* Wildtrack Publishing, Sheffield.

Smith, B.M. (2002) A Palaeoecological Study of Raised Mires in the Humberhead Levels. *British Archaeological Reports*, **336**.

Taylor, M. (1987) *Thorne Mere and Old River Don.* Ebor Press, York.

TMIDBP (Thorne Moors IDB Partnership) (2010) *Thorne, Crowle and Goole Moors Site of Special Scientific Interest Water Level Management Plan March 2010 Final Report.* [Online available at: http://www.thornepeatland.org.uk/media/509/thorne_moors_sssi_wlmp_final.pdf [Accessed 31 August 2014].

*The Doncaster East Internal Drainage Board Order 2012*. SI 2006/1027, Stationary Office, London.

# Chapter 13. Exmoor Mires Project: Initial analyses of post restoration vegetation monitoring data

**David M. Smith[1, 3], Conrad Barrowclough[2], Andrew D. Glendinning[3] and Anne Hand[3]**
South West Water [1], First Ecology (Somerset Wildlife Trust) [2], Exmoor Mires Project [3]

## Summary

The initial analyses of seven years of pre- and post-restoration vegetation monitoring have revealed short and medium term effects of peatland restoration by ditch blocking on the botanical communities of damaged peatland. The vegetation data are interpreted in terms of National Vegetation Classification (NVC) communities at site and quadrat level, by the application of Ellenberg's indicator values and by employing indicator species lists.

Site level NVC communities for five of the seven re-surveyed sites show a change in botanical composition indicative of rewetting of the underlying peat. The analysis of Ellenberg values, applied to the species found in all quadrats both before and after restoration, provides a detailed measure of change and suggests that restoration has led to significant peatland re-wetting. At site level, significant changes in Ellenberg values suggest successful restoration at four of the seven resurveyed sites, contradicting the site level NVC assessment for one site. Changes in the list of selected indicator species support the findings of the site level Ellenberg value analyses and highlight the underlying changes in species occurrence. Our analyses suggest that site level NVC analysis has some value but missed important detail which was picked up during the subsequent analyses.

Where restoration structures have remained intact, botanical communities have significantly changed, reflecting rewetting of underlying peat at all but one site. This indicates that the use of ditch blocking to re-wet peatlands is a successful hydrological rehabilitation strategy.

Vegetation community changes can also be used as indicators of changing greenhouse gas fluxes from peatlands as a result of restoration. These results enable the Exmoor Mires Project (EMP) to move towards the verification of the carbon emissions savings from peatland restoration on Exmoor, an essential step in the establishment of a Payment for Ecosystem Services (PES) reward scheme. A key EMP objective is to enable upland farmers and landowners to earn sustainable incomes from the provision of multiple ecosystems services.

**Key Words:** Exmoor, mires, peatland, re-wetting, vegetation, monitoring, Ellenberg, NVC, indicator species, PES.

## Introduction

The Exmoor Mires Project aims to deliver multiple ecosystem service outcomes by restoring peatland areas of Exmoor previously drained as part of historic conversion to agriculture or during peat cutting activities (Exmoor Mires, 2010). Restoration is achieved through ditch blocking and water management measures designed to re-wet peat sites where drainage has led to the drying of peat and an associated change in vegetation communities.

The MIRE (Moorland Improvement and Restoration on Exmoor) Project was initiated in 1998 as a pilot project, focused on habitat restoration and river headwater management by means of ditch blocking techniques. A small partnership of the Exmoor National Park Authority (ENPA), the Environment Agency (EA) and Natural England (formally English Nature) (NE) initiated pre-restoration monitoring of the vegetation and hydrology at two moorland sites at Exe Head and Blackpitts (on Exmoor). This was followed by small scale (12-ha) ditch blocking restoration action at the sites in the period 2001-3. In 2006 South West Water (SWW) joined the partnership and co-funded the Exmoor Mire Restoration Project (EMRP) a four year programme of restoration and monitoring on fourteen sites and 325 ha of restoration (ENPA, 2010). Since 2010 SWW have led the Exmoor Mires Project (EMP) a further phase of restoration through their progressive 'Upstream Thinking' initiative which promotes innovative ecosystem services (clean and sustained water supplies) from catchment management projects (Grand-Clement *et al.*, 2013). By the end of March 2014, the EMP had undertaken 1,015 ha of restoration at thirteen sites, with a target of 2,000 ha by April 2015. This scale of landscape restoration is targeted at achieving extensive habitat changes across these degraded peatlands. The ongoing vegetation monitoring programme reflects a need to develop an effective and efficient method of monitoring these changes.

SWW have a business interest in blocking historic moorland drainage ditches and peat cuttings as re-wetted peat provides regulatory ecosystem services (Bonn *et al.*, 2009). Restored areas are known to increase storage capacity for rainfall on moorlands and promote gradual release into catchment watercourses (Wilson *et al.*, 2010). Initial post restoration monitoring on Exmoor has confirmed these predictions with less peak flow runoff during periods of precipitation, reduced water colour (Dissolved Organic Carbon, DOC) and sustained base flows from the re-wetted peat (Luscombe *et al.*, 2014).

Ecosystem services-focused peatland restoration has been proven on Exmoor to recreate active peatland communities (Langton, 2009; Hand, 2009; Glendinning, 2013) which are now rare as a result of centuries of agricultural drainage (Bray, 2014). These changes are under reported in the literature. A recent evidence review of ditch blocking practice by NE found few citable papers. This investigation of the Exmoor Mires vegetation monitoring data seeks to redress this imbalance and present some initial findings with a view to developing further analyses over time.

Integral to the EMP has been the comprehensive and high resolution monitoring both before and after restoration in order to track the resulting changes in hydrology, greenhouse gas fluxes and biodiversity (Arnott, 2010; Luscombe, 2014; Hornibrook, 2014; First Ecology, 2012, 2014). A key part of the biodiversity monitoring has been the post restoration monitoring of botanical assemblages, which can be used to infer underlying changes in the peatland hydrology (Bellamy *et al.*, 2012; Lunt *et al.*, 2010).

This paper focuses on identifying the post restoration changes in the botanical communities at the restoration sites, which can be used in conjunction with the other ongoing monitoring programmes to indicate the underlying hydrological and greenhouse gas changes (Ramchunder *et al*., 2009; Couwenburg *et al*., 2011) across the whole of the 2,500 ha restoration area. The EMP is developing a rapid assessment method for monitoring hydrological change across the moorland landscape based on the proxy measure of ongoing vegetation changes. Demonstrating success is a pre-requirement of the EMP funding arrangements and a necessity if the greenhouse gas emissions savings arising from the restoration work are to be verified under the newly emerging Peatland Code (IUCN, 2013).

Somerset Wildlife Trust and its consultancy, First Ecology have been involved in the botanical monitoring of the restoration sites since the baseline monitoring was initiated in 1998 at Blackpitts and Exe Head (SERC, 1998). Since 2011, First Ecology has been contracted to lead the annual monitoring and reporting campaigns, supported by the project team and volunteers (First Ecology, 2012, 2014).

## Field survey

Seven post-restoration sites were re-surveyed during the 2013 survey season. The sites are presented in Table 1 and Map 1

**Table 1: Site summary 2013, with National Grid References**

| Site Name | Transect NGR | | Quadrats | Re-survey |
|---|---|---|---|---|
| | Start | End | | |
| Alderman's Barrow | SS8429242504 | SS8433242495 | 40 | x |
| Broadmead | SS7197441280 | SS7197241275 | 32 | x |
| Comerslade | SS7341037384 | SS7337637362 | 40 | x |
| Homer Common | SS6812042820 | SS6814842813 | 30 | x |
| Roosthitchen Phase 1 | SS7203740125 | SS7201940134 | 30 | x |
| Roosthitchen Phase 2 | SS7176440482 | SS7178940460 | 15 | x |
| Verney's Allotment | SS7781034640 | SS7777634663 | 40 | x |

## Map 1: Site locations for the 2013 surveyed transects

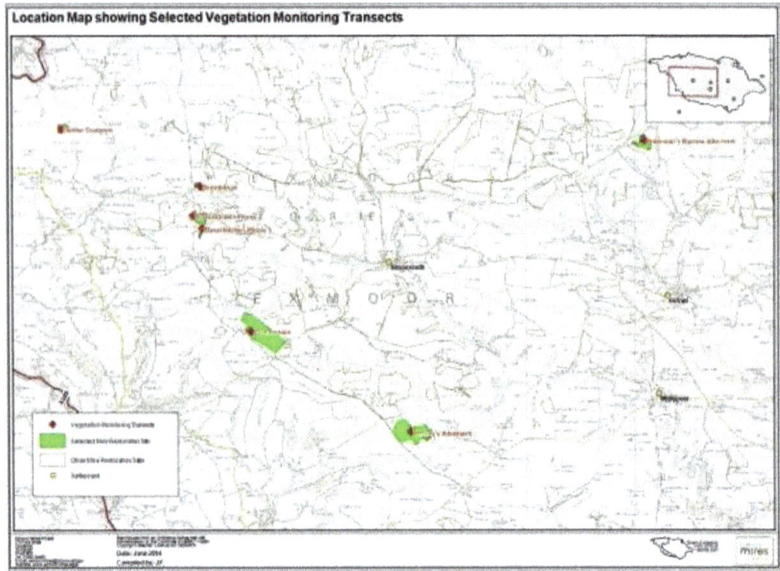


A field survey methodology was developed designed to collect accurate and comparable species data across the timescale of the project. The central objective was to enable the analysis of community change at re-surveyed sites in terms of the following:

- National Vegetation Classification communities; both for the site as a whole and at quadrat level where possible.
- Ellenberg (1974) values; this method allows for finer scale interpretation and comparison of results between years, based on several different parameters.
- Indicator species, using groups of species agreed by the project staff as being typical of "rich" and "poor" sites.

Consistency in data collection is particularly important, although changes to data collection have been made over the duration of the project to improve quality (e.g. movement from presence/ absence data to percentage cover). The field method employed in 2013 mirrors that employed the previous year and is broadly as follows.

- Sites are selected by the project staff for restoration, and a mapped ditch is targeted for blocking, across which the transect will be established. The site is visited prior to restoration and the transect marked out by measuring 15 metres perpendicular to either side of the ditch, with the transect ends being marked by two short wooden pegs one metre apart. The total length of the monitoring transects has varied from site to site depending on the original baseline surveys, and whether it was necessary to monitor both sides of the ditch, but 15m each side is the default length.

- When the site is surveyed, either to establish a baseline or to make a post restoration monitoring visit, a 30-metre measuring tape is run across the transect and tied off tight at either end. Along the length of this tape the 1m square quadrat is placed, totalling 30 separate samples for a standard 30m transect. The quadrat itself is subdivided into 4 sub-quadrats, and all species occurring in each sub-quadrat are recorded separately on a percentage cover basis. Species not identified in the field were taken back to the office for identification using light microscopy. Standard reference texts were used.

Surveys were conducted between June and November, with the majority of sites being visited in July and August when most plants are flowering and can be identified rapidly. For non-flowering species vegetative identification should allow accurate recording of the vast majority of species present and inter–year variation in the timing of surveys is not considered likely to compromise the accuracy of results significantly.

## Data analysis

## Allocation of NVC communities

The National Vegetation Classification system (Rodwell, 1991) is widely used to categorise dominant British vegetation in homogenous stands. It has been employed as part of this analysis both because it allows a broad classification of vegetation types and therefore underlying hydrological conditions, and because it is an accepted system which allows comparison of this study with others.

While the traditional method of assigning NVC communities usually employs hand-keying homogenous stands in the field, for this analysis we wanted to apply a consistent and impartial method of classification for all sites, some of which had been surveyed and hand-keyed several years ago. The most commonly used approach for this kind of problem is to employ a computer program such as MATCH (Malloch, 1990), TABLEFIT (Hill, 1991) or MAVIS (Smart, 2000), which allocates NVC communities to data entered and supplies 'goodness of fit' values for how closely data matches the standard NVC community types.

TABLEFIT and MAVIS were both employed in our analysis, dependant on the nature of the data to be classified. For the 2013 surveys, for which species data was collected in percentage-cover values, TABLEFIT was used to generate a whole site NVC community, a process then repeated using MAVIS to check both programs agreed. TABLEFIT was then used to generate NVC communities for every quadrat across the length of each transect, giving a finer scale picture of variation.

During initial comparison of 2013 NVC communities to historic NVC records for the same sites, it became apparent that this had limited value since many of the older NVC classifications (2006-2010) were generated using hand keying only in the field. This meant that it wasn't possible to confidently compare repeat surveys of the same sites due to the additional element of human interpretation. To make comparisons more reliable, the older site surveys were re-classified using the methodologies employed with the newer data.

An additional complication was that the data collected prior to 2010 was collected in a presence/absence format, as opposed to the percentage cover system used subsequently. Nevertheless, MAVIS can still be used to generate constancy values for each species based on occurrence in quadrats across whole transects from which NVC communities could confidently be generated. One limitation of this older presence/absence data is that it lacks the granularity needed to generate NVC communities at quadrat level, but whole site comparisons can be more confidently made once reclassification using MAVIS has taken place.

## Application and interpretation of Ellenberg's indicator values

Ellenberg's indicator values (referred to as Ellenberg values henceforth) are values allocated to individual species in a set of five scales: light; moisture; pH; nitrogen; and salinity. Given the anticipated nature of change in botanical communities after restoration, moisture, pH and nitrogen scales have been employed in this analysis. The values generally range from 1 to 9 (higher in some revisions) and are designed to indicate what the species in question reveals about that particular element of its environment. A species with a nitrogen (N) value of 1 for instance is indicative of extremely N poor sites (e.g. *Drosera rotundifolia*), whereas a species with an N value of 9 is indicative of heavily enriched or polluted sites (e.g. *Rumex obtusifolius*). The system was developed by Heinz Ellenberg (1974) and the values used in this analysis were revised specifically for the United Kingdom by Hill *et al.* (1999).

Applying Ellenberg values to the botanical data circumvents the problems caused by data being recorded in different formats between years. Ellenberg values for wetness (F from the German Feuchtigkeit), reaction/pH (R) and nitrogen (N) were applied to every species within each quadrat for all transects. These values were then averaged to give F, R and N values for each quadrat. Ellenberg values were included in the calculations for each quadrat on the basis of presence of a species in any single sub-quadrat, regardless of coverage; this allows direct comparison of the more recent percentage cover values with the older presence/absence data.

A number of comparisons were then made to detect changes in these indicator values as a result of restoration works. Paired T-tests were used to compare the pooled F, R and N values of all sites prior to restoration with the values from the most recent re-surveys to detect significant ($p < 0.05$) changes. Additionally, the same process was performed for each site individually to find significant changes which would further refine site level NVC designations.

## Indicator species analysis

A streamlined list of mire habitat indicator species (Table 2) has been drawn up by project staff over the course of the project and continually refined based on field observations. It is designed to allocate species to one of five categories: acid grassland/dry heath, wet heath/acid mire, meso-/minerotrophic mire and fen, agricultural grassland and woodland.

**Table 2: Indicator species lists developed by the project for analysis of changes at the sites re-surveyed in 2013**

| Positive Indicators | Negative Indicators |
|---|---|
| *Narthecium ossifragum* (Bog asphodel) | *Calluna vulgaris* (Ling) |
| *Carex demissa* (Common yellow sedge) | *Potentilla erecta* (Tormentil) |
| *Carex echinata* (Star sedge) | *Vaccinium myrtillus* (Whortleberry) |
| *Carex panicea* (Carnation sedge) | *Agrostis spp.* (Bent grasses) |
| *Eriophorum angustifolium* (Bog cotton-grass) | *Festuca spp.* (Fescues) |
| *Sphagnum capillifolium* | *Molinia caerulea* (Purple moor grass) |
| *Sphagnum cuspidatum* | *Rhytidiadelphus squarrosus* |
| *Sphagnum papillosum* | *Pleurozium schreberi* |
| *Sphagnum palustre* | *Hypnum cupressiforme* |
| *Sphagnum subnitens* | |
| *Sphagnum denticulatum* (Broadmead only) | |
| *Sphagnum fallax* (Broadmead and Homer Common) | |
| *Viola palustris* (Marsh violet, Broadmead only) | |
| *Carex rostrata* (Bottle sedge, Broadmead only) | |
| *Juncus bulbosus* (Bulbous rush, Homer Common) | |

This list was applied to the species recorded in the 2013 monitoring surveys and their comparable baselines to provide broad scale indication of directional change in terms of site wetness. To reconcile the different data formats between years, species occurrence has been scored based on presence of the species in all sub-quadrats within each transect, so for a 30-quadrat transect, occurrence is scored out of a potential maximum of 120.

Whilst the application of a bespoke indicator list may lack the rigour of the NVC community and Ellenberg indicator methods, it does have some advantages. Firstly, it keeps a graphical record of species occurrence across multiple years, which can be used as an adjunct to the NVC classifications to better understand changes. It also allows tracking of individual species fluctuations more easily, something which is inevitably lost in the 'noise' of the NVC community classification. Finally, evolving a list based on field observations allows a highly tailored approach to vegetation monitoring within the project area, which considers any variation from national norms which might be particular to the Exmoor area.

## Results and Discussion

## NVC community analysis - Site level

Classification of the 2013 re-survey data and re-classification of comparable baseline surveys generated results that indicate movement at the whole site level from drier to wetter communities at five of the seven sites re-surveyed in 2013. Results of the classification process are given in Table 3, followed by a brief description of each community. Note that where two different communities are given for a single year (e.g. M15d/M17c) this is because the TABLEFIT and MAVIS analyses returned goodness of fit values within one point of each other for both of the communities listed.

**Table 3: NVC communities for all sites re-surveyed in 2013, N.B. Community names only are listed and Rodwell (1991), should be referred to for their descriptions**

| **Site Name** | **Monitoring Year** | | | | |
|---|---|---|---|---|---|
| | **2006** | **2007** | **2008** | **2010** | **2013** |
| Alderman's Barrow | | | M25 **Restored** | | M25a |
| Broadmead | M25a | **Restored** | | M6a | M6a |
| Comerslade | | M15b | | **Restored** | M15b/M17 |
| Homer Common | | | | M15d **Restored** | M15d/m17c |
| Roosthitchen Phase 1 | M25 | **Restored** | | M6d | M6b |
| Roosthitchen Phase 2 | | | M15 **Restored** | M15 | M15d |
| Verney's Allotment | | M15d | **Restored** | M15d | M15d/M17c |

M25 *Molinia caerulea – Potentilla erecta* mire
M25a *Erica tetralix* sub-community
M17 *Scirpus cespitosus – Eriophorum vaginatum* blanket mire.
M17c *Juncus squarrosus – Rhytidiadelphus loreus* sub-community
M15 *Scirpus cespitosus –Erica tetralix* wet heath
M15b *Scirpus cespitosus –Erica tetralix* wet heath. Typical sub-community
M15a *Carex panicea* sub-community
M15d *Vaccinium myrtillus* sub-community
M6 *Carex echinata – Sphagnum recurvum/auriculatum* mire

M6a *Carex echinata* sub-community
M6b *Carex nigra – Nardus stricta* sub-community
M6d *Juncus acutiflorus* sub-community

It is immediately apparent from Table 3 that Broadmead, Comerslade, Homer Common, Roosthitchen Phase 1 and Verney's Allotment all appear to have undergone changes in vegetation composition at a site level which indicate rewetting of the underlying peat. Some of these changes are particularly pronounced, Broadmead for example moved from a degraded M25a community to a mesotrophic poor-fen community in just three years following restoration in 2007. This site has undergone repeated cycles of work to facilitate restoration, and the botanical changes reflect the impact of these efforts on the underlying hydrology of the site. Roosthitchen Phase 1 has also undergone a large change in the dominant vegetation type having moved from degraded M25 vegetation to a M6b community in the six years since restoration.

However, there have also been sites at which vegetation change is less obvious. Verney's Allotment and Homer Common for instance have only changed slightly from M15d communities to M15d/M17c intermediate communities since restoration, although this does suggest some level of rewetting. The reasons for this cannot be determined from this analysis alone, the key may lie in the complexities of the site hydrology. However, it should be noted the baseline survey of these two sites recorded a less degraded community than was found at some other sites, M15d rather than the M25 which is often associated with the drained areas of the moor. In this sense, these sites are unlikely to have such marked vegetation changes as might be seen when restoring areas more severely degraded.

Two sites, Roosthitchen Phase 2 and Alderman's Barrow, showed little appreciable change in dominant vegetation. However, reasons for this may lie in failures of restoration structures at these sites, rather than indicating a problem with the restoration methods in general. At Alderman's Barrow for instance, it was noted during the 2013 survey that a large portion of the ditch block had come away, and the site continued to be drained as a result. Roosthitchen Phase 2 has had similar problems, with part of the ditch block failing. Postrepair surveys should demonstrate whether further rewetting of the peat and corresponding vegetation change can be achieved. If so, the sites would demonstrate the importance of the integrity of the restoration structures.

## NVC community analysis - quadrat level

Due to the differing ways in which past survey data has been collected, it is not possible to allocate NVC communities at quadrat level to sites initially surveyed prior to 2010. This process has been conducted for all of the 2013 surveys however, and the results demonstrate variation across quadrats on a fine scale when compared with the classification at site level. Tables 4 and 5 present quadrat level NVC communities for both Broadmead and Comerslade.

These tables show that the distribution of NVC communities varies widely across the sites, despite the site level classification. At Broadmead for example, which was classified as M6a at site level, one side of the transect appears significantly drier than the other, based on the prevalence of M25a communities on that side. This demonstrates how the hydrology and resulting vegetative communities vary over short distances.

Looking at the results for Comerslade, which was classified as M15b/M17 at site level, variation across the site is also apparent. For example, surrounding the restoration feature, M6 and M6a communities are found, logical since this is the wettest part of the site. Elsewhere, away from the ditch, the site is characterised by M15b/M17 communities in tune with the site level classification.

These 2013 quadrat level classifications will serve as a valuable baseline. Recording and handling the data in this way in the next monitoring phase of the project will give a fine scale picture of developing changes in vegetation across whole sites.

**Tables 4 (left) and 5 (right): Demonstrating the allocation of NVC communities within transects at two sites surveyed in 2013, Broadmead and Comerslade. Note in both instances the bold central line indicates the ditch blocked during restoration**

| BROADMEAD |
|---|
| M6 |
| M6 |
| M6a |
| M6 |
| M6d |
| M6a |
| M6 |
| M6a |
| M6a |
| M25 |
| M25a |
| M6 |
| M6a |
| M6 |
| M6 |
| M6a |
| M23 |
| 100% water |
| 100% water |
| M25 |
| M25 |
| M13a |
| M25a |
| M25a |
| M6a |
| M25a |
| M25a |
| M25a |
| M25a |
| M25a |
| M25a |
| M25a |

| COMERSLADE |
|---|
| M15 |
| M15d |
| M15b |
| M15a |
| M1 |
| M17c |
| M15b |
| M15 |
| M15b |
| M15b |
| M15a |
| M6a |
| M6a |
| M15a |
| M15b |
| M6 |
| M6 |
| M17c |
| M15b |
| M6 |
| M6a |
| M15b |
| M21b |
| M15b |
| M15 |
| M15b |
| M15b |
| M15b |
| M15b |
| M15b |
| M21b |
| M17 |
| M15b |
| M15b |
| M15b |
| M17c |
| M15d |
| M15b |
| M15d |
| M15d |

## Ellenberg's indicator value analysis – Landscape scale

The seven sites re-surveyed in 2013 comprised a total of 224 individual quadrats. The quadrat mean Ellenberg values for all 224 quadrats were first compared to their pre-restoration equivalents. Grouping the sites in this way has both advantages and disadvantages. The large sample size increases the power of any comparison, since anomalous results which might occur as a result of mis-identification should have less effect on the mean, and a larger sample will always generate a sample mean more representative of the population mean. Conversely however whilst it can more confidently be said that restoration works are having an effect on sites if statistical tests reject the null hypothesis of no difference between years, we cannot identify, using this method, at which sites change may be less obvious or even non-existent. A paired-samples t-test was therefore conducted to compare quadrat mean Ellenberg F, R and N values at all restored sites to equivalent values at the same sites prior to restoration.

The results of the landscape scale analysis of Ellenberg values before and after restoration are:

- A highly significant increase in mean F values after restoration (baseline mean F = 6.88 SE ± 0.04, restored mean F = 7.07 SE ± 0.04; paired t-test: $t(223) = -4.96$, $p = < 0.001$).
- A significant decrease in mean R values after restoration (baseline mean R = 3.02 SE ± 0.03, restored mean R = 2.96 SE ± 0.03; paired t-test: $t(223) = 2.50$, $p = < 0.01$), and
- A highly significant decrease in N values after restoration (baseline mean N = 2.33 SE ± 0.03, restored mean N = 2.24 SE ± 0.03; paired t-test: $t(223) = 3.89$, $p = < 0.001$).

The implication of these statistics is that restoration work has made the sites wetter, more acidic, and has lowered nutrient levels. These changes further suggest that restoration is having the desired effect of rewetting the peat, as the changes in pH and nutrient level can both logically be associated with increased wetness and decreased lateral flow of water across site.

However, whilst this is very encouraging, several factors must be taken into consideration when interpreting these results. Firstly, it must be noted that these significant results only relate to Ellenberg values, and not real world hydrological change. These results are not direct evidence of re-wetting, but rather a botanical proxy measure. Whilst this may seem an obvious point, it is important to understand we are not measuring real world botanical parameters when using Ellenberg values, but rather imposing a set of values developed to monitor environmental change.

Additionally, the lack of comparable controls at each site makes it difficult to say with confidence that the observed changes in Ellenberg values can be attributed to the restoration work alone. Ideally, each site would have an additional control transect straddling an adjacent ditch which had not been restored. Comparison of the results between the two transects could then be used to support any conclusions that changes in Ellenberg values were due to restoration rather than local hydrological changes for example. Future survey and analysis should seek to include control transects to support these results.

Finally, controls which take account of regional scale variation and the inclusion of climate data from the project area covering the period of monitoring, could ascertain the impact of any link between changing Ellenberg values and broader climatic patterns. This could further support the conclusions relating to the success of restoration.

## Ellenberg's indicator value analysis – site level

The comparison of quadrat mean Ellenberg values at site level has the inverse advantages and disadvantages of the landscape scale comparison. Namely statistical power decreases due to the smaller effective sample size, but assessment of the impact of restoration per site is possible. Paired t-tests were conducted again, this time to compare quadrat mean Ellenberg F, R, and N values for each restored site to equivalent values at the same site prior to restoration. Results are summarised in Table 6.

**Table 6. Comparison of Ellenberg F, R and N values at each site before and after restoration work**

| Site | Ellenberg wetness (F) | Ellenberg pH (R) | Ellenberg nitrogen (N) |
|---|---|---|---|
| Alderman's Barrow | No change | Significant decrease in acidity (Baseline R=3.23 SE ± 0.09, restored R=3.37 SE ± 0.08; paired t: $t(39)=-2.83$, $p=<0.01$) | No change |
| Broadmead | Significant increase in wetness (Baseline F=6.82 SE ± 0.16, restored F=7.68 SE ± 0.08; paired t: $t(29)=-5.84$, $p=<0.001$) | No change | No change |
| Comerslade | No change | Significant increase in acidity (Baseline R=2.85 SE ± 0.03, restored R=2.63 SE ± 0.04; paired t: $t(39) = 4.96$, $p =<0.001$) | No change |
| Homer Common | Significant increase in wetness (Baseline F = 6.86 SE ± 0.07, restored F = 7.14 SE ± 0.12; paired t: $t(29) =-2.25$, $p = 0.02$) | Significant increase in acidity (Baseline R = 2.88 SE ± 0.05, restored R = 2.52 SE ± 0.05; paired t: $t(29) = 4.98$, $p = <0.001$) | Significant decrease in fertility (Baseline N = 2.40 SE ± 0.05, restored N = 2.02 SE ± 0.03; paired t: $t(29) = 7.86$, $p = <0.001$) |

| Site | Ellenberg wetness (F) | Ellenberg pH (R) | Ellenberg nitrogen (N) |
|---|---|---|---|
| Roosthitchen Phase 1 | Significant increase in wetness (Baseline F = 6.88 SE ± 0.05, restored F = 7.20 SE ± 0.06; paired t: $t(28)$ =-5.54, $p$ = <0.001) | No change | Significant decrease in fertility (Baseline N = 2.62 SE ± 0.07, restored N = 2.38 SE ± 0.06; paired t:$t(28)$ = 3.55, $p$ = <0.001) |
| Roosthitchen Phase 2 | No change | Significant decrease in acidity (Baseline R = 2.91 SE ± 0.05, restored R = 3.06 SE ± 0.04; paired t: $t(14)$ = -2.56, $p$ = 0.01) | No change |
| Verney's Allotment | Significant decrease in wetness (Baseline F = 6.92 SE ± 0.06, restored F = 6.87 SE ± 0.06; paired t: $t(39)$ = 1.81, $p$ = 0.03) | No change | No change |

Referring to Table 6, results for the site level comparison of quadrat mean Ellenberg values are generally favourable, and to some extent correspond with the site level NVC classifications. Alderman's Barrow, a site which has not changed in terms of NVC classification since restoration work, unsurprisingly showed no favourable change in any of the compared Ellenberg values. Indeed, the quadrat mean Ellenberg acidity values have actually moved significantly toward the alkaline end of the spectrum, indicating a possible further decline in acid mire condition. As previously mentioned, the lack of botanical community change at the site is probably due to the failure of the restoration structures on site. This effectively makes Alderman's Barrow an unintentional control site in our analysis. Roosthitchen Phase 2 showed similar results, which are probably also attributable to the structural failure of the restoration structures on site.

Broadmead showed a significant ($p$ =<0.001) increase in mean Ellenberg wetness values post-restoration, as might be expected given the site level NVC community changes previously outlined (Table 3). The magnitude of change in Ellenberg wetness values at this site was also larger than at any other site. Interestingly, there was no significant change in quadrat mean Ellenberg pH or nitrogen values, which might be expected to accompany peat rewetting. However, Broadmead is a distinctly mesotrophic site, a fact reflected in the abundance of species such as *Carex rostrata* and *Viola palustris*. In tune with this fen-like character, a drop in pH would seem less likely as part of restoration at this stage, and nutrient levels are probably sustained by a spring, and a high level of lateral flow across the site which remains despite restoration structures.

Roosthitchen Phase 1 was the other site which showed dramatic changes in site NVC communities (Table 3), and this is supported by the results of the Ellenberg value analysis (Table 6). Significant increases in the mean wetness indicator values and decreases in mean nitrogen indicator values both add weight to the conclusion that restoration at this site is progressing successfully. No significant change in Ellenberg pH indicator values was recorded, with an apparent change indicative of increasing acidity falling just short of significance ($p$ = 0.09). At Comerslade, comparison of quadrat mean Ellenberg values revealed significant change in indicators of acidity only, although this could be regarded as a potential indicator of restoration success. The NVC classification for the site was also rather inconclusive, showing possible change to an intermediate community only.

At Homer Common, however, another site with a relatively subtle change in site NVC communities, significant change suggestive of restoration success was identified in all three types of Ellenberg value analysis. This was unexpected and may suggest that site level NVC assessment is lacking as a tool for measuring community change. Further examination of the site botany using the project indicator species lists may provide a better assessment of the situation at the site.

Finally, Ellenberg value analysis at Verney's Allotment show a significant decrease in quadrat mean wetness values, and no change in either quadrat mean pH or nitrogen values (Table 6). NVC classification for this site was also somewhat inconclusive (Table 3), and again reference to changes in indicator species abundance may help to elucidate botanical changes at this site and determine whether restoration has been successful or unsuccessful so far.

## Indicator species analysis

Examination of the occurrence of indicator species as detailed in Table 2 help to explain the botanical situation underlying both the NVC and Ellenberg value analysis results. Detailed results from two contrasting sites are presented below, in Figures 1 to 4 as an example of this analysis. The units on the y-axis represent the number of sub-quadrats in which the species concerned was recorded.

**Figure 1. Positive indicator occurrence at Alderman's Barrow over three surveys; 2008 (pre-restoration), 2010 and 2013.**

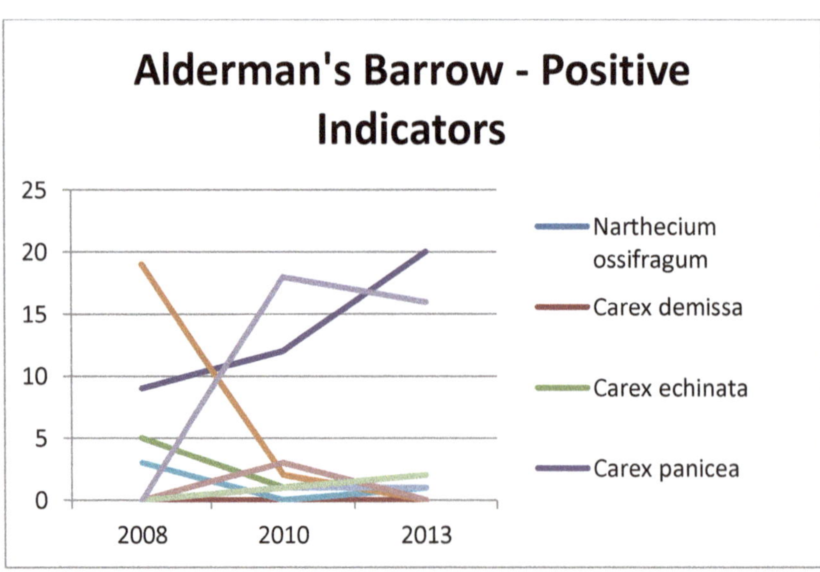

**Figure 2. Negative indicator occurrence at Aldermans Barrow over three surveys; 2008 (pre-restoration), 2010 and 2013.**

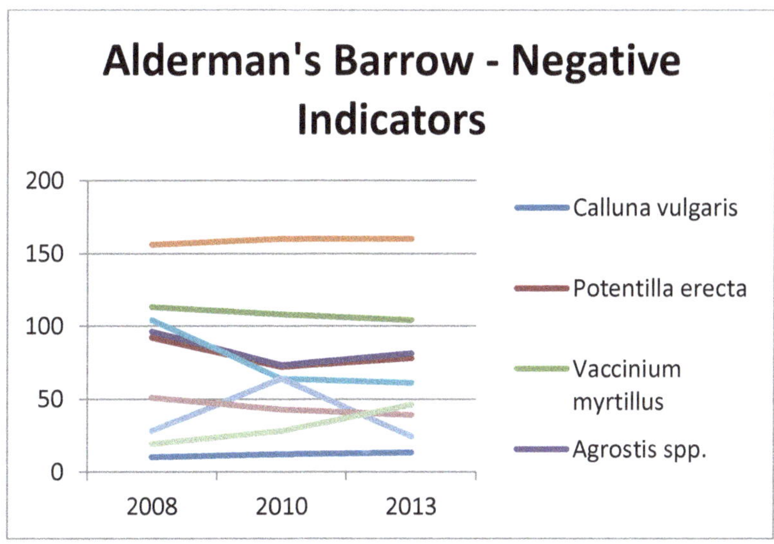


Indicator species occurrence results for Alderman's Barrow largely reflect the lack of change identified in the site NVC and the quadrat mean Ellenberg value analysis. The decrease in positive indicators, particularly *Sphagnum capillifoilium*, suggests the site is continuing to dry due to failure of the restoration structure.

**Figure 3. Positive indicator occurrence at Broadmead over four surveys; 2006 (pre-restoration), 2008, 2010 and 2013.**

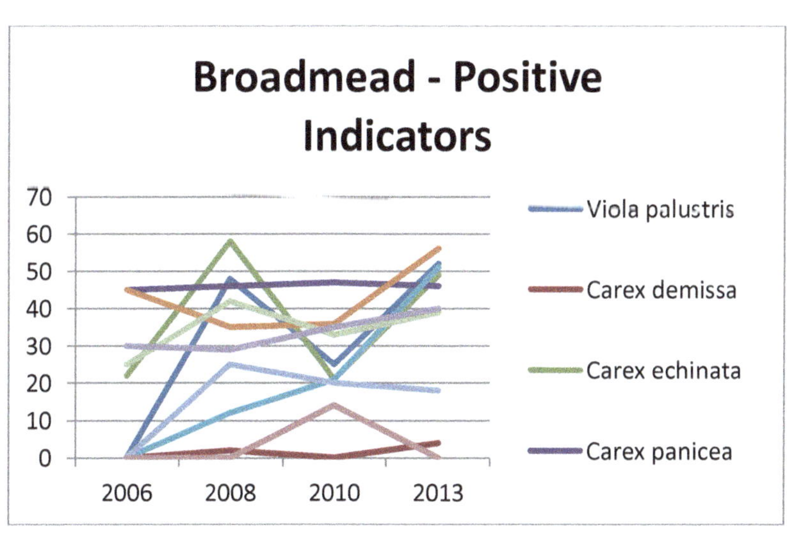

**Figure 4: Negative indicator occurrence at Broadmead over four surveys; 2006 (pre-restoration), 2008, 2010 and 2013.**

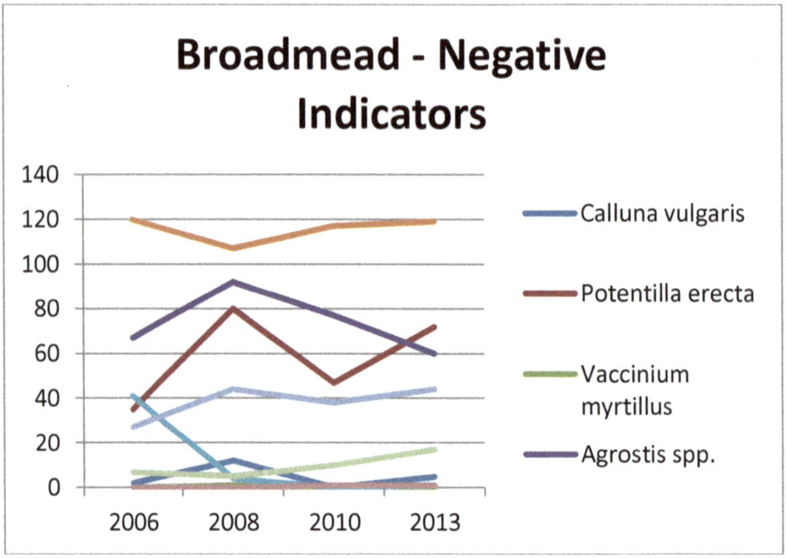

Broadmead - Negative Indicators

140
120
100
80
60
40
20
0

2006 2008 2010 2013

Calluna vulgaris
Potentilla erecta
Vaccinium myrtillus
Agrostis spp.

The indicator species occurrence changes at Broadmead differ from Alderman's Barrow but equally supports the NVC and Ellenberg value analysis results. A progressive increase in most of the positive indicator species can be observed, with several species increasing in occurrence markedly since 2010. Negative species however remain broadly constant, although *Agrostis* spp. appears to be in decline since restoration.

The indicator species occurrence at the remainder of the sites is in line with the findings outlined in the two examples above. This helps to explain the variation in results of the Ellenberg value analysis for the sites, which is only partially reflected in the NVC assessments. However, despite overall trends the fluctuation of species between years can still be very marked.

## Conclusions and recommendations

The results presented permit a number of conclusions relating both to the success of the project restoration work to date and the effectiveness of analytical methods employed.

1. At five of the seven restoration sites re-surveyed in 2013 there has been measurable change in the dominant NVC

community at site level, suggesting a re-wetting of the underlying peat. Some of the community changes were however particularly subtle, with several sites appearing to move toward intermediate communities rather than entirely distinct wetter NVC types.

2. Analysis of pooled quadrat mean Ellenberg values across all sites showed significant changes in the values associated with wetness, pH and nitrogen levels after restoration. Ellenberg values for restored quadrats suggested that the restored sites were significantly wetter, more acidic and less nutrient-rich than before restoration.

3. Analysis of quadrat mean Ellenberg values at site level proved particularly valuable, and provided additional detail not shown in the site NVC assessments. Of the seven sites re-surveyed in 2013, four demonstrated significant changes in Ellenberg values associated with rewetting, namely Broadmead, Comerslade, Homer Common and Roosthitchen Phase 1. Three sites returned results suggesting negative change and site drying, namely Roosthitchen Phase 2, Alderman's Barrow and Verney's Allotment. The two latter sites were not expected to show positive change because of the failure of the restoration features. The Ellenberg analysis which indicated drying at Verney's Allotment was however unexpected and contradicted the broader site level NVC analyses which indicated a change to a wetter community.

4. Application of the project indicator species lists to the data supported the Ellenberg value analysis fairly accurately, and visualised the changes in species occurrence which are central to the significant changes in quadrat mean Ellenberg values. This was a particularly useful tool for detecting fine scale changes between monitoring years and its continuation is recommended.

5. It is therefore judged that whilst site level NVC approaches may in many cases give appropriate indication of change, finer scale examination of results is necessary to discern changes which may be missed. The Ellenberg value analysis employed here provides a more complete picture and would be worth taking forward in future analyses. The quadrat level NVC approach which was applied to the data from 2013 also

highlighted the complexity of botanical communities across transects and should be applied to botanical data in forthcoming surveys.

6. Considering the results outlined above, it is possible to make some central conclusions about the effectiveness of the restoration methods used by the Exmoor Mires Project:

- At a landscape scale, restoration via ditch blocking results in an increase in species associated with re-wetting of underlying peat, increased acidity, and a decrease in nutrient levels.
- At a site level this holds true for four of the seven re-survey sites from 2013, Broadmead, Comerslade, Homer Common and Roosthitchen Phase 1, and
- Failure of restoration structures has had an appreciably negative effect on the recovery of botanical communities at two sites, Roosthitchen Phase 2 and Alderman's Barrow.

## Ongoing work

A further ten post-restoration sites have been selected for re-surveying in the 2014 survey season, including control sites and the two sites (Blackpitts and Exe Head) first surveyed in 1998. This data will add considerable depth to the existing vegetation data base in term of temporal and spatial distribution. The initial analyses developed here will be further advanced with this data to develop more robust conclusions regarding the amount, distribution and rate of post-restoration vegetation change on the Exmoor Mires.

## Application of the results

The vegetation monitoring outlined in this paper forms part of the comprehensive EMP restoration monitoring programme. Understanding post-restoration changes in a wide range of ecosystem services including hydrology, greenhouse gas fluxes and biodiversity is a key project outcome. The monitoring of botanical assemblages is examined here in detail in order to understand if this can be used to indicate underlying changes in the peatland hydrology and greenhouse gas fluxes.

This information will be used to develop a rapid assessment (proxy) method for monitoring successful hydrological change across the moorland landscape based on vegetation change monitoring. The development of this system (based on the GEST methods of Couwenberg *et al.*, 2011) is part of the ongoing work to verify the greenhouse gas emissions savings arising from the restoration work under the newly emerging Peatland Code (IUCN, 2013). Verification will enable the project to develop carbon off-setting and ecosystem service payments (PES) for the delivery of clean and sustained fresh water supplies. This is part of the EMP strategy of providing sustainable incomes in the uplands from multiple ecosystems services.

## Acknowledgments

Thank you to the land-owners and managers on Exmoor for their support of the project and for access to the sites. The continued assistance of the outstanding EMP volunteers is also much appreciated, their role in support of the botanical survey team at First Ecology cannot be understated.

## References

Arnott, S. (2010) *Exmoor Hydrological and Hydrogeological monitoring plan for the Mires-on-the-Moors project.* Environment Agency. http://www.upstreamthinking.org/media.cfm?mediaid=5779

Bellamy, P.E., Stephen L., Maclean I.S., Grant M.C. (2012) Vegetation: response to ditch blocking. *Appl. Vegetat. Sci.*, **15**, 129-135.

Bonn, A., Rebane, M. and Reid, C. (2009) *ESS of peatlands as driver for conservation.* In: Bonn, A., Allott, T., Hubacek, K. and Stewart, J. (eds) *Drivers of environmental change in uplands*, pp. 448-474. Routledge, London and New York.

Bray, L. (2019) *Mire restoration and the historic environment (Exmoor).* In: Rotherham, I.D. and Handley, C. (eds) *In the Bog.* Wildtrack Publishing, Sheffield. (This volume part 1)

Couwenberg, J., Thiele, A., Tanneberger, F. *et al.* (2011) Assessing greenhouse gas emissions from peatlands using vegetation as a proxy. *Hydrobiologia*, **674**, 67–89.

Ellenberg, H. (1974) Zeigerwerte der Gefässpflanzen Mitteleuropas. *Scripta Geobotanica*, **9**, 1-97.

Exmoor Mires Project (2010) *Delivery Plan 2011-2015 and Indicators of Success* Exmoor Mires http://www.exmoormires.org.uk/media.cfm?mediaid=5432

ENPA (2014) *Mire Restoration Project (2006-10)* web page http://www.exmoor-nationalpark.gov.uk/environment/moorland/mire-project

First Ecology (2012) *Exmoor Mires Project Botanical Data analyses 2011/12.* First Ecology http://www.exmoormires.org.uk/media.cfm?mediaid=6341

First Ecology (2014) *Exmoor Mires Project Botanical Data analyses 2013.* First Ecology http://www.exmoormires.org.uk/media.cfm?mediaid=6341

Glendinning, A. (2012) *The continued effect of damming moorland drainage channels on Exmoor Mire vegetation.* Unpublished dissertation report for FdFc in Countryside management, Bournemouth University, Bournemouth. http://www.upstreamthinking.org/media.cfm?mediaid=5777

Grand-Clement, E., Anderson, K., Smith, D.M., Luscombe, D., Gatis, N., Ross, M., and Brazier, R.E. (2013) Evaluating Ecosystem Goods and Services After Restoration of Marginal Upland Peatlands in South-West England. *Journal of Applied Ecology*, **50**, 324-334.

Hand, A. (2009) *Upland Mire Restoration in Exmoor National Park: using bryophyte species as indicators of mire hydrology.* Advanced Diploma in Environmental Conservation 2008 - 2009 Oxford University Department for Continuing Education http://www.upstreamthinking.org/media.cfm?mediaid=5100

Hill, M.O. (1989) Computerized matching of releves and association tables, with an application to the British National Vegetation Classification. *Vegetatio*, **83**, 187-194.

Hill, M.O. (1991) *TABLEFIT program manual (version 1)* Huntingdon: Institute of Terrestrial Ecology.

Hill, M.O., Preston, C.D. and Roy, D.B (2004) *PLANTATT - attributes of British and Irish plants: status, size, life history, geography and habitats*. Centre for Ecology & Hydrology, Abbotts Ripton.

Hill, M.O., Mountford, J.O., Roy, D.B. and Bunce, R.G.H. (1999) *Ellenberg's indicator values for British plants* ECO FACT Volume 2 technical annex. Institute of Terrestrial Ecology, Huntingdon.

Hornibrook, E. (2014) *Progress Report for the Exmoor Mires Project* University of Bristol http://www.exmoormires.org.uk/index.cfm?articleid=8702§ionid=10720

IUCN (2013) *Pilot UK Peatland Code* IUCN Peatlands Programme http://www.iucn-uk-peatlandprogramme.org/peatland-gateway/uk/peatland-code

Langton, S. (2009) *Response of vegetation to raising the water table as part of the Exmoor Mire Restoration Project.* School of Biosciences, University of Exeter, Prince of Wales Road, Exeter EX4 4PS, UK Proceedings of the Royal Society B: Biological Sciences http://www.upstreamthinking.org/media.cfm?mediaid=5088

Littlewood, N., Anderson, P., Artz, R., Bragg, O., Lunt, P. and Marrs, R. (2010) *Ecological benefits of peatland restoration-* IUCN Peatland Biodiversity Scientific Review http://www.iucn-uk-peatlandprogramme.org/work-commission/peatland-biodiversity

Lunt, P., Allot, T., Anderson, P., Buckler, M., Coupar, A., Jones, P.S. and Worrall, P. (2010) *Impacts of peatland restoration*. In: Evans, M. (eds) *IUCN Technical Review*. http://www.iucn-uk

Luscombe, D., Grand-Clement, E., Anderson, K., Gatis, N., Ashe, J. and Brazier, R.E. (2014) Short-term effects of restoration on the hydrology of shallow blanket peatlands in the South West UK. *EGU General Assembly Conference Abstracts*. **16**.

Luscombe, D., Smith, D., Grand-Clement, E. and Brazier R.E. (2014) *Initial changes in hydrology and water quality following restoration of a shallow degraded peatland in the South West* Water@Leeds/Upland Hydrology/BHS meeting 10/03/2014 http://www.uplandhydrology.org.uk/uhg-meetings/

Malloch, A.J.C. (1990) MATCH. *A computer programme to aid the assignment of vegetation data to the communities and subcommunities of the National Vegetation Classification*. Unit of Vegetation Science, Lancaster University, Lancaster.

Rodwell, J.S. (ed.) (1991) *British Plant Communities. Volume 2: Mires and heath* Cambridge University Press.

Ramchunder, S.J., Brown, L.E. and Holden, J. (2009) Environmental effects of drainage, drain-blocking and prescribed vegetation burning in UK upland peatlands. *Progress in Physical Geography*, **33**, 49–79.

Shepherd, M.J., Labadz, J., Caporn, S.J., Crowle, A., Goodison, R., Rebane, M. and Waters, R. (2013) *Natural England review of upland evidence - Restoration of Degraded Blanket Bog*. Natural England Evidence Review, Number 003, Peterborough.

Somerset Environmental Records Centre (1988) *Baseline vegetation survey prior to drainage reversal on blanket mire, Exe-Plain, Somerset*. Unpublished

Smart, S.M. (2000) *Modular Analysis of Vegetation Information System (MAVIS) Plot Analyser, Version 1.0.* Centre for Ecology and Hydrology, Merlewood, Cumbria.

Wilson, L., Wilson, J., Holden, J., Johnstone, I., Armstrong, A. and Morris, M. (2010) Recovery of water tables in Welsh blanket bog after drain blocking: discharge rates, time scales and the influence of local conditions. *Journal of Hydrology*, **391**, 377–386.

# Chapter 14. Mires, Men and Mechanisation

**Darren Whitaker**
JBA Consulting.

## Background

JBA Consulting was commissioned to write and deliver a water level management plan (WLMP) for Thorne Moors Site of Special Scientific Interest (SSSI) on behalf of Doncaster East Internal Drainage Board. Thorne Moors is England's largest terrestrial SSSI and consists of a degraded lowland raised mire covering a total area of 1,920 ha. The site is also designated as a National Nature Reserve (NNR) and Special Area of Conservation (SAC) due to its important degraded lowland raised mire habitats capable of restoration, and a Special Protection Area (SPA) due to the high numbers of breeding European Nightjar *Caprimulgus europaeus*.

The project has been funded by a £3m grant from the Environment Agency. The site has also received additional funding, secured as part of the Humberhead Levels Nature Improvement Area (NIA) scheme and, in the future, a LIFE+ project. The NIA and LIFE+ funding is directed towards the clearance of birch and rhododendron scrub, for which funding was outstanding.

The site has a long history of peat winning, dating back hundreds of years, with hand graving through to, latterly, machine milling being used to extract peat. The peat has been removed from site in a number of ways, ranging from horse drawn canal barges through a system of canals, and more recently by diesel powered narrow gauge railway and articulated-lorries.

The landscape of the site is a matrix of open flat undulating plains and scrub-covered cutting and baulk systems characteristic of hand dug sites. The site is cut roughly in half by a loose stone road installed to allow harvested peat to be removed, it was originally constructed from limestone in the late 1980s; it is now restored periodically with granite and other stone of an acidic nature.

## Initial Planning

The varied topography resulting from years of peat winning was assessed using LiDAR (Light Detection and Ranging) data (Figure 1). This was then analysed to produce an outline water level management plan proposing a series of peat bunds and plastic pile dams that isolate undulating sections of mire, allowing water to be impounded at the ideal level to permit the growth of peat forming vegetation. The LiDAR data was ground-truthed using a Leica Smart Rover Digital GPS (DGPS), to produce an overall plan enhancing the existing restoration work carried out on the site over the last fifteen years.

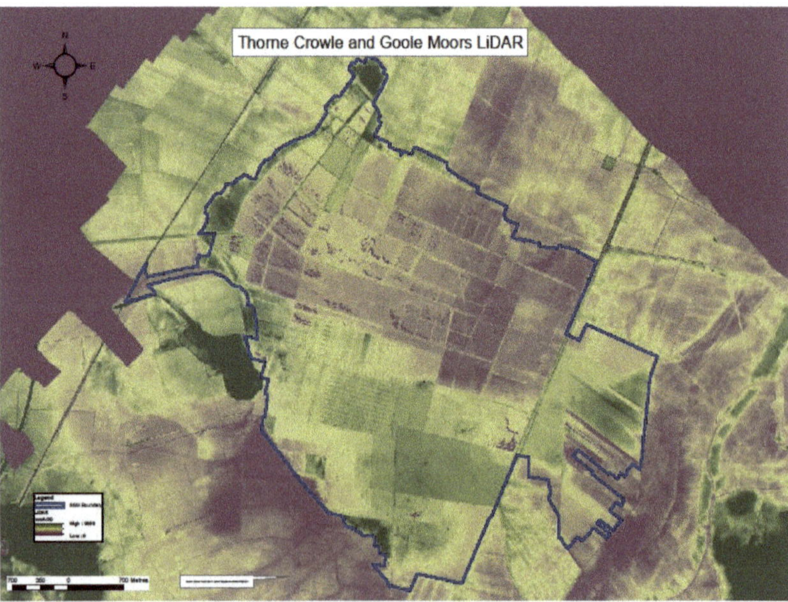


**Figure 1. Thorne Crowle and Goole Moors LiDAR Map**

A series of data loggers was also installed across the site to monitor fluctuations in water levels. These were analysed to determine the hydraulic gradients across the site and this data has been used to inform the locations of the peat bunds on-site.

The larger arterial drains are currently controlled via a series of steel pile structures with penstocks to allow water to be drained from specific compartments as the need arises. These structures will be retained and supplemented with a series of new steel pile dams, incorporating tilting weirs. These allow the water in the drains to be maintained at specific levels and opened as necessary to allow excess water to leave the compartment, maintaining favourable water levels. The installation of this series of steel pile dams in larger drains and fitting these with telemetry-controlled tilting weirs will allow water to be discharged from the site whilst keeping water levels at the desired level.

Water can be discharged from the site using an Archimedes screw pump partially powered using renewable energy in the form of solar panels or a small wind turbine. The electricity supply at the pump itself will be provided by the use of a generator to allow water movements at peak times. The system links into the existing telemetry network of the surrounding pumped drainage districts to make sure the discharge from the Moors does not overwhelm the local pump capacity, potentially resulting in increased flood risk to local properties.

## Implementation

A large section of this site is designated as open access land under the Countryside and Rights of Way Act 2000 (CROW) with several way-marked routes crossing the site; these are permissive routes and are not designated as Public Rights of Way. Public access to this high profile site has to remain open throughout the works. There are a number of sections of bunding that will be installed adjacent to the trackways and the tracks are kept open by installing bypasses, controlled by banks-men, to keep the work progressing and visitors safe.

The site has been out of peat production for many years, leaving much of the hand-cut areas as a mosaic of wet cuttings and dry baulks, covered with mature birch and bracken. As a result, the site now supports, not only species associated with mires, but also other, drier peatland species. As part of the WLMP process consideration was given to any interesting features that were likely to be affected by the works. Habitats Regulation Assessments were carried out where necessary, along with more general species surveys and, where practicable, provision was made to safeguard these features and improve the area for specific species e.g. the site has a significant population of Adder *Viper berus.* When areas are cleared of scrub prior to bunding, log piles are left in strategic areas and often these will be covered with peat to provide hibernacula for overwintering reptiles.

The site is difficult to reach by road: the only feasible access for large vehicles is at the north-eastern corner along a privately owned farm track. Access to other areas has been achieved using temporary roadways and bridge structures to cross over the boundary drain. Bog mats were then used to protect the tracks. Throughout all of the work undertaken the sensitive cultural heritage of the site has been considered and all planned works are agreed and overseen by archaeologists.

## Challenges

The varied topography of this site presented a number of challenges to restoration, including:

- The size of the project requires that the works adhere to the requirements of CDM (Construction, Design and Management Regulations, 2007).
- Areas have to be selected to allow the erection of site compounds, to safely store tools and materials and allow for the provision welfare facilities on site.
- The size of the site and the ground conditions requires that the main, large compound has to be established at the edge of the site. This is close to the workshop areas used by the peat company, giving a firm base and reasonable access for deliveries of heavy plant and materials.
- The fragile nature and the narrow linear track system dictates that sub-compounds have to be used to facilitate work and incorporate the welfare facilitates. The drive between the main compound and the smaller compounds can be up to 45 minutes, if the areas are within the interior of the site.
- In places the ground conditions may also require the use of low ground pressure vehicles, running on a temporary low impact trackway to allow access to work sites.

## Summary

The plan involved installing a series of steel pile dams in larger drains and fitting these with tilting weirs to discharge water from the site, controlled by a telemetry system acting in real time to keep water at a desired level within the cells.

Linking the system to the discharge point where water will either be discharged by gravity or be pumped out of the site using an Archimedes screw pump. This is partially powered using renewable energy in the form of solar panels or a small wind turbine for the electricity supply at the pump itself and supplemented by the use of a generator.

The system links into the existing telemetry of the surrounding drainage districts to make sure the discharge from the mire does not overwhelm the local pump capacity.

# Chapter 16. Can upland land use changes be used to predict bird populations? Investigations of farm-scale ecological change

**Dan Wildsmith and Ian D. Rotherham**

## Summary

Land-use changes on inbye and surrounding upland heathland can be attributed to many factors over many years. Factors include the rise of industrialism and populations in peripheral towns and cities, advancement in agricultural technologies, increase in agricultural intensity including drainage and improvement, conservation designations, national and European upland land policies and changes in the use of these areas as social resources. Land use change has an immediate impact on the vegetation of the landscape.

This study set out to examine some aspects of landscape change on selected bird populations of the Peak District uplands. A range of declining upland bird species such as lapwing, snipe, curlew, twite, skylark, meadow pipit, reed bunting, and others are clearly affected by land-use change. Furthermore, the loss of smaller upland farmsteads and cottages over the twentieth century is largely unrecognised. This demise of smallholdings, it is argued, has influenced declines through the loss of associated hay meadows, rushy pastures, and of weedy arable cultivation particularly oats, which were a part of a subsistence farming system.

## Introduction

The Peak District has witnessed a 'millennium' of significant change as populations waxed and waned and subsistence farming methods developed through time, albeit slower in comparison to more fertile and preferential lowland areas. However, it was the rapid rise of eighteenth and nineteenth century industrialisation and the partitioning of common lands under the various enclosure acts that accelerated land-use change in the Peak Park area.

The Dark Peak area is unique amongst upland bog and heath areas due to being surrounded by major industrial centres. The changes this has brought about through land use and vegetation change have been profound and has resulted in a restricted floral diversity in comparison to other areas. The feeding and clothing of increasing numbers of workers in these industrial centres, and the influence this had on the introduction of new intensive farming methods was also dramatic.

Many small farms which used mixed farming methods, and were on the whole good for biodiversity, were lost as farming practices benefitted larger farms, concentrating on rearing predominantly sheep, losing arable crops of oats and roots to improved pasture and meadow. Elsewhere, the vegetation reverted back to heathland assemblages or was lost to timber plantations and inundation of water from reservoir construction. Other drivers of farm abandonment in the nineteenth and early twentieth centuries were the loss of the cottage weaving industry to larger textile mills and policies of clearing catchments to provide clean water for reservoirs prior to chemical treatment of potable water.

## Research approach

This research project applied the study of ecological and landscape history, in conjunction with mapping and bird/vegetation modelling data, to predict the response of upland birds to vegetation changes on inbye and peripheral habitats. The consideration of faunal species, particularly birds, to land management decisions can be lengthy and complex. The study investigated whether groups of birds can be considered by using one methodology instead of individual bird species to provide an overall view of the likely effects to upland birds from vegetation change, thus highlighting the importance of recognising broad habitat-matrix conservation for birds.

(Source: Peak District National Park, 2013)

**Map 1. Location of the Peak District National Park, the Dark Peak occupying the northern area of the park.**

Three case studies of upland farm abandonment in the eastern Dark Peak were investigated to indicate the farm-scale ecological changes that have occurred since abandonment. These were located near Holme and Langsett, all are situated on the fringes of open moorland. The composition of historic vegetation was obtained by researching nineteenth and early twentieth century academic literature and associated maps.

Historic Ordnance Survey maps were also used, along with local archive materials, such as tithe maps and assessments, enclosure awards, maps and parish records to give a good approximation of the acreage of farms and the ratio of acid or neutral pasture/meadow and other vegetation to arable crops. The likely changes to the vegetation on peripheral heathland was obtained either from the historic accounts of past management on heath in the Dark Peak or from contemporary literature.

**Figure 2: Holme Cliff ruin with bilberry heath and acid grassland mosaic (Source: Wildsmith).**

The nature of contemporary vegetation was obtained by field visits. The historic and contemporary vegetation were assigned to phase 1 survey habitat descriptions, for example, semi-improved acid grassland, dry acid dwarf shrub heath. This gave the farm-scale changes in vegetation since abandonment in and around the peripheries of the farms (Figure 2).

Previous work on modelling the association of upland birds with the structure and composition of upland vegetation is available via the *Moors for the Future* project archives. Using the changes in vegetation at these farms, the predicted responses of ten upland bird species, whether positive or negative, to these changes could be deduced and tabulated. These were then depicted graphically using radar diagrams for each farm. See Figure 3.

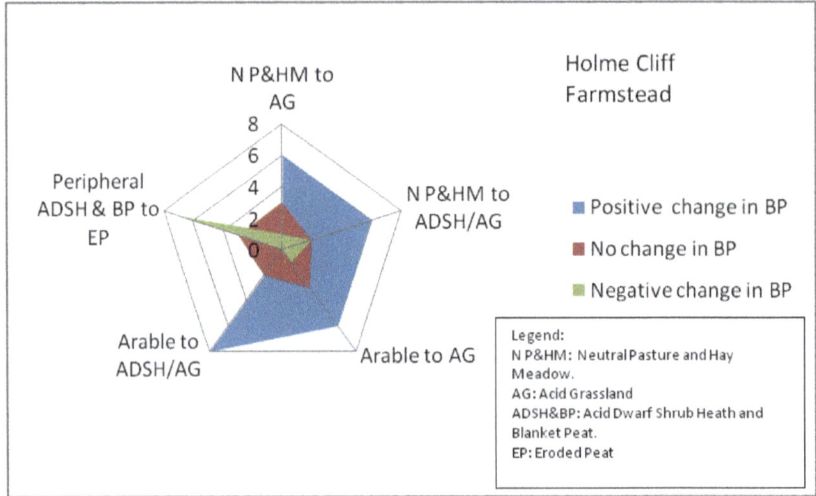


**Figure 3: Radar diagram for Holme Cliff farmstead indicating predicted positive changes in bird population for four changes in vegetation.**

These types of diagrams are used to display multivariate data with an arbitrary number of variables and can be used to assess which variables are dominant for a single observation. The radar diagrams give a diagrammatic representation of the predicted changes to groups of birds that may be affected by a particular change in vegetation at a particular farm. These changes can be either positive or negative for the 10 bird species studied.

A concept of 'directions' of vegetation change is discussed to indicate whether certain types of vegetation change are beneficial or deleterious to groups of birds that share multiple habitat preferences. For example, for Holme Cliff farmstead (Figure 2), the vegetation change to acid grassland, or a mosaic of acid grassland and acid dwarf shrub heath was predicted to be most beneficial to most birds with only two bird species being affected negatively. This can be described as an overall positive direction of vegetation change. The change from acid dwarf shrub heath and blanket peats to eroded peat gave a predicted negative direction of vegetation change for most birds. One case study indicated an overall positive change for all changes in vegetation and could be described as 'unidirectional'.

A very large area of species rich pasture, hay meadow, and arable with abundant weed species has been lost via farm intensification, culminating in an overall negative effect on the distribution of most bird species investigated. Birds that utilised inbye for one or more habitat associations were affected the most. However, not all farm abandonments were deleterious to bird populations, especially if the vegetation has reverted back to heathland habitats. Future work would include comparing local bird data to the case study areas to see if the predictions are accurate, using rose diagrams instead of radar diagrams to gain a better graphical representation of predictions and using more bird species in the analysis.

Predicting bird distribution change as a result of land-use/vegetation change is complex due to the multiple habitats birds utilise and the differing ways that vegetation changes after abandonment. However, these associations could be used to predict how groups of faunal species would respond to land management and policy decisions in the future. The incorporation of ecological and landscape histories are not usually utilised in conjunction with contemporary conservation studies. However, if the archive materials are adequate, a great amount of information can be acquired on the quality and quantities of past habitats and how these have changed both spatially and temporally.

The higher level farmsteads had various impacts such as localised shifts in nutrients effectively from an out-field to an inbye through management of stock and animal dunging. Bracken was manged by local farms up until the 1920s as an important part of the farming cycle, used as animal bedding in winter. However, in terms of the bird species in question the main impacts in terms of these smaller fam units were the maintenance of hay-meadows and oat-fields to feed stock animals, the inefficient farming which allowed species-rich, seed-rich weedy swards, and limited drainage. All of these would benefit the bird species in question, and within this system the presence of small patches of ploughlands were beneficial to species such as lapwing.

## Conclusions

The full review was never completed, but some broad conclusions can be drawn. A survey of lower-lying moorland and moorland fringe areas confirmed significant numbers of abandoned farmsteads and cottages at altitudes of around 1,000 feet. These still show signs of inbye enclosed fields and wider enclosure boundaries long-since abandoned and often reverted to heather-dominated or bracken-dominated moorland, or else to short, sheep-grazed acid grassland. Some of the sites on the fringe of the moorland blocks have clearly been 'improved' to either arable or pasture during the later twentieth century. There is also anecdotal evidence of widespread drainage and re-seeding of old, wet, rushy pastures from field ornithologists working locally from the 1960s to 1990s, and a parallel decline of birds such as snipe and lapwing (John Lintin-Smith pers. comm.).

Furthermore, field observations whilst working on ecological aspects of the Sheffield City Council estate in the 1980s and 1990s, confirmed a number of smallholdings that continued with hay-meadows and unimproved pasture as part-time farmers previousy with the local water companies or water boards. This was a way of offering part-time employment when needed on the reservoirs and water-gathering grounds at a modest cost since it was offset against a cottage and a bit of land. These then passed to the local authority when the water authorities were established. Such smallholdings were then the only areas of traditionally-managed farmland along the moorland fringe and ecological surveys highlighted their value for birds, flowering plants, and insects. Around former water company cottages and land on the Eastern Moors Estate in North Derbyshire, there was the last regional site for breeding twite until around the early 1990s.

More recent observations around the National Trust Longshaw Estate (North Derbyshire) have confirmed the recovery through sensitive management of enclosed meadows close to the moorland fringe. These have proved beneficial to orchids such as common spotted orchid, and to lapwing, curlew, and barn owl. On the moor higher up the slope there is again evidence of former farmsteads. It is suggested that many of these higher level farms and cottages were abandoned in the late 1700s and early 1800s when many of the moorland blocks were enclosed for grouse shooting and sheep rearing.

The research highlights the potential for linking historical spatial data on ecological and land-use aspects of upland moors but concludes that much more needs to be done. Human settlement patterns do include major incursions uphill and into the peatland and moorland blocks during the period from the 1600s to the 2000s. However, counter-intuitively, on the higher moors the farmsteads and cottages are being cleared and settlement shifts downslope. There is a shift in land-use associated with these changes which removed diversity of habitat availability, and this may have contributed to the loss or decline of threatened bird species.

## Bibliography and references

Anderson, P. and Shimwell, D. (1981) *Wild flowers and other plants of the Peak District*. Moorland Publishing, Ashbourne.

Ardron, P. A., Rotherham, I.D. and Gilbert, O. (1999) An evaluation of the South Pennines peatlands with reference to the impact of peat cutting. *Peak District Journal of Natural History and Archaeology*, **1**, 67-75.

Bownes, J.S., Riley, T.H., Rotherham, I.D. and Vincent, S.M. (1991) *Sheffield Nature Conservation Strategy*, Sheffield City Council, Sheffield.

Howkins, C. (1997) *Heathland Harvest*. Pub. Chris Howkins, Addlestone, Surrey.

Moss, C.E. (1913) *Vegetation of the Peak District*. The University Press, Cambridge.

Parry, M.L.(1977) *Mapping Moorland Change: A Framework for Land-Use Decisions in the Peak District*. Peak District National Park, Bakewell, Derbyshire.

Rotherham, I.D. (1995) Urban Heathlands - Their Conservation, Restoration and Creation. *Landscape Contamination and Reclamation*, **3**, (2), 99-100.

Rotherham, I.D. (1996) Habitat Fragmentation and Isolation in Relict Urban Heathlands - the ecological consequences and future potential , Abstract paper in: *The Proceedings of the 28th International Geographical Congress. August 1996.* The Hague, The Netherlands.

Rotherham, I.D. (1999) Peat cutters and their Landscapes: fundamental change in a fragile environment. In: Peatland Ecology and Archaeology: management of a cultural landscape. *Landscape Archaeology and Ecology*, **4**, 28-51.

Rotherham, I.D. (2005) Fuel and Landscape – Exploitation, Environment, Crisis and Continuum. *Landscape Archaeology and Ecology*, **5**, 65-81.

Rotherham, I.D. (2013) *War & Peat: exploring interactions between people, human conflict, peatlands, and ecology*. In: Rotherham, I.D., & Handley, C. (eds) (2013) *War & Peat.* Wildtrack Publishing, Sheffield, 7-44.

Rotherham, I.D., Egan, D. and Ardron, P. A. (2004) Fuel economy and the uplands: the effects of peat and turf utilisation on upland landscapes. *Society for Landscape Studies Supplementary Series*, **2**, 99-109.

Simmons, I.G. (2003) *The Moorlands of England and Wales*. Edinburgh University Press, Edinburgh.

Webb, N. (1986) *Heathlands*. Collins, London.

Webb, N.R. (1998) The traditional management of European heathlands. *Journal of Applied Ecology*, **35**, 987-990.

Wildsmith, D. (2013) Can upland heath land-use change and farm-scale ecological changes on inbye can be used to predict bird populations in the Dark Peak area. Unpublished MSc dissertation, Sheffield Hallam University, Sheffield.

# The conference was organised and supported by the organisations shown below

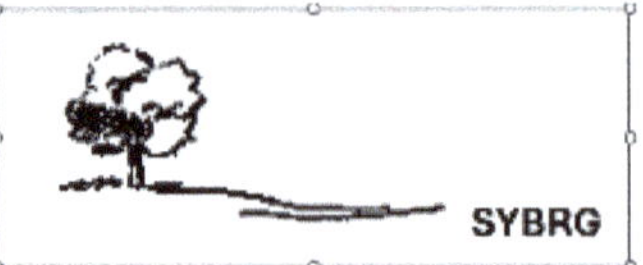

www.ingramcontent.com/pod-product-compliance
Lightning Source LLC
Chambersburg PA
CBHW040148270326
41929CB00025B/3423

*9781904098751*